HEGEL OR SPINOZA

HEGEL OR SPINOZA

Pierre Macherey

TRANSLATED BY SUSAN M. RUDDICK

University of Minnesota Press
MINNEAPOLIS · LONDON

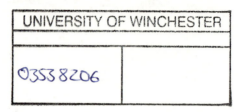
Originally published as *Hegel ou Spinoza*. Copyright 1979
Librairie François Maspero, Paris; copyright 1990 Éditions La
Découverte, Paris.

Copyright 2011 by the Regents of the University of Minnesota

Translator's introduction copyright 2011 by Susan M. Ruddick

Published by the University of Minnesota Press
111 Third Avenue South, Suite 290
Minneapolis, MN 55401-2520
http://www.upress.umn.edu

Library of Congress Cataloging-in-Publication Data

Macherey, Pierre.
  [Hegel ou Spinoza. English]
  Hegel or Spinoza / Pierre Macherey ; translated by Susan M.
Ruddick.
    p. cm.
  Includes bibliographical references and index.
  ISBN 978-0-8166-7740-5 (hc : alk. paper)
  ISBN 978-0-8166-7741-2 (pb : alk. paper)
1. Hegel, Georg Wilhelm Friedrich, 1770–1831. 2. Spinoza,
Benedictus de, 1632–1677. I. Title.
  B2948.M1513 2011
  193—dc23

                    2011028085

Printed in the United States of America on acid-free paper

The University of Minnesota is an equal-opportunity educator
and employer.

17 16 15 14 13 12 11   10 9 8 7 6 5 4 3 2 1

Contents

Translator's Introduction:
A Dialectics of Encounter

Hegel or Spinoza first appeared in 1979 after an eight-year near-hiatus in Macherey's work. As Warren Montag argues, it marked a divergence in the philosophical paths of Pierre Macherey and his mentor and colleague Louis Althusser, each responding in his own way to the violent misreading of their work as a so-called structuralism and the resurgence of humanism (or, perhaps more correctly, an anti-antihumanism) in France at the time. Montag suggests that *Hegel or Spinoza* began a new phase in Macherey's work, one that could be viewed as "a displacement, neither a rejection of nor a return to the past, but instead the attempt to discover new points of application from which one might speak about certain problems and questions without being drowned out by a chorus of commentators."[1]

What possible interest could the book hold, we might ask, except for a limited audience concerned with obscure points of philosophy? But to view the work this way is to miss entirely its critical relevance both to contemporary philosophy and to politics. Although stylistically the focus of the book eliminated "all but the most serious of readers,"[2] this was not a strategy of retreat. It is a rigorous and precise text that exposes the legacy of a Hegelian misreading of Spinoza, a misreading that arguably undergirded the post-1968 humanist backlash. And it is a seminal engagement with the work of Spinoza itself that has informed political philosophy going forward, neither a break nor a retreat from political engagement but rather an elaboration of a cluster of philosophical problems that invested Macherey's thinking through the early 1960s, which persisted after 1968 and remain central today.

This is a pivotal and arguably prescient work. The questions it addresses speak not only to the historical legacy of Hegel in France but to persistent fault lines and potential points of convergence in contemporary social theory and political philosophy. These include questions about the role of the dialectic and the negative in the work of Negri and Althusser; questions about the politics of ontology and how we conceive of multiplicity, a point of contention between Deleuze and Badiou; and questions about the immanence of expression and the role of representation in the play of difference, a point of divergence between Deleuze and Derrida. *Hegel or Spinoza* offers us a clear understanding of the exact points of divergence of readings—and indeed often of misreadings—of Spinoza's *Ethics,* misreadings that undergird contemporary philosophical debates and their implications for how we envision societal struggle and social transformation.

The decision to reengage on the terrain of philosophy after the failure of political projects of the 1960s, then, was not a turn *away* from politics by Pierre Macherey toward a different object—the "consolation of philosophy"—but rather a reengagement of politics *through* philosophy.[3] As Macherey argues in a different context, "philosophy . . . is not before you as you imagine, but behind you, in that element of the always-already over which the veil of ignorance is usually drawn. . . . It is not a problem of not knowing enough philosophy but, in a very particular sense of the word 'know' which comprises a relation with non-knowledge, of knowing it already too well, in forms whose confusion needs to be unraveled, necessitating an intervention that will trace within them their lines of demarcation."[4]

What forms of knowledge and nonknowledge continue to haunt contemporary debates, and in what ways were they "known too well" in the aftermath of 1968 to precipitate the falling out of favor of Marx and Marxism and the recasting of Macherey along with the rest of Althusser's circle as "structuralist dinosaurs"? And what might we learn from the staging of this encounter between Hegel and Spinoza, in terms of both the specific points of application and the method of inquiry?

Macherey offers an answer to these questions, not only in *Hegel or Spinoza* but also in a series of articles addressing Hegel's prior uptake in France, an engagement that had solidified tendencies in Hegel that were also, not coincidentally, the points of Hegel's misreading of Spinoza. Read together, they offer us a fuller picture of the long shadow cast initially in Hegel's misinterpretation of Spinoza and amplified subsequently in the uptake of Hegel in France.

This is not to offer a reading of a "good" Spinoza set against a "bad" Hegel. To proceed in that way would be to suggest it would be possible to undertake a reading (or a writing) that was not tethered to the material conditions of its production and that certain texts might therefore operate entirely free of ideology.

Hegel or Spinoza is first of all an interrogation, with surgical precision, of the exact points of misreading of Spinoza by Hegel—an interrogation that attests, contra Hegel, to the immanent power of Spinoza's work. It begins by challenging the teleology of Hegel's project, a teleology that situates Spinoza's work in a progression within modern philosophy, in which Spinoza's work marks a crucial beginning, but one that, because of the nature of Spinoza's "arrested thought" one must "pass through," ending finally with Hegel's own corpus.

Macherey reveals the necessity of Hegel's misreading in the kernel of thought that is "indigestible" for Hegel, that makes the Spinozist system move in a way that Hegel cannot grasp, exposing the limited and situated truth of Hegel's perspective, one that reveals more about Hegel himself than his object of analysis. Thus, as Macherey remarks in his "Soutenance,"

> When Hegel reads Spinoza, which he does with great care, it is as if he were prevented by the appearance of his philosophical problematic from seeing—even before setting himself the question of understanding it—what Spinoza had actually been able to say: Hegel is then obliged to set up an imaginary form of thought, or that which is, at the very least, a product, indeed a figure of his own doctrine.[5]

Against Hegel's characterization of Spinoza's work as immobile, Macherey offers a reading of a lively alternative that upsets the comfortable historical progression of philosophical knowledge. Against Hegel's view of the geometric method of *Ethics* as a formalism precluding the movement of thought, Macherey offers evidence of a method that is only apparently geometric and Cartesian and instead expresses an immanent philosophy that is not subordinated to the guarantee of an a priori truth: in Spinoza's work truth emerges through exposition rather than being fixed at the outset as a set of formal principles.

Against Spinoza's supposedly immobile substance (which for Hegel lacks a subject and finds only degraded expression in its two attributes), Macherey finds in Spinoza's work a relation of substance and an infinite variety of attributes (of which we can know only two), neither set in dialectical opposition nor subordinated to substance but emerging simultaneously as the expression of substance rather than sequentially as its degradation.

And against Hegel's distillation of Spinoza's entire corpus to the misattributed phrase "all determination is negation," whereby the finitude of determinate beings can approach the infinite only via an endless (and impossible) mathematical aggregation, Macherey uncovers a misinterpretation of a geometric progression, which in fact demonstrates the infinite movement inherent in a bounded and finite object—a mobile expression of conatus, a purely positive essence that encounters the negative not as essence but as existence.

What was the significance of this pairing in *Hegel or Spinoza* at the time of its first appearance, when interest in Hegel was on the wane, or for our own time, when the overwhelming influence of Spinoza all but eclipses Hegel? *Hegel or Spinoza* discloses the operative "non-knowledges" that were active in the violent misreading of Macherey and Althusser's philosophical projects in the mid-1960s. These non-knowledges were arguably the effects of a long legacy of Hegel that haunted *that* present. And it can be read in relation to our own present—in relation to our own questions about the role of the negative (and the positive) in the politics of ontology and the ability to renew Marxism not as a science but as a theoretical practice and a philosophy.[6]

Hegel or Spinoza provides a clarity of interpretation around some of the more difficult aspects of Spinoza's thought that subtend contemporary debate around the nature of method and the politics of ontology. And it offers a way of renewing dialectical thought, a dialectic that certainly did not belong to Hegel and could never be found in Spinoza but emerges, as Macherey argues (in the second preface to *Hegel or Spinoza*), within a space that belongs properly to neither but is produced in the passage between the two.

The Spinozist Turn

To turn, or perhaps more properly re-turn, to Hegel as Macherey did in the late 1970s might be thought an unusual maneuver at the time. In the mid-1960s Hegel was "firmly on the intellectual agenda," a centrality secured in part, ironically, by the vociferous attack on Hegel by Althusser and his circle.[7] It was Spinoza who was notable for his absence at this time: before the mid-1960s, emerging Spinoza scholars in France by some accounts had little to turn to for guidance in a French tradition of Spinozist scholarship except the turn-of-the-century work of Delbos.[8] But by 1968, thanks largely to the works of Guéroult and Deleuze, Spinoza had made a "thunderous return"—shifted from the margins of discourse as an "anomaly or curiosity" to a "decisive key to understanding contemporary problems."[9] And by the mid-1970s, arguably the turn to Spinoza was well under way, although, as Read notes, the diversity of engagements with Spinoza's work renders the idea of a singular turn problematic.[10] It was Hegelianism (at least in explicit form) that was "on the wane," and the "3 Hs" (Hegel, Heidegger, and Husserl) had arguably been abandoned in favor of Marx, Nietzsche, and Freud. To return explicitly to Hegel in 1979—even if to "surpass" him—was in part to exhume a corpse, to demonstrate the ways in which Hegel continued to haunt philosophy. *Hegel or Spinoza* was a response to the long and still active legacy of what we might call (borrowing from Macherey) Hegel á la Française.

Hegel à la Française

As Michael Hardt remarks in *Gilles Deleuze: An Apprenticeship in Philosophy,* for the generation of Continental philosophers writing in the 1970s, explicit engagement with Hegel was not without its dangers. The issue was not simply to avoid Hegel and risk a mere repitition of "the Hegelian problematic" nor even "to make Hegel the negative foundation of philosophy," a difficult task in itself because "anti-Hegelianism, through a dialectical twist, becomes a position more Hegelian than ever."[11]

From the 1920s on, Hegel had constituted something of a lure in French thought, the subject of a second of Macherey's projects that might be read alongside *Hegel or Spinoza*: a series of articles that excavate the conceptual and ideological coordinates of Hegel's thought, divergent currents that surfaced and resurfaced from the 1920s through the 1950s and 1960s.

The extraordinariness of this event—the resurgent interest in Hegel's thinking in France of the 1920s and 1930s—can best be understood when contrasted with his uptake in the previous century. In the nineteenth century, Hegel was first used (or perhaps rather abused) in France by Victor Cousin in support of a state science and later by Vacherot as a bulwark for pantheism.[12] As Macherey notes, Cousin and Hegel had a shared political project and adversaries in common in the form of clerics and conservatives.[13] But the philosophical framework that Cousin developed was a "corrected, toned down version" bearing "only a formal resemblance to Hegel," a conception that had "no place for any kind of dialectic."[14]

In this reading, a position later elaborated by a rather "mediocre" and "inoffensive" translation by Bernard, the dialectic was reduced to the passage from a spontaneous form of reason whereby "the popular conscience of Caliban, infested with superstition, the stock and trade of the clergy," was corrected and clarified by its alternate pole: intellectual elites who were to exercise influence over civil society through a system of public education. In this formula, Cousin eviscerated the middle term of Hegel's dialectic of all negative attribution: "in Cousin's spirit there was never any doubt—the negative, was contestation, disorder and, in the end revolution, that is to say the system of sovereign intellect overwhelmed by the ignorant masses, in brief a return to confusion and popular violence to be avoided at all costs." It was this, Macherey argued, that was the "grounding reason (political in the last instance) for Hegel's expulsion from the cultural dispositif in France, condemned to the role of shadow."[15] And it was also the moment at which philosophy in France began to be "integrated into the functioning of the state and its apparatuses," a development that has characterized French philosophy to this day.[16]

In the 1920s, however, what surfaced was the Hegel of phenomenology rather than of science, the Hegel of Wahl, of unhappy consciousness; the Hegel of Kojève, whose dialectic of the master–slave relation took the form of anthropomorphized struggle; and finally

the Hegel of Hyppolite, whose provision of both translation and commentary allowed the French public, finally, to engage Hegel on their
own terms.[17]

In the aftermath of World War I in France, Hegel's *Phenomenology*
offered

> the vision of an active and creating human subject, a journeying
> subject empowered by the work of negation, serv[ing] as a source
> of hope during these years of personal and political crisis. Hegel
> provided a way to discern reason in the negative, to derive the
> transformative potential from every experience of defeat . . . the
> destruction of institutions and ways of life, the mass annihilation
> and sacrifice of human life.[18]

The subsequent Hegelian inflections of Marxist humanism in the
1950s and the distortion of Hegel in the service of a Marxist version of humanism, the "occultization" of Hegel, which Macherey
contended with in his own time, was therefore not a new event.[19]
Kojève's rendition of Hegel's *Phenomenology* supported an anthropomorphized dialectics of class struggle and vision of the end of history.
Here Hegel played a role not as a historical figure in philosophical
thought but as a "partner in a hermeneutical encounter," an encounter
dominated by Kojève's intercession, rather than Hegel's own work.[20]
As Macherey notes in *The Object of Literature*, "In each of his lectures
Kojève would read a few lines from the German text then supply a
commentary in the shape of a translation or a translation in the shape
of a commentary . . . a strange language that was neither quite French
nor quite German . . . Kojèvean . . . in which speculation and narrative
were constantly merged" (60).

Striking a responsive chord to the mal de siècle that followed World
War I, Kojève's courses on *Phenomenology of the Mind*, taught between
1933 and 1939, were a "pretext," less perhaps about Hegel than about
the development of a common language around affect and emotion,
centering on death, praxis, negativity, satisfaction, and wisdom (ibid.,
59–61). But Kojève's vision (presented in lectures later transcribed
by Queneau) was his own version of Hegel, authorizing a reading
that emptied the text of all movement. It evaded Hegel's idealism by

anthropomorphizing both class struggle and the dialectic, inverting the relationship between human desire and metaphysical order, with an atheist, anthropomorphic, and heroic notion of the human spirit at the center of dialectical struggle,[21] a move that merely inverted but did not resolve the idealist–materialist split. And it treated Hegel's own corpus as "the end of history" to the extent that his philosophy represented the ultimate synthesis and reconciliation of any contradiction.

As Macherey argued, Kojève's rendition of Hegel embodied a teleology in which Hegel himself represented the pinnacle of thought and the end of history (the search for wisdom recast as wisdom itself), a closed totality within which all human activity could be situated:

> Human reality has realized its full potential and has achieved the idea by giving it concrete incarnation. . . . After this nothing can happen which does not already figure in the total system that gives history its rational meaning. . . . There is a necessary relationship between the final form of this narration and its content . . . namely the idea that certain contemporary events represented the final realization of human destiny in a universal absolute empire. Kojève's original model was Napoleon. He was later replaced by Stalin.[22]

The ontological dualism on which Kojève founded his anthropology, which Kojève falsely attributed to the lineage of Hegelian thinking,[23] is arguably the same ontological dualism that Macherey later confronted in the French Communist Party (PCF) of the early 1960s.

Moreover, as Macherey later recounted, these lectures, attended by the likes of Bataille, Lacan, Breton, Weil, Merleau-Ponty, Aron, Klowoski, and others, were to have an impact "far beyond their immediate reception," speaking in turn to subsequent developments of "Marxism, psychoanalysis, phenomenology, surrealism and existentialism (yet to be born but already in gestation)."[24] And it was to reverberate more subtly in Lacan's use of dialectical syllogism.[25]

Kojève's highly edited version of Hegel—the "hallucinatory gloss" of his lecture–commentary on the master–slave relation in the 1930s, an imposed and impossible distortion on Hegel's original text—constituted one of the earliest variants of a Hegelian humanism.[26]

Substantively, the echo of Kojève's Hegel in its crude form might be read in the humanism of Marxism in the 1950s and 1960s. But it also haunted early renditions of Althusserian structuralism, whereby "theoretical humanism was displaced but in a way that left its form intact . . . still a spiritual whole even if it did not take the form of what Althusser called an expressive totality," a concept that Macherey distanced himself from early on in his work with Althusser.[27] It was Hyppolite's engagement of Hegel that provided the first opportunity for a properly indigenous reading in France.[28] Hyppolite focused on the "unhappy consciousness" in Hegel, extending and deepening a line of inquiry begun by Koyré and Wahl, and continued in the work of Sartre, Derrida, and even Lefebvre.[29] This particular inflection of Hegel resonated with the sentiment of the time, a sentiment that deepened in the French experience of, and need to grapple with, the fact of German occupation. As Simone de Beauvoir later remarked, "we turned to Hegel in 1945 at Hyppolite's urging. . . . We had discovered the reality and the weight of history, now we were wondering about its meaning."[30]

The Cercle d'Ulm and the PCF

Although it is clear that Hegel haunted a range of intellectual projects that continued after World War II, in the late 1950s and early 1960s Macherey's most immediate confrontation with the legacy of his thinking was perhaps in relation to the PCF.

From the 1950s through the 1960s, the intellectual left in France (aided in part by the emergence of French Maoism) expressed a growing dismay over the atrocities of the Stalinist regime and dissatisfaction with the crass empiricism of Stalin's dialectical materialism, all forming the basis of diverse critiques of the PCF, which, despite this dissatisfaction, continued to be aligned with Moscow. We might say that Hegel's ghost appeared here first in the form of a teleological reading of class struggle in the PCF's early endorsement of Stalin and then in the very humanism that was invoked in the act of his exorcism.

This appeal to humanism—the attempt to present "Marxism with a human face"—was spearheaded by Semprun, Garaudy, and others in a continued alignment with the Soviets. As Perry Anderson writes, "[r]ebels of 1956 appealed to the humanism of young Marx against

Stalinism. . . . Debates in post-56 Europe largely revolved around the antithesis Stalin/Young Marx . . . the values of humanism were extolled from the balconies of the French Politbureau and its major ideologue, Garaudy, while in the USSR Kruschev's new party program for the CPSU declared 'everything for Man.'"[31]

As early as 1953, Althusser had sought to combat the "spectre of Hegel" in Marx's works and the theoretical poverty of the PCF in order to further the scientific basis of materialism, a historical materialism.[32] In terms of political practice this took the form of an internal debate within the PCF and a larger discussion among philosophers on the left. Along with the students of the Cercle d'Ulm, he sought to develop a scientific basis of, and a theoretical antihumanism for, Marxism. For those who chose this path, it was Hegel and Feuerbach and their residual influence on Marx, particularly the early Marx, that were seen to act as the ideological bulwark for the persistence of humanism, teleology, and the counterposing of idealism and materialism, theory and practice, philosophy and politics.

The broad contours of the project and Macherey's seminal role within it will be well known to this readership.[33] Macherey came to the École in 1958 and in the early 1960s, together with Balibar and Regnault,[34] he approached Althusser to read the early works of Marx. This collaboration culminated in *For Marx* and *Reading Capital*. Although this was a decidedly philosophical project, there were political consequences to their efforts, not only in the increasingly strained relationship of the students to the Union des Étudiants Communistes, the student wing of the PCF, but in the series of reprimands that Althusser and students of the Cercle d'Ulm endured for their rejection of humanism.[35] These reprimands emanated from within the circles of communist philosophers, in a conference at Choisy-le-Roi—directed by largely by Garaudy at an absent Althusser and vociferously contested by Macherey—and more formal reprimands within the PCF itself.[36]

This is not to say that one can treat this enterprise and its participants as an undifferentiated whole.[37] As Montag notes, early on Macherey expressed some discomfort with Althusser's concept of a structured whole, and the early influence of Macherey's own Spinozist framework can be found in theses exchanges.[38]

For Macherey the struggle between humanism and antihumanism

took less the form of a debate that "would need at the very least to share terms in common" than a rupture, expressed not only between humanism as an ideology ("theoretically a false problem, because it is badly posed") and antihumanism as a science, but also between two very different conceptions of practice, conceptions that "slide over each other . . . belonging to different, incompatible universes."[39]

In the years after 1968, reactions to the antihumanist project, in the form of anti-antihumanism, gathered force. The British variant was launched as an attack against the presumed formalist and functionalist application of the dialectic itself, culminating in the vitriolic exchanges between Louis Althusser and E. P. Thompson through the 1970s, which characterized and caricatured for the Anglo-American world the reaction against French so-called structuralism. Only one year before the publication of *Hegel ou Spinoza,* Thompson accused so-called structuralists of fitting the dialectic with a gown fashioned from the cloth of over-determination, one to fit so tightly that she could not move and declared "that the understanding of dialectics can only be advanced if an absolute embargo is placed on the mention of Hegel's name."[40]

A Dialectics of Encounter

In *Hegel or Spinoza,* Macherey addresses Hegel's own philosophical encounter with the work of Spinoza in specific points of application, points that arguably had formed the basis for amplification distortions of Hegel's framework in the history of successive engagements of Hegel in French thought and that simultaneously occluded the possibilities of thinking otherwise—that is, of grasping the productive possibilities of Spinoza. But it also produces something more.

This is not the sanitized dialectic of Cousin in which all contestation and disorder have been eviscerated, nor the anthropomorphized and teleological dialectic of Kojève, nor the Hegelian inheritance of the dialectic of Marx, but a different kind of dialectical engagement. Macherey's revisioned Marxian dialectic, purged of its Hegelian inheritance, is posed as a problem at the end of the text, but its form is to be found in the underlying structure of the text itself, in the encounter Macherey organizes between Hegel and Spinoza, a dialectic rendered from a Spinozist lens.

Rather than simply authorizing a particular reading, a "good" Spinoza against a "bad" Hegel, *Hegel or Spinoza* initiates an encounter that produces something new: an understanding that is proper to neither but shared by both, a common truth that emerges from this encounter, existing "in the interval that separates them." Neither Hegel nor Spinoza is cast strictly as the negative of the other; each is read in terms of his own adequate truth. What is inadequate in Hegel is his *necessary* misreading of Spinoza, a reading that situates Spinoza from Hegel's point of view, that separates Spinoza's philosophy from what it can do, the adequate truth that is Spinoza. But what becomes activated in the encounter is a dialectic that could never be found in Spinoza alone.

What becomes active in *Hegel or Spinoza* is a "material dialectic that does not presuppose its accomplishment in its initial conditions through the means of a necessarily ideal teleology," nor, one might add, within a presupposed subject. It is rather a dialectic effected in the encounter, an unscripted space that emerges between the two systems of thought. The possibilities this dialectic offers for rethinking our praxis—the questions it allows us to ask and the new problems it invites us to think in relation to the creation of a common space, not solely in philosophy but also in relation to a social field that is increasingly fragmented—surely speaks to the most pervasive political challenges of our time.

Translator's Note and Acknowledgments

AS MACHEREY himself argues,

> The *word* itself can change as the same time as it displaces the
> concept, and this labour of language on itself, perhaps precedes,
> in fact definitely aids the mutation of meaning. . . . This plasticity
> of words, this almost "spontaneous" power they possess to move
> in order to welcome a new concept in advance, obviously finds
> its main reason in the image the concept conceals in itself only to
> expose it in the crucial moments of the history of ideas. The study
> of the *variations of language* leads, then, to a meditation about the
> function of the *imagination*.[1]

In this instance the different trajectories of thought engendered by
French and English translations laid this issue bare—although the
choice here was clear—to follow the meanings produced in the French
text and Macherey's subsequent labor upon them.

In some cases the gap between English and French interpretations
of Hegel's corpus is quite large. For instance, the characterization of
not yet and *already* that Hegel makes of Spinoza's work, key to Macherey's analysis and closer to the German, occurs several times in the
French rendition of Hegel's work, as translated by Labarriere and
Jankélévitch, but is not found at all in the English version by Wallace,
where it is translated simply as *falling short,* which captures none of the
sense of an anticipated framework to come, suggested but not fully
realized in Spinoza's text. Here the choice was obvious: while consult-
ing these English texts to maintain familiarity for an English audience, I
stayed as close as possible to a direct translation of the French because
it formed the basis of Macherey's analysis and was often closer to the
original. I have also followed Macherey's choice in the translation of

xix

Begriff as *concept* rather than *notion,* in order to remain true to his text. And the French translation of Hegel's *Logic* by Labarriere presented some challenges, as it appears to reference the edition revised in 1832 (when compared with the English translation by di Giovanni). Here at Pierre Macherey's request I reverted wherever possible to the best English translation. Where the text was close to unrevised editions, I consulted Miller and Wallace or, where possible, the comparable passages in di Giovanni's translation, and in a few instances I simply translated directly from the French.

But in other cases the choice was more difficult, particularly when meanings and emphases have wandered over time from the original or perhaps, to put it more adequately, the entire problematic that emerges in the attempts to characterize the history of philosophy echo in the act of translation itself. Here the choice of words in itself raises questions about the place that the translated text will invoke in the original context, as a bridge between two discursive trajectories, and as comparisons of French and English. In some cases the use of a particular word might invoke a not-yet-existing discourse or distinction, such as the distinction between *pouvoir* and *puissance* in the work of Spinoza.

More challenging are questions of double entendre and nuance. For instance, *Meprise,* a word that crops up often in characterizing Hegel's assessment of Spinoza's thought, translates as both *misunderstanding* and *mistrust.* In such cases I have sometimes included an adjective to capture this double meaning when an equivalent word is not available in English. In particular, where the French is in the active voice I have chosen this over a more conventional passive voice in English, particularly in discussions about cause in itself.

There are also nuanced distinctions that do not always translate: *emporter* and *transporter* both mean *carry,* but one suggests an inner dynamic and the other an external cause, a significant distinction in Macherey's discussion of the concept of cause. Here I have moved from direct translation to something that better invokes intention, rendering them as *propel* and *compel* to try to capture this distinction. In instances where I thought there might be several choices of English, which would inflect the translation in a variety of productive ways, or where I have deviated from a standard practice in the text (e.g., translating *puissance* as *power* instead of as *capacity*), I have included the French in square brackets. I have also included English clarifications in square brackets where the use of the demonstrative pronoun alone might introduce ambiguity into the English text. Any text in parentheses with Latin or German equivalents appeared in Macherey's original work. In all cases I have attempted to stay closer to the meaning in the French text rather than resort to conventions within English. Although this has sometimes stretched convention, my preference has been to avoid domesticating the text in favor of better capturing the distinctions in Macherey's argument.

I WANT ESPECIALLY TO THANK Warren Montag for his enthusiastic support of the project, from initial encouragement and generous response to my many questions and later feedback on drafts; Ted Stolze for providing feedback on points of translation and allowing generous consultation on his previous translation of "The Problem of Attributes," which appeared in *In a Materialist Way*; Hasana Sharp for her reading of an early draft; Caroline Desbiens and Annie Ferrat for occasional consultation on particularly puzzling idioms; and two research assistants, Simran Karir and Meaghan Morris, for tireless tracking down of secondary sources; as well as Pierre Macherey himself for his willingness to respond to my queries from across the water. I also thank the University of Minnesota Press, particularly director Douglas Armato and editorial assistant Danielle Kasprzak, for their dedication to the project and tirelessness in replying to my many questions. Any faults in this book remain mine.

HEGEL OR SPINOZA

Preface to the Second Edition

TO DEVOTE A STUDY to the relationship of two major and historic philosophers such as Spinoza and Hegel is to be confronted indisputably, beyond the limits of a formal comparison (which is both academic in its undertaking and indifferent to its content), with certain stakes that are fundamental to the approach [*demarche*] to philosophy in general.

Spinoza and *Hegel*: these expressions indicate for us, first of all, two systems of thought that have value in and of themselves and are connected to the personal existence of their authors, which immediately name them, that is, at the same time designate them and sign them. Moreover, if you take the enterprise of philosophical thought seriously at all, you must grant it a relative autonomy with respect to such procedures of identification, which under the pretext of singularizing them actually disperses them, and tendentially make them disappear in an indistinct plurality of doctrines by privileging certain speculative "points," which constitute concrete positions, incarnated in the empirical reality of systems of authors. But to strip them of the link of speculative engagement [*jeu*] between individual discourses that traverse them is, at the same time, to risk deadening the enterprise of thought and submitting it to an abstract and atemporal evaluation, whose universality in the end risks an existence without content. This is why it is not possible to extract this enterprise entirely from its doctrinal origins; the work of philosophical reflection would then be transformed into a "putting in perspective," which would assign the position of philosophers, to the extent that these create the conditions of their elaboration, their expression, and even their interpretation. The truth of philosophy is as much in Spinoza as it must also be in Hegel; that is, it is not entirely in one or the other but somewhere between the two, in the passage that is effected between one and the other. To say this somewhat differently, philosophy is something that moves, that passes, and that takes place [*qui passe, et qui se passe*], in a place where the connection between thoughts gestates, which, in the works themselves, escapes the specific historical conditions of their authors' undertakings, and the understanding of this process diminishes the interest we might extend to their systematic intentions, because this process grasps them dynamically in the anonymous movement of a sort of collective project, appropriating a given philosophy to the ensemble of philosophy and not only to one or another among them.

When two systems of thought as well described as those of Spinoza and Hegel react to one another, that is, at the same time one against the other and one with the other, something must emerge, which coming from both belongs properly to neither but rather to the interval that separates them, constituted as their common truth.

And yet, in the exact case of these two philosophies, if their confrontation seems particularly fertile, it is because it is not an intellectually neutral encounter between two philosophies that confront each other while remaining external to one another; it is rather a reciprocal and ultimate test, which while it causes them to speak to each other opens up each system within itself and exposes each to an internal challenge, which gives rise to the recognition of its limits. Thus we cannot escape this double existence: to read Spinoza in Hegel and to read Hegel in Spinoza, in the manner of two mirrors that reflect, respectively, their images.

The expression "Hegel or Spinoza"—used here to express this confrontation—carries a semantic ambiguity that suits it, if not to explicate [*lever*] this ambiguity, at least to emphasize it, the better to characterize it. In the French language the use of the conjunction *or* merges two forms of evaluation that other languages distinguish from each other; it is thus that this *or* of the French offers an indistinct translation of *vel* and *aut* of Latin, which expresses things that are apparently contrary to one another. *"Aut . . . aut"* is the expression of opposition and exclusion: it is (either) one or the other but not the two at the same time. If "Hegel or Spinoza" were expressed in this way, *"aut* Hegel *aut* Spinoza," that is, either Hegel on one hand or Spinoza on the other, this would lead us to present them as two irreducible forms of thought, constituting the terms of a choice that it would not be possible to leave suspended indefinitely. And yet, in privileging an order of names that reverses the chronological succession, in order to signal the incontrovertible character of an alternative, in making

Spinoza come after Hegel and not before him, we seem to be engaged immediately in such a choice, because we have by this fact implicitly rejected the evolutionary logic that constitutes the heart of the Hegelian system, according to which that which comes after necessarily engulfs and includes that which, in coming before it, can only act in anticipation or as a preparation. Thus we have inverted the perspective that demands the Hegelian reading of Spinoza by subordinating it to that of a (necessarily hypothetical) Spinozist reading of Hegel, whose speculative power from that moment appears to transport it. Beyond a reciprocal consideration of systems, which makes them depend on this relationship, this game of "either–or" appears thus to lead, more or less dogmatically, to a resolution of the crisis initiated by their confrontation, and by choosing to place Spinoza as an alternative to Hegel, and not the inverse, it seems that we must look on the side of the former for the conditions of this resolution, through a decision whose necessity remains thus to be established and justified.

But we must not forget that "Hegel or Spinoza" can also be translated as "Hegel *vel (sive)* Spinoza," which apparently signifies the opposite. The *or* here is an expression of identity and equivalence. It is the one we find in the well-known expression so often attributed to Spinoza, although he never wrote it in exactly this form, *Deus sive natura*, in which "God" and "nature" are presented as two different forms but also indifferent, for one and the same thing. Are not *Hegel* and *Spinoza* also equally two names for the same thing, which would be this thing they designate indistinctly? For this question, we would do well to conserve the interrogative character for as long as possible, without pretense that we might resolve it definitively. It is this question, from start to finish, that sustains the work we will read. Following the spirit of this interrogation, it is evident that if it is unavoidable to read Spinoza and Hegel in opposition to one another—this is the "*aut . . . aut*" side of the *or*—it is also no less necessary to think about them, one with the other, as if they would lend their elements or parts to a single unique discourse, in the interior of which their respective positions would be indistinguishable, because their meaning could be explained only in their interaction, and here it is the *sive* side of the *or* that we would bring to light.

The debate that arises between these two forms of thought has no necessity and is of no significance if these two forms do not partake of a single truth, whose process belongs neither to one nor to the other, because it is produced at the intersection of their respective journeys. This suspended truth, emerging from contestation and conflict, by this act no longer has the value of an arrested thought; it is rather that of a critique and a proof whose object is philosophy itself, as it expands across the ensemble of its own history, in the problematic element of difference and debate.

—Pierre Macherey
June 1990

The Alternative

On July 30, 1816, the Pro-rector of the University of Heidelberg wrote to Hegel, then principal of the Gymnasium of Nuremberg, to offer him a chair as tenured professor. He explained his offer in the following manner: "Heidelberg, for the first time since the founding of the university, will have a philosopher—Spinoza received a call from Heidelberg, but in vain as you undoubtedly know." Actually, we are familiar with the letter of March 30, 1673, "to the very illustrious and very distinguished Dr. Louis Fabritius, professor of the Academy of Heidelberg and advisor of the Elector Palatine" in which Spinoza declined the invitation that would have enabled him to occupy the professorial chair because he feared that by dedicating himself to the education of youth, he would have to renounce his personal philosophical projects; above all, he feared that his freedom as a philosopher would be limited by the need to respect the established laws and precepts of religion. His clearly motivated refusal concluded in this manner: "what stops me is not at all the desire for a better fortune, but the love of my tranquility which I believe I must preserve in some way, by absenting myself from public lessons." Hegel was aware of this incident, which he related as follows in his *Lectures on the History of Philosophy*: "Spinoza (in his published letters) very wisely declined this offer, however, because 'he did not know within what limits his philosophical liberty would have to be constrained in order that it would not appear to disturb officially established religion.'"[1]

On August 6, 1816, Hegel responded to the Pro-rector with zeal: "out of the love of academic studies" he accepted his proposition even though other opportunities were open to him from the University of Berlin. He asked only that their offer to him be augmented, that they provide him with free lodging, and that the costs of his moving be reimbursed. A little later, on August 20, when these material questions had been dealt with to his satisfaction, Hegel returned to his nomination to "express his gratitude, in part for the interest that [the

Pro-rector] had taken in his cause, and in part for the sympathy he showed for the state of philosophy in Germany and other universities." He added, "Equally pleasant to me is the kindness with which you view both my past works—and more—the benefaction of your hopes for my activities in the university. In no other science, in effect, is one as solitary as in philosophy, and I sincerely long for a livelier circle of activity. I can say that this is the greatest desire of my life. I likewise feel all too acutely how unfavorable the lack of living exchange has been for my works thus far." Hegel remained in Heidelberg for one year, where he simultaneously composed and taught his *Encyclopedia of Philosophical Sciences*. In 1817 he finally accepted the post he had so desired at the University of Berlin.

Beyond what these circumstances suggest anecdotally, something significant is already apparent. In this history, Hegelians maintain above all that Hegel occupied the place that Spinoza had left vacant, through this "replacement" filling a task that the other was not able or did not want to complete. Nothing can escape its own time: the moment had not come for Spinoza, when the real philosophy would make itself publicly known. Others whom we might well call Spinozist, on the contrary, see a point of divergence here, an irreducible separation, if not between two systems at least between two conceptions, that is, two practices, of philosophy.

In the Hegelian system an argument is constructed and evolves while its author, with great good fortune, navigates the stages of a university career (from private instructor at the University of Berlin, passing through all intermediate steps). One is reflected in the other, reciprocally, and gives it its truth; is he not rightly destined, in this hierarchical organization, to be acclaimed within the body of an academic institution? Jacques Derrida expresses it very well: "Hegel does not conceive of the school as the consequence or image of a system, as its *pars totalis*: the system is, itself, an immense school, the thorough-going auto-encyclopedia of the Absolute Spirit in Absolute Knowledge. And a school which one does not leave, a mandatory instruction as well: that mandates itself, since its necessity can no longer come from outside."[2]

In contrast, even though it would become well known for giving political concerns a proper place in philosophical speculation (see not only the *Treatise* but also *Ethics,* a key text), the Spinozist doctrine would have found such an official rendition profoundly repugnant. This doctrine reveals the point of view of a recluse, a reprobate, a rebel, transmitted by word of mouth. To be acclaimed, the doctrine risks entering into a contradiction with itself by accepting a place in this mechanism of intellectual and material oppression, which subordinates everything to the point of view of the imagination. Spinoza's philosophy vanquishes fear and ignores obedience; it cannot therefore be taught publicly. The philosophy of Hegel is instructed from on high to pupils below; Spinoza's philosophy is transmitted to disciples in an egalitarian manner. Here a difference emerges that we must take seriously.

Nevertheless, this is a common ground that connects Spinoza and Hegel, because an obvious familiarity exists between them. We cannot read Spinoza today without thinking about Hegel, perhaps because between Spinoza and us, there is Hegel, who intervenes or intercedes. Hegel himself never stopped thinking about Spinoza, or rather thinking him, in order to digest him, to absorb him, as an element dominated by his own system. But the fact that Hegel never ceased to return to the problem that was posed for him by Spinoza's philosophy indicates that he found something there that was indigestible, a resistance he continually needed to confront anew. Everything transpired as if Spinoza occupied a limit-position in relation to Hegelian discourse, which he rejected even at the moment of its inclusion.

This is why the task of comparing the philosophies of Spinoza and Hegel is fundamentally deceptive. In effect, it is necessary to understand what such a comparison is about; the systems, that is, discourses organized formally according to an internal principle of coherence, between which we could attempt to establish a correspondence, would be interpreted as a relationship of lineage, or a difference, which excludes all possibility of understanding one through the other. Thus, in an annex to his monumental study of Spinoza analyzing Hegel's interpretation of Spinozism, Guéroult concludes there is a radical "misrecognition" founded on a "confabulation": those who adopt Hegel's interpretation "do no more than project into Spinoza's doctrine an entire world of concepts conceived elsewhere and with no relationship to it."[3] As we will show in a detailed study of the texts

Hegel devotes to Spinoza, it is difficult not to credit Guéroult with this at least: the search for a supposed homogeneity, resemblance, or evolutionary relationship between the two philosophies, if not absolutely fated to fail, leads to uninteresting results. Quite simply, it tends to transform the two doctrines into a common model, which authentically represents neither one nor the other.

But if we must go against the inclination of more obvious comparisons that proceed by analogy and reject the temptation to look for the similitude of a global common meaning between Spinoza and Hegel (through which the commonality or the convergence of the two systems of thought would manifest itself), it would be no less absurd to decree that this is a case of two forms of philosophical reflection that are radically exterior to one another and restore them to their independence. In effect, it is incontestable that Hegel and Spinoza met one another, even if their encounter on Hegel's part took the form of an extraordinary misunderstanding. If Spinoza and Hegel do not travel the same path, together or one behind the other, it remains a fact that their paths crossed, connecting at certain moments in order to separate in strongly opposing directions. From this point of view, rather than compare the systems—an attempt doomed to failure or to too easy success—it might be significant to look for singular points of intersection between these two philosophies. It is these that explain the strange feeling of familiarity all Hegelian readers of Spinoza experience, as do all Spinozist readers of Hegel.

In his *Essays in Self-Criticism*, Althusser talks of "the repetition of Hegel anticipated by Spinoza."[4] Let us list a few points justifying this assertion: the refusal of a relativist conception of knowledge and the idea that there is, within reason, something of the absolute that connects it [*l'apparente*] to the real; the discovery of the formal character of all finite representation, dedicated to abstraction; the critique of the "bad infinite"; and the idea that knowledge is a real process that carries within itself the conditions of its objectivity. On all these points, even if they reflect on them using very different conceptual elements, even if they derive opposing consequences from them, evidently Spinoza and Hegel have something in common that distinguishes them from everyone else. This rapprochement must be explained.

We will address this question by applying ourselves to the reading that Hegel himself derives from Spinoza. This reading is very instructive, not because it would manifest the truth of Spinozism, finally laid bare by Hegel, but on the contrary because it is based on a formidable misreading; everything transpires as if Hegel were given the means to construct an interpretation of Spinozism that permits him to ignore its essential lesson, insofar as this bears exactly on something related to his own system. This interpretation appears as a sort of obstinate defense, set against a reasoning that destabilizes Hegelian philosophy itself. This produces a paradoxical effect: Hegel is never so close to Spinoza as in the moments when he distances himself from him, because this refusal has the value of a symptom and indicates the obstinate presence of a common object, if not a common project, that links these two philosophers inseparably without conflating them.

To take into account this conflictual relationship is to depart from a formalist conception of the history of philosophy, which suppresses all historicity within itself, segmenting it into irreducible and arbitrary unities, whose dispersal becomes ever more the object of descriptive commentary; moreover, this is more exhaustive than if it immediately contained itself within the limits of the internal coherence of a system, eliminating all interrogation of a historical position. The significance of this dissipation is all the more [*tout au plus*] aesthetic, to the extent that it makes doctrines into works of art. Against this, we must come to think a certain form of unity, a link, between these diverse philosophies: the entire question is to know whether this is possible without falling back into the confusionism, which purely and simply identifies different philosophies within the fiction of a common truth.

To simplify, we could say that this problem is that of the dialectic. But it would be absurd to discover in Spinoza a rough draft or promise of a dialectic that is manifestly absent in his work. Nevertheless, this does not prevent us from beginning with Spinoza ourselves to be able to think of the dialectic anew, that is, to ask it these questions that Hegel rejected from his own system because they were unbearable for him. In the mirror of Spinozism, without a doubt Hegelian discourse brings into view its own limitations, or even its internal contradiction. Spinoza in Hegel: this does not imply that it is necessary to read *Ethics* as the failed beginning of *Logic,* as Hegel reads it himself, but that it is necessary to search for the conflictual unity between these two philosophies, which explains the astounding phenomenon of a simultaneous mistrust and recognition [*méconnaissance* and *reconnaissance*], which links them by opposing them to each other. Hegel or Spinoza: it is a unity that divides itself in two.

We say "Hegel or Spinoza," and not the inverse, because it is Spinoza who constitutes the true alternative to Hegelian philosophy. Therefore, the discussion we will undertake has more than one objective. It will not only make the limits of the Hegelian system apparent, a system whose universality is necessarily historical; it will allow us at the same time to extricate ourselves from the evolutionary conception of the history of philosophy, which is also the heritage of Hegelianism. According to this conception, Hegel proposed himself as the only possible alternative to Spinozism, the forerunner that ceded its place to that which came afterwards, in this movement of ascension that comes ever closer to the spirit itself. But here we would like to subvert the potency of this unitary and progressive interpretation of the history of philosophy, which is only apparently dialectical.

According to Hegel, Spinoza's thought is not yet dialectical enough. And what if it were too much—or at least, if it were so in a way that was unacceptable to Hegel? The denial of this dialectic—let us say, to move ahead quickly, of a dialectic without teleology—toward which Hegel proceeds via the intermediary of Spinoza is his way of addressing an insurmountable obstacle in the development of his own thought: that of a discourse that we must not say is *not yet* Hegelian but is so *no longer*. And it is here that the evolutionist presentation of the history of philosophy lies in ruins: because Spinoza himself also refutes Hegel, objectively.

⇒ 1 ⇐

Hegel Reads Spinoza

The Point of View of Substance

For Hegel, everything begins with the realization that there is something exceptional and inescapable in Spinoza's philosophy. "Spinoza constitutes such a crucial point for modern philosophy that we might say in effect that there is a choice between Spinozism and no philosophy at all *(du hast entweder den Spinozismus oder keine Philosophie)*."[1] It is necessary to "pass through" Spinoza, because it is in his philosophy that the essential relationship between thought and the absolute is developed, the only point of view from which reality in its entirety is revealed and in which it appears that reason has nothing outside itself but contains everything within it. Thus all philosophy, all of philosophy, becomes possible.

For Hegel, therefore, Spinoza occupies the position of a precursor: something begins with him. But he is not just a precursor: what begins in him does not end there, in the manner of an arrested thought, which is prevented from the possibility of achieving an objective to which it nevertheless aspires. This is why Hegel discovers in Spinoza's work all the characteristics of an aborted project, hindered by insurmountable difficulties that it engenders by itself in its own development. This fundamental but broken knowledge therefore has no significance except a historical one: in the entire body of philosophy, Spinoza occupies a very particular position, from which the absolute is perceived but grasped restrictively as a substance. To some extent, we acknowledge Spinoza and his effort to think the absolute, but the historical limits of this thinking make it impossible to go further, in the anticipation of a final point of view, where Hegel is already situated and from which he interprets all previous philosophies retrospectively.

This analysis is illustrated by an altogether characteristic expression that arises whenever Hegel speaks of Spinoza. For example, in book I of *Logic*, "With Spinoza, substance and its absolute unity takes the form of an inert unity, of a rigidity in which one does *not yet* find the concept of a negative unity of self, a subjectivity."[2] Or again, in paragraph 50 of *Logic* in the *Encyclopedia*, "Substance according to Spinoza is *not yet* absolute spirit." And in the chapter of *Lectures on the History of Philosophy* dedicated to Spinoza, "Absolute substance is the true, but it is *not yet* the true in its entirety." Under this very particular modality of an "already" that is also "not yet," proper to all anticipation, Spinoza frees himself from the foundation of the entire history of philosophy, whose progression he underscores by bringing it to a standstill.

In addition, because in the introduction of the third book of *Logic*, "Concerning the Concept in General," Hegel unveils the conditions that allow him to interpret philosophical doctrines and to explain their concrete significance, he could do no better than return to the example of Spinoza: "the only possible refutation of Spinozism must therefore consist, in the first place, in recognizing its standpoint as essential and necessary and then secondly by elevating that standpoint to a higher level."[3]

To take up a well-known formula in the preface of *Phenomenology*, this point of view is that of substance, insofar as this is "not yet" subject: "substance is an essential stage in the evolution of the Idea, not however the Idea itself, not the absolute Idea, but the Idea in the still limited form of necessity."[4]

Spinoza's oeuvre is significant because it tends toward something that it does not achieve: to master its meaning is to follow this tendency beyond the limits that impede it, that is, to surpass it by resolving its internal contradiction.

To achieve this, there must be a change in viewpoint, located in the view of an absolute that is not only substance but also subject. And yet this passage from one point of view to another depends on historical conditions: history is an irresistible and irreversible process that transforms points of view not only in the sense of their gradual expansion but also in the real movement of their decomposition, followed by their reconstruction on new foundations: thus one "elevates oneself" continuously to a superior point of view. It could even be said that Spinoza was Hegelian without knowing it, and thus incompletely, whereas Hegel would be a Spinozist conscious of the limits of this singular point of view, from which he knew how to extricate himself once and for all, locating himself in the point of view of the universal.

This is why Hegel's interpretation of Spinozism does not lead him back to the quest for a fully realized meaning. If there is a "truth" to the doctrine (which makes all attempts at external refutation of this doctrine laughable because such a refutation arbitrarily opposes an independent point of view to its own viewpoint), this truth is relative to a very particular situation that confines Spinoza within the whole process of the history of philosophy, and this truth cannot be detached from it. Grasped from the inside, in this tension and limitation that it imposes on itself, this point of view is for itself simultaneously its own justification and refutation: if it is returned to its internal movement, it is evident that it destroys itself in the process of its own construction and by these same means because this movement transports it outside itself. It is therefore not a question for Hegel to "return" to Spinoza to discover, there, the abstract form of a complete, coherent, and autonomous truth; on the contrary, it is necessary to make this immanent transformation manifest, this "passage" that already compels this system toward another system and incites us to read it as the draft or outline of a new and pending meaning, which has not yet encountered its conditions of realization. In this manner, the Hegelian reading of Spinoza is to a certain extent doubled: it searches within the doctrine for the signs of a truth that announces itself, and at the same time it discovers the real form of its absence, the obstacles that block its manifestation and that oblige us to talk about it only as a lack.

To understand Spinozism is thus first to identify the contradiction on which it is founded. As we will see, this contradiction is manifest immediately. We have said that the profound truth of Spinozism consists in his effort to think the absolute. Even if, in the history of philosophy, this problem doesn't begin with him—there are precedents that we will discuss—he establishes it for the first time as the object of development and an attempt at a systematic resolution. With Spinoza there is an orientation toward an absolute understanding, and what it corresponds to [*et ce qui le représente*], according to Hegel, is the concept of *causa sui*, which gives the entire doctrine its rational foundation: "the first of Spinoza's definitions is that of *causa sui*, conceptualized as this [*ce*] 'cujus essentia involvit existentiam' . . . the inseparability of the concept from being is the main point and fundamental hypothesis in his system."[5]

In effect, with the *causa sui* an identity is immediately posed between what is and what is understood [*conçu*] between being and thought, which is for Hegel the condition of an absolute thought that has nothing outside itself and that consequently develops itself within an immanent and universal reflection. Returning to these definitions in his historical remarks in book II of *Logic*, dedicated to Spinoza, Hegel talks of these concepts that are so "profound and correct."[6] And, more precisely still, he says, "If Spinoza had been more attentive in developing that which is contained in the *causa sui*, its substance would not have been rigid and unworkable *(das Starre)*."[7] Thus the specific contradiction of Spinozism appears immediately: his first concept contains within it the promise and the failure of a truth, for which he provides only one point of view, in an incomplete understanding.

Before making explicit what, according to Hegel, is lacking in the concept of *causa sui* and prevents it from overcoming its own limitations, we can immediately make a comment that clarifies the style of this interpretation and reveals the gap in which it immediately positions itself, in relation to the doctrine it works on. First of all we can show, as Guéroult does, that the concept of *causa sui* does not really have an initial foundational value for Spinoza: it does not represent a kind of first truth, a principle in the Cartesian sense, from which the entire system can be developed, as if from the starting point of a germ of truth. The *causa sui* is a property of substance and is explained through it [*et s'explique par elle*]. But there is no question, for Spinoza at least, of defining a thing (whatever it is) by its property: to proceed this way is to fall into serious confusion, subordinating the essence of God to his capacity, which is the key to all finalist theologies that rely on the imagination. It is therefore inadequately and as a matter of convenience that we restore substance to the *causa sui* because, on the contrary, the concept of the latter does not truly clarify itself except by way of substance: "si res in se sit, sive, *ut vulgo dicitur,* causa sui" *(De intellectus emendatione)*. It is thus only in a manner of speaking that substance is assimilated to the *causa sui*.[8]

But it is possible to go further still: what Hegel presupposes here is less that the *causa sui* is the fundamental concept of Spinozism, which already adds to the controversy, as we will see, than the fact that Spinozism admits a first concept from which it proceeds. This signifies that the enterprise of an absolute understanding that Spinoza undertakes develops by way of an absolute beginning and that this is also the real point of departure of his interpretation. It is not astonishing, then, that Hegel himself would be engaged in the enterprise of a critique of Spinozism: one of the crucial ideas of his own system is, in effect, that absolute understanding does not begin, or rather that it cannot begin absolutely; its infinity reveals itself exactly in this impossibility of a first beginning that is also a true beginning or a beginning of the true. So, whatever the actual truth of the concept of *causa sui* (which "resides in it," to take up the terms of Hegel), the very fact that he gives a beginning to Spinoza's system is sufficient to mark the limitation of this system.

Here we can begin to be astonished: does Hegel ignore that this aporia of beginning—which sets his *Logic* in motion, this impossibility of grounding the infinite process of knowledge in a first truth which in itself as principle or foundation—is also an essential lesson of Spinozism, the principal objection that he himself opposes to the philosophy of Descartes? In such a sense that it is only "ut vulgo dicitur," "so to speak," the geometric exposition of the *Ethics* "begins" with definitions, which for that matter do not have an effective sense, except at the moment when they function in demonstrations or they really produce the effects of truth: Spinozist thinking precisely does not have this rigidity of a construction relying on a base and pushing its analytic to a end point, which would find itself thus limited between a beginning and an end. It does not obey the model of the order of the reasons.

But what is surprising here is less that Hegel has misunderstood an important aspect of Spinozism—everyone can make mistakes, even Hegel, who pretends to be able to escape this common condition—than the unexpected content of this error. What Hegel has not seen in Spinoza is this new truth, which he claims himself to discover and which he uses to guarantee the final form of his philosophy and the success of its ultimate realization. Hegel thus ignores in Spinoza that which he is better placed than anyone to recognize, because he thought of it himself: it could be said that he proceeds from the denial of that which might be Hegelian in Spinoza, or at least that he does not seek to exorcise his own Spinozism. Is it not because he fears that Spinoza was not only already Hegelian but above all that he was more profoundly so and with greater consequence than he himself? Thus the inadmissible presents itself. The historical evolution that subordinates that which comes before to that which comes after and that leads successively from one to the other—making the key to all of philosophy into a teleology—is turned away from its inescapable meaning.

Having made these remarks, which we will need to return to, we can now indicate what is "lacking," according to Hegel, in the concept of *causa sui* and compromises its development in Spinoza. The *causa sui* is based on a substantial principle that "lacks the principle of the personality."[9] It thus constitutes a substance that cannot become subject, which fails in this active reflection of self, which would permit it to undertake its own liberation through its own process. If he did not grasp or was not able to develop the concept of the *causa sui* it is because this concept, as he defined it, contained nothing other than an abstract and indifferent identity of self to self, in which the self is nothing other than that which is already in its beginning, without the possibility of real passage toward self, of an immanent movement that would not be that of its pure and simple disappearance. The point of view of substance expresses the absolute in its own manner, without the life that animates it and that causes it to exist. This is an arrested and dead spirit, which is nothing but that self in an original restriction, which condemns it from the beginning.

In addition, even as it announces itself, the point of view of substance creates the conditions of its own destruction: its immobility is apparent because it is the precarious equilibrium that results from an internal conflict, which is impossible to contain indefinitely. The limits of the system, even if they are truly real for the thought that they impede, are fictitious from the point of view of the absolute because the absolute opposes the violence that is done to it with a violence that is greater still, and it propels the system beyond the illusory limits that impose on it the conditions of its formal coherence. Immanent negativity undermines the doctrine from the inside and forces it to declare that which it refuses nevertheless to declare itself: here exactly, in this confession, is the substance that becomes subject.

Once this initial contradiction is revealed, the philosophy of Spi-

noza can be understood absolutely, in an inverted sense to the one that
it professes. According to Hegel, the discourse of Spinoza is entirely
marked by this destiny, which condemns it and absolves it, simultaneously declaring its disappearance and its resurrection in the living
body of absolute knowledge, where it realizes itself. To *really* read
Spinoza, for Hegel, is to reconstruct the edifice of his thought, causing
the conditions of another form of knowledge to appear from what is
only the unachieved form or the anticipated ruin, because in Spinoza,
the effort to link knowledge to the absolute resolves itself only in a
broken promise.

A Philosophy of Beginning

As we shall see, the interpretation Hegel gives Spinoza foregrounds the
idea of beginning. As the beginning of philosophy, Spinozism is also
a thinking of beginning. Following the method of the *Encyclopedia,*
it is "the fundamental establishment of all real subsequent development." And again, in the *Lectures on the History of Philosophy,* "It is
therefore worthy of note that thought must begin by placing itself at
the standpoint of Spinozism; to be a follower of Spinoza is the essential
beginning of all Philosophy."[10] Thus is forged the link that unites the
philosophy of Spinoza with all thinking of beginning.

Here Hegel engages in a form of reasoning that is quite paradoxical: at the same instance he presents Spinoza as a point of departure,
which he views as the point of departure of philosophy, and he places
him in the company of all those who have understood beginning but
who knew only that, without (through their efforts) being able to
complete the effective discovery of the true.

> God is in truth assuredly the necessity or, as one might say as
> well, the absolute thing, but also at the same time the absolute
> person, and on this point we must agree that the philosophy of
> Spinoza falls short of the real concept of God, which forms the
> content of religious consciousness in Christianity. Spinoza was
> by descent a Jew, and it is in general the oriental view according
> to which all achieved finite being appears only as transient being,
> as being that disappears, that has found in its philosophy an ex-
> pression that conforms to this intellectual system. It is certainly
> true that this oriental view of the unity of substance forms the

basis of all real further development, but one can't stop there; it continues to be marked by the absence of the occidental principle of individuality.[11]

Spinozism is thus at the same time a point of departure and its conclusion, because in that which begins there should also be something that finishes. The singularity of Spinozism affirms itself in the perpetuation of an entire tradition, whose dynamic it encapsulates: what dominates within it once again, but here for the last time, is an "oriental intuition." Thus begins the chapter of *Lectures on the History of Philosophy* dedicated to Spinoza: "this profound unity of his philosophy such as it is expressed in Europe, his manifestation of Spirit, the identity of the infinite and the finite in God, a God that does not appear as a Third, is an echo of the Orient."[12] This is what gives this philosophy its unmistakable character: it completes the discourse of origins.

In Hegel, the Orient is the visible figure of that which begins; this figure is more mythical than historical, but is not myth the most appropriate form of exposition for origin? It is the moment where the absolute is affirmed for the first time, in substance that excludes the individuality of a subject:

> In oriental thought, the principal relationship is as follows: the single substance is as such the true, and the individual in himself is without value and has nothing to gain for himself insofar as he maintains his position against that which is in itself for itself; he cannot, on the contrary, have any real value without confounding himself with this substance, the result of which is that substance ceases to exist for the subject and that the subject itself ceases to be a conscious being and vanishes within the unconscious.[13]

The sublimity, the immensity of this representation, which in one stroke absorbs all reality in a single being or a single idea, remains a formal representation because it coincides with the laughable poverty of the external manifestations of this substance, which are effectively nothing more than an empty exteriority:

> The finite cannot become truth expect by immersing itself in substance; separated from it, it remains empty, impoverished,

determined for itself, without internal connections. And as soon as we find a finite, determined representation in their view (the Orientals), it is nothing but an exterior, dry enumeration of the elements—something very labored, empty, pedantic, flat.[14]

Having considered the absolute for a single instance, this thought can do nothing subsequently beyond this but abstractly enumerate its manifestations, between which, if we detach them from their origins, any real form of unity disappears.

Here the call to an absolute knowledge, which would not be solely the knowledge of the absolute, realizes itself in an immediate ecstasy, whereby all consciousness is necessarily abolished; it is the knowledge that realizes itself in the form of its own negation. But in Spinoza himself, behind the appearances of a geometric rigor that are nothing for Hegel but a mask (a form without content), we find once again, for the last time, this abyss of the unconscious, which excludes a rational discourse:

> Just as in Spinozism it is precisely the mode as such that is untrue and substance alone that is true, such that everything must be restored to it, resulting in the submersion of all content in the void, in a purely formal unity, without content, thus too is Siva once again the great whole, no different from Brahma, but Brahma himself, that is to say the difference and the determinateness only vanish again, without being preserved, without being sublated, and unity does not become a concrete unity, nor does division become reconciliation. The highest goal for man placed in the sphere of coming to be and ceasing to be, of modality generally, is the submergence into unconscious, unity with Brahma, annihilation of self: it is the same thing as Buddhist Nirvana, Nibban, and so forth.[15]

"It is the same thing": this extraordinary historical syncretism is for Hegel without limits, apparently because it is still relevant to explain certain aspects of "occidental" thought.

Commenting in the *Lectures on the History of Philosophy*, the famous speech of Parmenides on being and nonbeing, Hegel discovers once again the same collusion of a pure affirmation and a radical negation, which found its ultimate exposition in Spinoza: "here is the matter in brief, and negation in general comes under this void, and under a more concrete form of the limit, the finite, the boundary: 'omnis determinatio est negatio' is the grand dictum of Spinoza. According to Parmenides, whatever form the negative takes, it is nothing at all."[16]

The inaugural form of oriental thought still haunts the doctrine of Eléates, a form with which even Spinoza must maintain a privileged relationship: the One, pure and immediate being, is at the same time the dissolution of all determined reality, the disappearance of the finite in the infinite, the abolition of all individuality and all difference. As Plato had already remarked in his last dialogues, relying himself on a dialectical point of view, the discourse in which this absolute or initial totality is expressed (to the extent that it excludes all negativity, to the extent that it refuses to grant the existence of nonbeing) is an impossible discourse.

Note that in the chapter of book I of *Logic* on measurement, Hegel makes this same connection to Parmenides, but this time in order to discover within his work the indices of difference:

> The Spinozist mode, exactly like the Indian principle of change, is that without measure. The Greeks realized, albeit in an imprecise manner, that everything had a measure, to the point that Parmenides himself introduced necessity after abstract being as the ancient limit that imposed itself on everything. We find there the beginning of a concept that is much superior to that contained in substance and its difference with the mode.[17]

There is therefore more than one kind of beginning: there are beginnings that begin over a longer period of time than others and those that on the contrary already begin to differentiate themselves from pure beginning. Nevertheless, despite his position as a latecomer in the chronology of philosophy, Spinoza is grouped with those who begin absolutely, among the real primitives of this thought, and this is why, because it is necessary to note his singularity, it is the orientalist metaphor that persists with Hegel.

In Spinoza's biography, which Hegel includes in the *Lectures on the History of Philosophy*, he notes, "It is not insignificant that he is preoccupied with light (optics): because in the material world *(in der Materie)*, this is absolute identity itself, which constitutes the basis of oriental view of things."[18]

This inaugural light is the element of immediate thought. It is significant that Hegel finds the same image in the first chapter of *Logic* to represent the illusion of pure being, which is itself also "without measure":

> It happens that being comes to be represented in the image of pure light, as the clarity of untroubled vision, whereas nothing-ness is represented as pure night, and we attach their difference to this well known perceivable diversity. But, in fact, if we represent this vision in a more exact fashion, it is easy to understand that in absolute light [*clarté*] we see as much and as little as in absolute darkness, that one of these forms of vision is just as good as the other, pure vision is a vision of nothingness. Pure light and pure darkness are two voids that are the same thing.[19]

The indeterminate brilliance of the immediate is profoundly obscure, like the night: like the night, it absorbs, effaces, and dissolves all contours, which would be for its infinity again a limit. Likewise, the pretension of seizing being in itself, in its instantaneous identity with itself, not yet contaminated with a relationship to another, resolves itself immediately in an inverse purity and is formally equivalent to an absolute nothingness, the contradiction of beginning that is the initiation of all passage.

From this point of view, we might believe that the privileged place in *Logic* where Hegel must have recalled his interpretation of Spinozism is the first chapter of book I, where the immediate itself refutes its own illusion. But in this celebrated text there is not a single reference to Spinozism! Without doubt this is because Hegel wanted to avoid this too simple connection, which, taken literally, would turn easily into a consolidation. As we have already noted, Spinoza's philosophy is not a beginning like the others: less developed than the Greeks in terms of its intrinsic excess, it anticipates broadly enough the most modern aspects of rational thought. We might say that it is a discourse that is fundamentally anachronistic, misplaced, a beginning that is not at a beginning but already finds itself displaced elsewhere.

In fact, it is remarkable that in order to present the point of view of substance in his ensemble, Hegel has chosen the chapter on "actuality" (die Wirklichkeit), which is found at the end of the second part of Logic. It is a key argument, which is a good indicator of the crucial significance that Hegel lends to Spinozism, in which the very destiny of philosophy is at stake, because it is at this moment in the articulation of books II and III of Logic that the passage from objective logic to subjective logic is addressed. According to the place it is assigned in the process of the ensemble of knowledge, it is clear that the point of view of substance represents a false beginning, a beginning that is itself the outcome and the recapitulation of a prior movement, a movement from the thought of Being to that of Essence. In the Spinozist sense it is thus the entire process of objective logic that is realized and encapsulated in substance.

Thus, in an analogical manner, the Spinozist consideration of substance has already appeared in rough form right at the end of the first book in the paragraph on "absolute indifference" in this internal articulation of objective logic, which is the passage from Being to Essence:

> As regards absolute indifference, which is a fundamental concept of Spinozist substance, we can recall this concept is the final determination of being before it becomes essence; but it does not attain essence itself.[20]

Spinoza is thus present at all the turning points in rational thought: as an absolute beginning, he could not be limited to a single beginning of one sort or another, but he had to reappear each time that something essential emerged in the development of the rational process. Spinoza haunts the Hegelian system throughout its unfolding. The obsession, of which he is a symptom, is not immediately undone; it reappears continuously in the discourse that itself never completely finishes with its beginning.

The Reconstruction of the System

There are numerous references to Spinoza in Hegel's work; they often take the form of incidental remarks, varying in precision or detail. But Hegel also proposed explanations of the entire Spinozist system: the chapter of Lectures on the History of Philosophy that is dedicated to him provides a sustained analysis based on a study of the text. Nevertheless, we will focus here on another commentary, which Hegel provides in the chapter of book II of *Logic* dedicated to the Absolute,[21] which is in a very different style: it consists of a global interpretation of the Spinozist doctrine, leading back to its general "meaning" and detached from its details. From the beginning of this text, which nowhere else explicitly names Spinoza, Hegel distances himself to the margins of Spinozism, where he liberally reconstructs the discourse following a logic of his own conception. This violence to the text corresponds to a very precise objective: it permits the revelation of the essential "movement" of the system, so to speak, because Hegel characterizes this philosophy above all in terms of its stasis. What is interesting in this apparently arbitrary reconstitution, in this reconstruction, is that it reveals the principal articulations of Spinozist thought as Hegel understands it, by isolating its principal categories and situating them in relation to each other. It is through this interpretation that Hegel then exposes his critique of Spinozism in an important "Historical Remark" dedicated to Spinoza and to Leibniz, which concludes this chapter. This general presentation is extremely interesting because it situates the constitutive elements of the doctrine and makes their articulation explicit.

The absolute, which gives its object to the ensemble of this development, is first of all characterized by "its simple substantial identity",[22] it appears to be confined in the interiority of substance, completely withdrawn into itself. And yet, as we will see, there is a process of exposition of the absolute: it is that of its exterior manifestation, which passes from initial affirmation of the absolute like substance toward its reflection in the attributes, then in the modes. It is this "passage"—we will see that it only has the appearance of movement—that organizes the point of view of substance in its singular disposition as it expresses itself historically in the work of Spinoza. We will follow this development in its successive stages.

This process begins with the absolute itself, which presents itself immediately as such. Hegel's argument consists of discovering the latent contradiction that haunts and secretly decomposes this apparent unity. In its initial constitution, the absolute presents itself as an identity that is undifferentiated from form and content and thus indifferent to itself. The absolute, which is absolute, is at the same time a subject in which all predicates have been posited and a subject in which all predicates have been negated; it is a point of departure, a base, that cannot be recognized as such except at the moment when nothing is based on it any longer and that is the basis for nothing. Hegel's entire reasoning here is built on a play on words that takes as its pretext the expression "zum Grunde gehen": to return to the foundation, which also means "to go to the abyss." The plenitude of the absolute, imprisoned in the radical interiority of substance, is that of the void.

Thus substance, which presents itself as a source of determinations, is also in itself a nothingness of determination because it is the indeterminate that precedes and conditions all determination. This is the contradiction that is peculiar to substance: it offers itself first in its absolute positivity, as that which is the most real, but at the same time, to guarantee this maximum of being, it must draw reality back to that which it is not, and it makes this reality dependent on it. In affirming its anteriority and its preeminence, substance emerges as that which is, in light of the appearance of that which is not also in this beginning, whence its essential function of *de-realization*, because it casts into a bottomless abyss of the negative, which is nothing but the negative, all that does not coincide immediately with its initial positivity. In substance, that which appears and vanishes at the same time is that which presents but also that which does away with actuality [*réalité*].

On the other hand, the self-sufficiency of substance that defines itself through itself in the absence of all determination makes the passage from subject to predicate, the relation of the foundation to that which it grounds, incomprehensible; the determinations that have a basis in the absolute cannot add themselves to it, except after the fact and from the outside, in an arbitrary manner, without immanent development. This is why substance, which is the object of all knowledge, is also unknowable. It is in itself a subject about which one can affirm nothing if not itself, and its relationship to the determinations it supports is incomprehensible; by the fact of its total self-sufficiency it has no need of these determinations, which are consequently adjuncts to it without necessity and without reason.

As absolute beginning, substance is thus also an end. In the plenitude of its own being, for which nothing is lacking, it has already exhausted all possibility of movement; what it initiates within itself is immediately fully realized. It is a beginning that begins nothing, where the immobile absolute constitutes the denial of all process. The system that begins with the exposition of the absolute finds itself immediately frozen: because it is itself given at the beginning of all reality, it cannot progress.

However, the Spinozist doctrine that is referred to implicitly in this analysis is not content to indicate the plenitude of the absolute through an initial definition. It presents it in an internal order, in a coherent manner, by clarifying its rational content. But the progression of this exposé cannot be anything but apparent; its formal development is in fact a regression, because the immediate identity of the absolute to itself forbids all subsequent advances. The illusory "process" of substance that inaugurates the exposition of the absolute cannot be the movement of a positive constitution, because everything is constituted immediately, but that of a degradation, which subtracts the elements of its reality successively from the absolute, by taking them away through extrinsic determinations, which cannot effectively add anything to it because it is completely sufficient unto itself.

This regression is manifest in the first "passage," which leads from substance to attribute, that is, from the absolute to the relative. The absolute that is absolute is also that which is *only* absolute; its primordial plenitude is also the inescapable form of its limitation. The perfection of the absolute is at the same time that which it lacks in order to be truly absolute being, the totality of determinations it had to negate in order to merge with itself, in order to be nothing but itself. The absolute that is nothing but absolute is also the negation of the absolute: "it is not therefore the absolutely absolute, but the absolute in a determinateness, or it is attribute."[23] The absolute-become-attribute acquires these determinations, but it therefore exhibits itself within a diminished reality.

The attribute constitutes the second moment, the middle term, of the apparent process of the absolute, that devotes itself immediately as such at the beginning, and whose progression finds itself hindered by this event: "the attribute is the merely relative absolute"[24] or, again, the absolute determined only as regards its form. Substance, which expresses itself in its attributes, by discovering that they are identical to it, is the absolute that reflects itself through its own exteriorization: precisely because, as such, it carries no determination at all within itself, it is incapable of immanent reflection. The absolute exhausts itself in this reflection, because its determination confronts it, opposes itself to the absolute like the inessential to the essential: there the absolute recognizes only its inanity. The attribute is the predicate that reflects the subject outside itself. It is the representation, the phenomenon; it provides only an image of substance.

The attribute is thus an empty form, because it describes substance from the exterior and without necessity; in it the absolute finds itself restrained, and diminished, to the extent that it establishes itself with the attribute as its own identical being. This restriction, which appears as soon as one reflects substance in an attribute, is reinforced when a multiplicity of attributes are proposed. Because of its exteriority and its contingency, one single form is not sufficient to represent the absolute; this is why it relies on the indefinite quest for new determinations, which oppose each other (as, for example, thought and extension). Through these it seeks in vain to recuperate its completeness. In the form of the attribute, the infinite necessarily takes the appearance of plurality: it separates itself, scatters itself, loses itself in the unlimited series of images that provokes the illusory movement of its exterior reflection. The passage from substance to attribute is the becoming-appearance [devenir-apparence] of the absolute, which calls its unity into question in the dissipation of pure difference.

Substance undoes itself, dissolves itself in its attributes, by projecting itself into a consciousness that is necessarily foreign to it. This is because it requires the intervention of the abstract intellect that decomposes identity of content into its multiple forms in order that the unity of substance can be determined in a diversity of forms. Faced with the pure objectivity of the absolute, that is nothing but absolute, it poses and opposes [se pose et s'oppose] the exterior form of a subjectivity that opens a perspective, evokes a manner of being, projects an appearance. Despite the abstract identity that links it to substance in a formal relationship of representation, the attribute taken as such detaches itself from this substance and distances itself as a simple modality; thus we have already "passed" from attribute to mode, which constitutes the third moment of the regressive process of the absolute.

The mode is still substance but held in the element of absolute exteriority: "the mode is being outside of the self of the absolute, the loss of self in the variety and the contingency of being."[25] Thus the absolute is no longer identical to itself; it has lost all its reality, it is diluted in its own appearance, in the unlimited facticity of that which no longer has a cause in itself. At the extreme limit of its manifestation, as the ultimate emanation of a perfume that evaporates, substance is worn out, exhausted in the swarming of aspects that manifest it in its decomposition, in the terms of a presentation that is purely negative. Inversely, if we reflect on the absolute, the immediately perceptible reality that results from the addition of all these modes converts itself into an appearance in the most critical sense of the term, because this appearance does not give the absolute anything more than an illusory expression in which it ends by disappearing, and at the same time appearance is engulfed in the absolute. In this moment when reality, immediately exposed within the absolute, is totally dissipated, the essentially negative "movement" of substance is achieved.

In the mode there is nothing left of what is given in substance; nothing is left except this nothing in which all reality does away with itself. In another passage, at the beginning of the third section of book I of *Logic*, "The Measure," Hegel writes about the mode in general: "if the third term were taken as a simple exteriority, then it would be a mode. In this sense, the third term is not a return to itself, but insofar as the second is the beginning of a relation with an exteriority, an exit [*sortir*] that still holds itself in relation to the original being, the third is the rupture, completed."[26]

Referring back to Spinoza he immediately specifies,

> With Spinoza, the mode is likewise the third after substance and attribute; he explains it to be the affections of substance, or that element which is in an other through which it is comprehended. According to this concept, this third is only externality as such; as has already been mentioned, with Spinoza generally, the rigid nature of substance lacks the return into itself.[27]

The "syllogism," which links substance to its affections through the intermediary of attributes and encapsulates the essential significance of the Spinozist system, is for Hegel an abstract syllogism: it does not describe the completion of the absolute but rather this progressive degradation, which distances it from itself.

From this reconstitution of the framework, the reason that the point of view of substance is characterized by its immobility now becomes clear. The movement that establishes itself beginning with the absolute, leading substance to the attributes and then the modes, is exactly the opposite of a real movement, of a process of the constitution of the absolute; this is why the efficacy of the real cannot be determined here except as a kind of caricature, in the derision of decline. It is the regressive movement of a successive degradation that leads from a maximum of being given at the beginning, toward its total depletion, in forms that are increasingly exterior to it and that, for it, rather than manners of being are manners of no longer being. This movement of descent, contained between a positive absolute origin and a definitively negative end beyond which there is nothing, is exactly the opposite of a rational cycle, of a dialectical process from which Hegel elsewhere establishes the principle of all reality: a process that exposes quite the opposite of what we have just described, the indeterminacy of its beginning, its apparent and provisional character, in order to direct itself progressively toward an end in which it realizes itself, through the total determination of an identity that cannot be affirmed except at the moment when it has become truly effective. However, the manifestation of the absolute that is only absolute has not taken place except within the empty repetition of a disappearance, of a diminution, of a loss of identity, in such a way that the progression is evidently formal, because it is determined by a "growing" lack of content.

The point of view of substance, which claims to embrace all of reality in a single concept, thus inverts itself in a negative understanding[28] [connaissance]: reality's absolute, which lays claim to substance, has as a counterpart the denial of reality borne by all that it is not and that succeeds it. The pure discourse of the absolute develops primarily the theme of the lesser reality of things, of everything that is not it; the becoming of the absolute can do nothing except distance itself from its initial integrity and cause it to wither. This is a skepticism of the substance, which absorbs in its formalism reality in its entirety; thus the negative is only a movement of subtraction, which leads to a disappearance, outside any real work of determination. This is expressed very well in a passage from Lectures on the History of Philosophy:

> As all differences and all determinations of things and of conscience are returned to the unity of substance, one can say that, in

the Spinozist system, all things in effect find themselves cast into the abyss of annihilation. But from this abyss nothing reemerges and the particular that Spinoza speaks about is not recaptured and recuperated except in representation, without finding its justification there. In order that it be justified, it would have been necessary for Spinoza to have derived it from his substance: but this substance does not open up, does not achieve life, or spirituality, or activity. . . . The misfortune that befalls this particular is that it is nothing but a modification of absolute substance, but that is not declared as such: moreover the moment of negativity is what is lacking for this immobile and rigid being, whose single operation consists of dispossessing everything of its determination and its particularity, in order to cast it back to the unity of absolute substance, where it disappears and where all life decays. This is what leaves us philosophically unsatisfied with Spinoza.[29]

The absolute opens up, but only as a pit where all determinations annihilate themselves, where all reality is lost in the irresistible abyss of the void.

The philosophy of Spinoza is thus for Hegel a completely abstract school of thought, in which all movement and all actualized life disappear. At the conclusion of a brief biography of Spinoza, which Hegel provides in his *Lectures,* we find this extraordinarily significant observation: "Spinoza died 21 February 1677, in his forty-fourth year, from consumption that he had suffered from a long time—in accordance with his system in which as well, all particularity, all singularity fades away in the unity of substance."[30]

Spinozism is a consumptive philosophy, declining progressively toward the disappearance of all effective reality, belabored in the affirmation of an absolute that it cannot represent except from the outside, inactive and without life.

The verdict of insufficiency, which was ordained in the encounter with this philosophy, and the point of view that supports it, thus finds legitimacy. As negative thought of a negative that is only negative, it unfolds only through the abolition of its content; it cannot therefore be revealed except negatively, according to its failures, its own inanity. Philosophy of beginning = philosophy of decline. It is only in going against this beginning, through the work of the negative that is not only negative, that thought can elevate itself above the abyss of substance, in order to discover the concrete movement of the actual. It is necessary to begin with Spinoza, it is necessary to pass through Spinoza, it is necessary to depart from Spinoza.

For this, it is necessary to submit the doctrine to a proof of a critique that does not rely solely on a global interpretation, such as the one that we have just followed, but that considers his argumentation in detail. In this way we will highlight the contradiction that is appropriate to his content. This analysis isolates three critical points in his system, three concepts, on which Hegel concentrates his argument: these are the problem of demonstration (designated by the famous expression *more geometrico*), the definition of attributes, and finally the formula *omnis determinatio est negatio*, which Hegel imputes to Spinoza and in which he concentrates his entire system. These are the three points we will now consider precisely.[31]

꞊ 2 ꞊

More Geometrico

Hegel and Method

Hegel critiques Spinoza first for the place he assigns method in philosophical knowledge and also for the particular content of this method. According to Hegel, Spinoza locates himself as a follower of Descartes by borrowing the procedures of demonstration from mathematics, a model of organization of rational discourse; in effect he subordinates philosophical truth to a guarantee of formal evidence, an exterior and abstract rule. In this way, even though he declares himself a monist in affirming the absolute unity of substance, he reestablishes a kind of dualism through the separation he imposes between form and content within knowledge itself. From the formal point of view of method the conditions of knowledge, whose universality is determined in a completely abstract manner, are indifferent to its object, and they can be specified outside of it. But this split does not recognize that which is specific in philosophical knowledge, the identity of being and of knowing such as they are effected in the concept:

> The Spinozist method of mathematical determination would appear to be nothing more than a simple defect in the form; but it is a fundamental defect, which characterizes the entire point of view of Spinozism. In this method, the nature of philosophical knowledge and its object are completely misconceived; because in mathematics, knowledge and method are merely formal knowledge, and therefore completely inappropriate to philosophy. Mathematical knowledge sets out its proof on the existing object as such, and not the object insofar as it is conceived; what is lacking, consequently, is the concept; but the object of philosophy is the concept and that which is understood through the concept. Therefore this concept as the knowledge of essence is simply

assumed and falls within the subject of philosophy; and nevertheless this is how the specific method of Spinozist philosophy
presents itself.[1]

This method privileges the formal, strictly reflexive aspect of deduction in the manner of ancient logic, whose point of view, according to
Hegel, is essentially unchanged from Aristotle to Descartes; the true
is thus relegated in the order of representation by reciprocal relations
that organize the constitution and succession of the propositions outside all real determination inherent in Subject that is expressed therein,
that is to say in Concept as such. It is because of this formalism, which
separates the effective content of thought from its forms of reflection
in discourse, that the Spinozist system is inscribed in the sphere of
essence, for which it constitutes a kind of absolute limit; this is why
Hegel dedicates a long historical remark to Spinozism precisely at the
end of the second book of the *Logic.*

Hegel does not limit himself to questioning the principle of the
Spinozist method; he objects as well to its effective unfolding. What
characterizes the "method," as we shall see, is its verbosity [*verbalisme*]:
it returns the conditions of all truth to a formal order of propositions.
From that point on, knowledge reveals itself in a succession of abstract
utterances whose validity must be established from its beginning, in
the first propositions from which all truth is derived and in some way
extracted; there is no knowledge except in relation to these propositions. After presenting the content of the definitions that inaugurate
the discourse of *Ethics,* Hegel writes,

> The entire Spinozist philosophy is already contained in these
> definitions, in spite of their completely formal character: in a
> general sense, the defect specific to Spinozism is that he begins
> in this manner with definitions. In mathematics, this method is
> merited, because it proceeds from propositions such as point, line
> et cetera; but in philosophy, it is the content that must be known
> in so far as it is in itself and for itself. One can from time to time
> recognize a nominal definition as correct, such as the manner in
> which the word "substance" is accorded a representation, which
> defines it; but whether the content that it indicates is true in itself
> and for itself is an entirely different matter. Such a question is

definitely not addressed in the geometric propositions, and yet it is, for a philosophical reflection, the first thing to be considered, and this is the very thing that Spinoza has not done. In the definitions that he proposes at the beginning, he simply explains simple thoughts, and he presents them as something concrete. Instead, he should have also investigated if their content was true. What is provided, apparently, is only the explanation of the word: but what matters is the content that is found there. It suffices that all other content is referred to it, in order to be established through it as intermediary; in addition, all other definitions are dependent on this first content, because it is the foundation from which all necessity derives.[2]

What we find here is Hegel's fundamental objection to the pretense of a subordination of knowledge to the prerequisite of an absolute beginning: the knowledge that results from such an approach is purely relative. The first propositions, for example the definitions, which seek to fix the sense of concepts and to regulate functioning within them, present themselves as the source of truth on which all subsequent knowledge depends, because it is nothing but the explanation of that which one finds immediately given in these definitions; the paradox is that the truth of these propositions, upon which all the rest depends, appears to raise no question exactly because it has been established at the beginning, thus without precondition. But the act that poses this initial truth cannot be anything but a formal decision in which the content remains only verbal: the recourse to the criteria of evidence gives this procedure an abstract and arbitrary guarantee of an essentially relative value, which grounds the extrinsic order of propositions and ensures their coherence without determining the content within them, that is to say the truth.

These objections evoke something very familiar for all scholars of Hegel. They refer back to his persistent demand for a new logic that is no longer a logic of representation and the formal conditions of its organization, but a logic of content itself; this concerns neither exclusively nor primarily the formal exercise of thought, but rather it exposes the effective movement of Concept and the necessity of this determination it gives to itself, in its immanent activity:

It is this objective thinking that forms the content of pure science. Therefore, far from being formal, far from lacking matter in light of a real and true knowledge, it is rather this content that has absolute truth, or, if we continue to make use of the word *matter,* it is its content that constitutes true matter, but matter in which the form is not something that is exterior to it, rather matter that is pure thought and consequently absolute form.[3]

From this point of view, it is the project of a methodology of knowledge that finds itself invalid. For example, Aristotle's *Logic* is nothing for Hegel but an empirical description, necessarily elaborated after the fact, from the unfolding of knowledge that it reduces [*qu'elle ramène*] systematically to the functioning of rules, to procedures exterior to all content: "the purpose at the core of this science is to learn to become familiar with the procedure of finite thought, and this science is considered exact if it corresponds to its presupposed object."[4]

A methodology presupposes its object, as a given exterior that it finds completely before it, because it is incapable of constructing it. This is why, remaining indifferent to the real movement of content or even of the thing, the method cannot be recognized as true in itself, but only because it is verified at the level of its application. Its ambition to condition truth itself thus appears laughable, to direct knowledge on the right path that links conformity to its formal procedures:

> The deduction of so-called rules and laws, above all syllogism, is thus no more worthwhile than a manipulation of sticks of unequal length with the goal of sorting and combining them according to their size—this game that children are absorbed by, and which, beginning from a puzzle cut in many ways, consists of investigating which pieces fit together. It is thus not incorrectly that we liken this thinking to calculating and this calculating, in turn, to this manner of thinking.[5]

Are the demonstrations of *Ethics* something else, for Hegel, than this futile and necessarily incomplete arrangement of scattered elements of a truth, which cannot be grasped as such through them, in necessity and totality?

In this case, there is no method that is preliminary to the exercise of thought, which can be studied for itself in order to begin, no "discourse of method" preceding that of the "application of this method." This would be nothing but a retrospective caricature of an effective science, in which the movement that has already actually been completed would only be reflected in the illusion of a general form of knowledge. If one can still talk about method, it is on the condition of specifying that this is inseparable from the knowledge in which it manifests itself, that is, it does not come either before or after it, but with it: "the method is nothing other than the structure of the Whole, presented in its pure essential form."[6]

It does not encapsulate the complete development of knowledge [*savoir*] in the formal condition of an initial rule; it is nothing other than this development itself, grasped in its concrete necessity, at the moment that it is carried out. This is what enables Hegel to add, "Considering what has prevailed upon this subject up until now, we should realize that the system of representation corresponding to this philosophical method belongs to a bygone culture."[7]

Because method no longer has any value outside the knowledge that fulfills it, "it is the exposition of logic that requires the most complete specifications of what can alone be the true method of philosophical science: because the method itself is the conscious form of its internal movement."[8]

It is nothing other than the knowledge of the self of knowledge, which recognizes what it is in the process in which it is made. From thereon, the "method," to the extent that this word still has meaning, has lost all formal and abstract character because "it is in no way different in relation to its object and its content."[9] It is no longer "a" method, that is, a recipe for knowledge, but knowledge itself, which reflects itself in its object, which reflects itself as its own object:

> In this way, method is not an exterior form, but the soul and concept of the content, from which it is no different except to the extent that the dynamic elements of the concept come, in their self-determination to appear as the totality of the concept. Since this determination, or the content leads itself, with the form, to the idea, this idea reveals itself as a systemic totality which is nothing

but an Idea whose particular movements are also completely implicit in this idea, one which they bring to light in the dialectic of the concept, the being-for-itself of the simple idea. The science concludes in this manner by grasping the notion of itself as of the pure idea, for which the idea is.[10]

The exposition of this method coincides with the deployment of understanding, whose movement it expresses in totality, as totality; it does not inaugurate the process of knowledge, in the act of an initial foundation, but it forms within it the conclusion, and a final recapitulation of that which has been completed. It is clear for Hegel the category of method has lost all autonomous signification; in order that it be conserved, it was necessary that its philosophical value would be completely distorted [*pervertie*].

But when Hegel discusses the notion of method and the project of a philosophical method, it is always in reference to the functioning of the method in mathematics. The privilege accorded to method in the unfolding process of knowledge and in the unfolding of truths has its source, if not in their mathematics themselves, at least in the idea, or the prejudice, that it offers a model of reasoning that is universally valid. A constant theme for Hegel is that mathematics can no longer lay claim to this regulatory function in the work of knowledge:

> It is not difficult to see that the manner of proposing a proposition, to put forward the reasons in its favor, and then to refute in the same way the propositions opposed to these arguments, is not a form under which truth can appear. Truth is the movement of itself within itself, whereas this method is a form of knowledge that remains exterior to its material. That is why it is peculiar to mathematics and should be left to it.[11]

If understanding is a necessarily determined process, it is no longer because of its conformity to a formal order of reasons, which regulates a sequence of propositions: philosophy, as the movement of autoproduction of the concept, is no longer subordinated to the ideal of an exact deduction.

If, in an earlier historical period, it was thought necessary to submit knowledge to this exigency, it is because there is much in common between philosophy and mathematics. What they share is the project of the determination of the real through thought, in knowledge that has the dignified status of general knowledge. But this common element is not essential, because it remains exterior to the content of knowledge and consists only of an abstract reflection: "scientific culture, then, shares its formal aspect with philosophy."[12]

This is why, between the truth of mathematics and the truth of philosophy, there can be nothing more than a superficial resemblance. It remains, then, to be seen what might legitimate this confusion that has brought them together, specifically in Spinoza's era; according to Hegel, it is a strictly conjunctural reason, which has thus lost all value in any other historical period. At a time when the enterprise of knowledge found itself hindered, crushed by the insurmountable authority of a dogma, mathematical reasoning might have appeared as the strongest weapon in a defensive battle against this oppression: on the side of philosophy and in a common movement, it represented the same effort "to think oneself,"[13] far away from all external constraints. But this time is past: along with its all powerful dogma, the necessity of making compromises against it has disappeared, compromises that, without these circumstances, quickly become ambiguous. In Hegel's time, a time of free thinking that could pursue its fulfillment to its limits, by its own means, what propelled it forward [l'emporte] by contrast was what separated philosophy from mathematics, with which it had had a very brief alliance.

This difference is essentially that between a science of the finite and a science of the infinite. It is clear that in these two cases the word *science* designates completely different realities: on one hand an abstract knowledge that always finds its object in exteriority, on the other a concrete knowledge that is itself its own content and is thus made absolute. If intellect—which is the locus par excellence whereby to know and to represent are formally identical—is a necessary determination of rational thought, a moment that has its place in the process of the body of knowledge, it exists exactly through the limitation that situates it somewhere in this unfolding, and the point of view that corresponds to it has no value except relative to this singular position, which is enough to deny it the right to a universality that it claims nevertheless.

The argument that permits Hegel thus to put mathematics in

their place is exposed in its clearest form in a well-known passage from the preface of *Phenomenology*, which we have already referred to several times. Hegel proceeds in quite an astonishing fashion in this text toward an amalgamation of mathematical and historical truths. He compares both with truths of fact in a manner characteristic of the "dogmatic form of thought" that separates the true from the false, once and for all:

> For such questions: when was Caesar born? How many feet are there in a stadium and so forth, one must give a clear-cut answer: just as it is true that the square of the hypotenuse is equal to the squares of the other two sides. But the nature of what one calls such a truth is distinct from the nature of philosophical truths.[14]

This comparison is very significant, because it shows that Hegel attacks mathematics simultaneously from the position of its formalism and from the position of its empiricism, because these are essentially convergent tendencies. Abstraction is not that which diverts us from the immediate; quite the contrary, it is what traps us there. As Lebrun wrote in his beautiful book on Hegel, "The drama of the thought of the intellect is that it detaches itself from the perceptible even as it continues to operate with the same naiveté and without calling into question the representations that arise from its ongoing relation with the sensible ('time' for example)."[15]

According to Hegel, this mathematical "naiveté" can be explained by the fact that formal reasoning is not capable of engendering its object. This object is thus necessarily granted it, existing outside of the movement within which it is thought; the object thus is in fact presupposed, exactly as all things that, for common knowledge, belong to experience. The object is only represented within the intellect, which remains external to it: "the process of mathematical proof is not part of its object, it is an operation external to the matter at hand."[16] Thus the form and the content exist in a necessarily finite manner, exactly because they are foreign to each other.

This finiteness not only characterizes the relationship between mathematical reasoning and the content that it addresses, it marks its very form: behind the apparently implacable progress of an irreversible and constrained order of demonstrations, Hegel detects a disarticulated series of independent elements that are simply added, one after another, without real communication, without necessity. In addition this demonstration offers nothing but the caricature of free thought, the illusion of knowledge in movement; the proof is only constructed through finite operations, which are realized in propositions that are artificially combined, which are laid out and arranged (see the metaphor of the puzzle already invoked), in a manner that leads only provisionally to the belief in, that is, the adherence to, a "subject" imbued with the feeling of the evidence, submitting itself to the operations of the "subject" as operator that imposes this arrangement on it, this constraint. Here again we cannot do better than recall the explanation of Lebrun:

> In isolating "thoughts" and linking them together as if they were simple objects of knowledge, the intellect gives credence to the idea that Knowledge is a "subjective" strategy. It follows from this that "thought" is by rights abstract, that these "knowledges" are by rights partial, that the domain of "knowledge" is disconnected from practice. The intellect accepts that something is true "in my head" and that "knowledge" reduces itself to a distribution of contents in an order which I can easily review [*parcourir*].[17]

Thus we find the pretense of the mathematician to produce an objective knowledge is defeated as well, but his subjectivism is that of an inert thought that allows itself to be fatally manipulated from the outside, following the technological prejudice that dictates the illusion of the free will of the individual; it is not the true and living subjectivity of the concept, which realizes itself in the effective mastery of self, which is also its knowledge. This is what separates the enterprise of the mathematician and that of the philosopher; *more geometrico, id est non philosophico*, and vice versa.

Therefore, the first fault of Spinozism is to have tried to import mathematical reasoning into philosophy and thus to have introduced the defect that is specific to his work, yet according to a particularly brutal passage in the preface of *Phenomenology*, it is "non philosophical understanding that envisions mathematical knowledge as the ideal that philosophy must do its best to achieve."[18] The point of view of substance itself depends completely on this fixation with an exterior model: "Spinozism is a defective philosophy because in it, reflection and its manifold determining activity is an external thinking."[19] Or again, "the defect in Spinozism is precisely that the form is not understood as immanent within it, and for therefore, approaches it only as an external subjective form."[20] The absolute desire for rigor that superficially characterizes Spinozism coincides with its powerlessness to develop in itself the necessary rationality effectively adequate to its objective and concrete content.

Even as it lends philosophy the appearance of formal coherence, geometry transmits to philosophy the arbitrator that is the foundation of all its procedures. In one addition to paragraph 229 of the *Encyclopedia,* Hegel notes that, "for philosophy, the synthetic method is much less well suited than the analytic method, because philosophy must justify above all else the subject of necessity of its objects."[21] But the synthetic method is exactly one of geometers, who construct their objects in these definitions, as Spinoza himself intended. But the geometric method, according to Hegel, has a limited validity, peculiar to its own domain, where it engages abstract realities, and as a consequence it is not at all suitable to try to apply it outside of this domain; in particular, this removes from philosophy all possibility of effectively addressing these objects, from which abstraction is excluded. This is what Spinoza did not understand: when he "begins with definitions and says for instance 'the substance is *causa sui,*' within his definitions he has revealed that which is the most speculative, but which is presented in the form of assertions."[22] It is clear from this that Spinoza, from the outset, places himself outside the domain of truth.

The Spinozist Reevaluation of Method

We will not ask ourselves whether these objections that Hegel formulates against the geometric method are well founded but rather whether they touch effectively on something in Spinoza's philosophy, and at what point this encounter occurs.

Let us begin with the definition Spinoza himself gives to the method: "it seems clear what a true method must be and what it essentially consists of, which is solely in the knowledge of pure intellect, to know its nature and its laws."[23] "If it is part of the nature of thought to form true ideas, such as we demonstrated before, it is necessary now to investigate what we mean by the forces and capacities of the intellect. . . . The principal task of our method is to understand as best as possible the forces of intellect and its nature."[24] This signifies that method is not a knowledge in the ordinary sense of the term; in effect, it knows nothing if not our power to know, the intellect whose nature is expressed. This distinction, which places method outside of the order of knowledges, represents par excellence the anti-Cartesianism of Spinoza.

What does it mean, in effect, "to know the forces and the nature of the intellect?" In no way does it mean, following Descartes, to circumscribe the limits of its use: because the power of the intellect is not determined a priori by conditions that would limit its activity, it is by contrast a constant theme in Spinoza, which we all know, which is to achieve a kind of absolute understanding exactly on the condition that we engage thought in a way other than that which Descartes has established, in relying on its "method."

In effect, as long as it concerns our power to know objects and not these objects themselves, the method presupposes the exercise of this power, and it thus has as a prerequisite the knowledges it produces, "whence it becomes apparent that the Method is nothing other than reflexive knowledge, or the idea of the idea, and, since there is no idea of the idea, if there is no idea in the first place, it follows that there would not be a method if there were not first an idea."[25] We see here that the traditional order of presences is inverted: the idea of the idea, the reflexive knowledge that has for an "object" the power of the intellect, is not the condition of the manifestation of the true but on the contrary, its effect, its result. The method does not precede the development of knowledges, but it expresses or reflects it. What this implies is that it is necessary to produce real ideas before being able to "re-cognize" [*re-connaître*], formally Hegel would say, the conditions of their understanding [*appréhension*]. This is the meaning of the famous parentheses of the *Treatise on the Emendation of the Intellect: habemus enim ideam veram,* we already have the true idea, without which we could not know that we have it, nor even what it is to have a true idea. But Descartes says exactly the opposite: before knowing in truth, and according to the order, it is necessary to provide yourself with the means for such a knowledge, that is to say it is necessary to know how to recognize the truth, where it is possible according to the rules—formal ones, Hegel would say—of its constitution.

The reversal that Spinoza undertakes has as a consequence a displacement and reevaluation of method. A displacement: if method is an effect, it should come after and not before knowledge, as we have already said. Thus, for example, we can explain an anomaly in the *Theological-Political Treatise,* whose composition has given pause for thought among its critics; it is only in chapter 7, after having completely developed the analysis of prophecies and miracles, that Spinoza makes explicit his "historical method" of the interpretation of the scriptures, which signifies that it is necessary to make a method function effectively even before being able to formulate it. It is knowledge that applies itself in the method and not the inverse.

A reevaluation, in fact a de-valorization. "To understand this, at least as much as the method requires it, it is not necessary to know the nature of mind through its first cause, all that is necessary is a small description *(historiolam)* of the mind or its perceptions in the manner expounded by Bacon *(Verulam).*"[26]

Reflecting on an already effective knowledge after the fact, method is nothing more than an empirical inventory of procedures, outside all determinations of real causes that guide its functioning. This means in particular that method has lost the juridical function of guarantee that it is assigned in the Cartesian theory of knowledge; it no longer has the power to assign its originary conditions to truth, but it engages some of its properties after the fact, some aspects, moreover, in a manner that is isolated and arbitrary. In this sense, it is necessary to read the *Treatise on the Emendation of the Intellect* as a sort of "Discourse against Method."

Along with method, the classical notion of order is itself also overturned: the development of rational knowledge is no longer subordinated to a strict hierarchy of successive operations, in which the sequence is fixed for once and for all. If *Ethics* is *ordine geometrico demonstrata,* as his subtitle indicates, "order" here designates something completely different from a relationship of presence between propositions. We know that Spinoza never stopped returning to and modifying the demonstrations of the *Ethics,* and there is no guarantee that the state in which he left them was definitive. It is not a case, then, of a rigid relationship, encased once and for all between a beginning and an end, proceeding in a straight line from one to the other by way of a linear sequence of arguments, as with Descartes. For Spinoza, the ideas of method and order cease to be formally determined by a criteria of priority; rather, they express the real movement of thought:

> Since truth has no need of a sign, but rather it is enough for it to grasp *(habere)* the objective essences of things, or, what is the same thing, their ideas, in order that all doubt be removed, it follows that the true method does not consist of seeking a sign of truth after acquiring ideas, but that the true method is the path *(via)* whereby truth itself, or the objective essence of things, or the ideas (all these terms mean the same thing) is to be sought in proper order.[27]

Returning to the original sense of the word *method,* Spinoza identifies this as the true path *(via)* of the true idea, which forms in the mind according to laws that are proper to its nature, independently of any exterior model. The order of ideas is thus that of their actual production; this order is necessary, not by virtue of a rule-bound obligation, which could only be satisfied in a contingent manner, but by reason of the intrinsic causality of the true idea, which determines the idea in the course of producing the totality of its effects, that is, all the ideas that depend on it.

All these considerations, far from distancing Spinoza from Hegel, move Spinoza closer to him: like Hegel he sees method, in its Cartesian sense, as an obstacle rather than an effective instrument for developing adequate thought. But, and this is particularly interesting, in undoing the traditional bond established between method and knowledge, Spinoza achieves a definition of method that is very close to that which Hegel proposes himself: it consists of a reflexive understanding [*connaissance*], in which "the form of interior self-movement" becomes self-aware in the course of which knowledges have produced (following Hegel) "the idea of the idea," which reproduces the real movement of the idea (following Spinoza). Thus, instead of discovering an oppositional motif in the position of the two philosophers as regards the notion of method, which would be a rigorous justification of Hegel's critiques, we see emerging out of his argument a kind of common line of thought that reconciles the doctrines, engaged in a struggle against the same adversary. We see things from closer up.

In an important passage of the *Treatise on the Emendation of the Intellect* (§30), Spinoza develops arguments that render the traditional conception of method untenable. In establishing the primacy of method in relation to the real development of knowledge [*savoir*], as Descartes has done (see *Rules for the Direction of the Mind,* rule 4), we lay ourselves open unavoidably to the refutation of Skeptics, who deduce very logically that the prerequisite conditions for knowledge pose the effective impossibility of all knowledge. In effect, if we need a method in order to know, we also need a method to establish the method itself, and thus in succession, in an infinite regression: we would thus prove easily enough that humans could never achieve any form of knowledge, because the means that we declare indispensable to the research of truth precisely prohibits our achievement of it.

To make this difficulty explicit, Spinoza takes up Descartes in a strange comparison, but he makes him say something completely different. In the eighth of his *Rules for the Direction of the Mind,* Descartes justifies his conception of method by comparing it to certain mechanical arts. The practice of forging requires tools, a hammer, an anvil, which must preexist the exercise of forging; one equips oneself with these instruments through means that come from nature (a pebble, a block of stone) before engaging in the production of finished objects (a helmet, a sword). In the same way, Descartes says, before engaging in the enterprise of understanding things we must set out the means that are indispensable to this activity, in using innate elements that appear immediately to our mind; this preliminary recognition is exactly the method.

In the passage referred to here in the *Treatise on the Emendation of the Intellect,* Spinoza literally reproduces Descartes's comparison but in order to arrive at exactly the opposite conclusion: there is no precondition in the enterprise of knowledge. In effect, just as the Skeptics, exploiting the traditional conception of knowledge, demonstrate the impossibility of attaining truth, one could demonstrate by the same regression toward the infinite the lack of capacity confronting humans in forging metal, because they needed instruments to do this, which they also had to create, using already existing tools, etc. But in this case, as with that of knowledge, it is practice that is definitive in revealing the fictitious character of the argument. Because humans forge the metal, "humans think" (*Ethics* IIA2); thus to transform nature, no threshold was needed for a first tool, and at the same time, to understand things, no threshold was needed for a first idea, nor a first principle in the Cartesian sense. Here at the same time, Spinoza resolves the difficulty posed by the Skeptics, and he completely does away with the critical part of their argument. This is effectively irrefutable if one relates it to its true object, which is the traditional conception of knowledge whose internal contradiction he reveals. To extricate oneself from this contradiction it is enough, then, to renounce the problematic of a truth that submits itself to preliminary conditions of possibility.

Paradoxically, Spinoza's comparison between the development of intellectual knowledge and the history of the technological transformation of nature functions to eliminate the instrumental conception of knowledge that, by contrast, dominates Cartesian thought.

Descartes reasoned as follows: to know it is necessary *first* to set out our tools, which we *then* use in order to know properly; thus we begin by establishing the right method. We know what we are able to know, on which ideas we can rely, and which route we can take to achieve this knowledge. The example that justifies this prescription for Descartes is interpreted inversely by Spinoza: in the history of knowledge (because there is a history of knowledge and not just an order of reasons) the "tools" do not intervene as prerequisite conditions because they themselves must be produced in the same movement that engenders all other processes of production, whether as a finite object or a true idea. Knowledge does not put these instruments to work except to the extent that it has elaborated them, themselves, without the privilege of rules dictating their usage, through the presupposition of an initial given. This indicates that the production of ideas is not regulated through a simple interplay of intellectual technology that would subordinate their validation to the precondition of method. But as indicated, the refutation of this traditional conception of method that leads to a manipulation of instruments is also essential for Hegel; it is even one of the arguments he makes against Spinoza.

But it is possible to go further still: if, according to Spinoza, the development of knowledge does not bring us back to the initiation of a procedure, it because for knowledge there is no absolute beginning. By contrast, for Descartes, the search for truth is placed exactly under this initial condition of rupture with anterior forms of thought, which are nothing but misrecognitions and which must be returned to the obscurity that confounds them. The reform of intellect determines this origin, which redirects knowledge at the moment of its birth, and from which all other ideas derive, on the correct path of a rational and necessary order. The Spinozist project of an *emendatio intellectus* (where one translates the original medical term, *emendatio*, with a notion that has meaning only in the context of religious or juridical reform), which appears to take up this concept, in effect arrests it, distorts it, posing the question of knowledge and its history on a completely different basis.

In effect, "the truly given idea," which for Spinoza permits an escape from the vicious circle implied by the instrumental conception of knowledge, is exactly the opposite of a principle in the Cartesian sense. Spinoza does indeed say that the mind needs an "innate instrument" to begin to know, but it is clear that for him this does not consist of a germ of truth, an originary knowledge in which all knowledge that must result from it preexists its actualization.

And it is here that the comparison with the history of mechanical arts, borrowed from Descartes, acquires the full force of its meaning, a meaning that necessarily escapes Descartes. The first hammer used by a blacksmith could *not* have been a real hammer, any more than the man who made it was himself a real blacksmith, but it was a stone collected from the side of a road, a "natural" instrument, in itself imperfect, which became an instrument only through the use that was made of it, in serving like a tool, which it was certainly not to begin with. Thus humans in this primitive era were able, with the aid of improvised instruments, to fabricate objects, at first very imperfect then increasingly perfected, from which arose a number of instruments that were better adapted to the function they were supposed to fulfill; in this manner they gradually embarked, *paulatim*, on a progressive road where eventually "they were able to complete difficult and numerous tasks with a minimum of trouble." In the same manner, the intellect had to first work with ideas that it had, serving as they did as authentic knowledges, in order to make them produce all the effects they were capable of, gradually refining their own activity; they thus arrived, by completing their intellectual labors *(opera intellectualia),* "at the summit of wisdom."

This analysis signifies quite clearly that there is no proper beginning for thought, which could engage it for once and all, whose orientation on the correct path can be traced from its beginning; this prejudice is entirely symptomatic of the persistence of the finalist illusion of Cartesian theory. Knowledge is by contrast an activity—this idea is essential for Spinoza—and as such never truly begins, nor begins in truth, because it has always already begun. There are always already ideas, because "man thinks" in accordance with his nature. This is why the argument of infinite regression, which we have already addressed, retains a certain validity, if at the same time we deny it the value of a refutation: it simply describes the conditions in which knowledge is produced, through a sequence of absolutely continuous ideas without any assignable beginning. The real problem is to know what becomes of these ideas that we in fact have *(habemus enim ideam veram),* how they are transformed, in the manner in which one might transform a stone to make a hammer. But this transformation does not pose a merely technical problem; it does not consist principally of knowing how to make use of these ideas, to the extent that they do not preexist their usage but on the contrary result from this usage. The ideas with which it is necessary to "begin" to arrive at knowing are not innate truths on which one can found once and for all an order of reasons, as if on a firm foundation; rather, they are a material to be worked on that must be profoundly modified in order to serve, subsequently, the production of truths.

Here we rediscover an argument whose importance we have already established for Hegel: the pretense to an original understanding, a foundation for knowledge, is laughable. In effect, it misrecognizes the necessarily fictitious character of beginnings to which the mind is condemned in its effective history: by definition all that appears at the beginning is precarious, unfinished, condemned to disappear, because it must give way to that for which it is only the precursor. These beginnings justify themselves only through their internal frailty, through their intrinsically contradictory nature, because this allows them effectively to act as the impulse for a movement that succeeds them and effaces them. If a knowledge is possible, it is precisely through this distance that it has established in relation to its beginning; it does not "emerge" from this to develop a content that is already positively given within it but to escape from its indeterminacy and its necessary abstraction. There is no introduction to understanding, no correct method to know, because it is only in its effective practice that thought can be considered, as a real activity of a mind that puts to work, and submits to proof, its own power [*force*] *(vis sua nativa),* which it forms in its practice.

If knowledge does not develop by conforming to an order of reasons by abstractly establishing a framework that persists only to organize it, it is because knowledge exists already in its real history, in its effective labor. Understanding is a process, we might call it the process of production of ideas, and that is what justifies its comparison to the process of production of materials. This explains entirely how we can talk of the causal sequence of ideas, which is the same as that of things: it is a single and same order, and a single and same movement, which expresses itself as real and as thought. This is why understanding should be presented as an activity and not as a passive representation, an idea that Spinoza returns to again and again: knowledge is not simply the unfolding of an established truth but the effective genesis of an understanding that nowhere preexists its realization. This is also why its progress is not subjected to the condition of an absolute origin, which guarantees truth within itself through its "founding"; contrary to a formal order, which is determined by its limit, a practice never really begins, because it has always already begun, in a manner that can thus never be "true." We can equally find in Spinoza the idea of a history of knowledge; this does not encounter truth as a norm that is fixed from the beginning, because it is inseparable from the movement through which it is constituted, and this movement itself is its own norm. Additionally, because Hegel rebukes Spinoza for having banished all movement from his philosophy, by constructing in advance the ideal and the model of an inert knowledge, frozen by its obligation to reproduce an inflexible order, we should be surprised to see him ignore, or falsify, an essential tendency in Spinozism.

An idea, any idea, is adequate in relation to its cause: in its intrinsic

determination the idea expresses the power to act [*puissance*] of the
soul in which it appears. But this capacity is not the abstract power
of a nature delimited by its conditions, natural light in the Cartesian
sense; it is the concrete project, one could say, almost, the material of
a thought engaged in the effort, the labor, of its own realization. In
Ethics Spinoza proposes to "lead us as if by the hand to the knowledge
of the human spirit and its supreme beatitude" (foreword to book
III) and to do this by following a necessary order of demonstrations
that we must follow, without being able to escape it. How does this
order differ from the Cartesian order of reasons? How does the path
that he has opened up differ from the rigid path, already completely
determined by the prerequisite of a method, which would lead us, as
we know, to the fiction of an all-powerful and truthful God?

Following the premises we have established, we must engage in a
reading of *Ethics* that is freed from all formalist prejudices, abandon-
ing the illusion of an absolute beginning. If the thesis of Spinozist
doctrine begins with definitions, axioms, and postulates, if it begins
with substance, if not with God, this does not signify in any way that
these primitive notions constitute a source of truth from which everything that follows can be simply deduced, according to a rigid and
predetermined development, in the form of a clarification. Substance,
attributes, modes, such as they appear in these preliminary principles,
are exactly equivalent to the rough-hewn stone that the first black-
smiths needed to "begin" their work; these are notions that are still
abstract, simple words, natural ideas that acquire no real significance
except at the moment when they function in the demonstrations and
where they produce real effects, thus expressing a capacity that they
did not have at the beginning. Perhaps it is even necessary to approach
Spinoza's *Ethics* in the same manner as Hegel's *Logic*. This is not a
linear and homogenous exposé, one that is uniform and true from
beginning to end, which explores an already established order step by
step, establishing its own ideal of conformity; rather, it is a real process
of knowledge that builds bit by bit, as it develops its own necessity,
in the effective movement of its self-conception, of its genesis. Thus
substance, or the *causa sui*, as it first presents itself to us in a geometric definition, at the beginning of book I of *Ethics*, is something that
comes close to Being in the Hegelian sense: a precarious notion and

untenable as such, which one must transform in order to understand it and master it.

Notwithstanding, this connection we have just outlined reaches its own limit quickly enough: what constitutes for Hegel the motor of rational development, the contradiction, is completely absent from the Spinozist demonstration, and it would do violence to the text to pretend to find it there. For Spinoza, the power of the intellect is, in his entire exercise, integrally positive, an affirmation of self, that excludes any retreat or failing; it does not incorporate negativity of any kind. Is it necessary to interpret this absence as a symptom of failure specific to Spinozism, as Hegel does? Because even as the contradiction that determines it is absent from the movement of this system, that is, an internal life that directs or returns mind to itself, it is exactly at this point where history and reason come together: the thought that aspires to a positive that is nothing but a positive is a lifeless and arrested thought. In contrast, the Hegelian concept is constantly tested by obstacles that it must overcome in order to advance: the history that it engages is all the more real and necessary to the extent that it is punctuated by these attacks, by these irritations and reversals that actually cause it to persist. And yet, if the Spinozist system treats knowledge as a process in its own way, this progresses in a very different manner than the Hegelian development, because it perpetuates this same absolute affirmation: does this demonstrate that it remains subordinated to the laws of an abstract temporality, an order that is at the same time simultaneous and successive, whose continuous progression is only apparent? If so, the discovery of a historical rationality within Spinoza would be, effectively, an illusion.

To overcome this difficulty, we should note that what a Spinozist history lacks is not only the motor of the contradiction but also the thing that is its most characteristic product: an orientation that directs the entire process toward an end that is the principal secret of all its operations. The fundamental aspect of the Spinozist argument is its radical refusal of all teleology. But, for Hegel, the contradiction is the means to create a history and at the same time to allow it to be superseded, pushing it to an endpoint in which all its aspects are totalized and reconciled. From this point of view, the Hegelian dialectic might well be nothing more than a substitute for the notion of classical order in which, through its renewal, it reengages the function of guarantee. In its recourse to negativity, by returning to itself, history advances at a cost that is as great as its detour, toward an end that is the same time its completion and its realization: it is a recurring history, because it is oriented, because it has a meaning, which affirms itself in a lasting manner at every moment. Thus the real successor of Descartes would not be Spinoza but Hegel himself.

Contrary to the development of the Hegelian spirit that is essentially completed, the process of knowledge, such as Spinoza constructs it, is absolutely causal. Therefore, it is at the same time necessary and free from all pre-established norms; its positivity does not presume any regulatory function, which would subordinate the activity of the intellect to an exterior model, independent of its completion. It is exactly for this reason that it excludes any relation to the negative: because it cannot be sustained within a teleological perspective that, for once and all, would establish the relationship between the positive and the negative, sharing a common intention and the promise of reconciliation. If there is a Spinozist history, it is totally independent of such a presupposition. It situates itself at a point where its necessary development, its material process, no longer requires the ideal sanctum of a meaning or an orientation in order to be understood; its rationality has nothing to do with the obligatory unfolding of an order, because it no longer has any goal to complete.

Knowledge by Means of Causes

What remains, then, for Spinoza himself in the procedure *more geometrico*? Doesn't his unswerving fidelity to a mathematical model of demonstration proceed in the opposite direction to the new path Spinoza embarks on, by substituting the formal determination of knowledge as order, with the presentation of knowledge as an active and open-ended process? To answer this question, we must understand what, exactly, Spinoza's reference to the procedure *more geometrico* signifies.

Here again, we will see that Hegel is completely disdainful of Spinoza's real thought, presupposing it is a continuation of Descartes. As a consequence, for Hegel the sequence of propositions that make up the *Ethics* can be nothing other than the application of the ideal of rigor formulated in the *Discourse of Method,* an example of these "long chains of reason, so simple and easy" that construct the geometries in order to directly achieve specific knowledges. But, quite the contrary, the procedure *more geometrico* is symptomatic of a fundamental divergence: far from aligning Spinoza with the Cartesian problematic of knowledge, it is what allows him to affirm a radical opposition to it.

To understand the nature of this opposition, we must return to Descartes's passage in his *Responses to Second Objections,* which Spinoza addresses, via his preface writer Louis Meyer[28] at the beginning of the *Principles of Philosophy of Descartes.* In this passage, Descartes distinguishes two "forms of proof." One follows an analytic order and returns effects to causes; it represents a *ratio cognoscendi,* which addresses its objects from the point of view of their representation in thought, according to a process that accompanies knowledge in its progress. This order is the one that Descartes followed in his *Meditations.* But this proof can also arise from causes to construct their effects from their starting point; thus, Descartes says, "it makes use of a long series of definitions, of postulates, axioms of theorems and of problems, in order that, if we deny any of its consequences, it would cause one to see how they were contained within the antecedents and they would wrest acceptance from the reader, however obstinate and opinionated he might be."[29] But this method, followed by the ancient geometers, "does not conform at all as well (as the analysis) to the subject matter of metaphysics . . . where the principal difficulty is to conceive first concepts clearly and distinctly." Undoubtedly, it is possible to convert one order of exposition to another: the *Second Response* is completed in the *Abbreviated Geometry,* in which the proofs of the existence of God are precisely *more geometrico dispositae.* The term *dispositae* is significant: the geometric order "disposes" the proofs; therefore, for Descartes, it is nothing more than an artificial order, appropriate only to address certain questions, but it remains external to the specific nature of the human spirit, a stranger to its natural light. The synthetic order leads back to a formal manipulation of ideas, and therefore it must be rejected in metaphysics for the benefit of an analytical order, whose exigencies are authentically rational. Because Hegel deems this method geometric, in order to disparage it, we see that he scarcely moves away from Descartes's conception of it.

But when Spinoza adopts the procedure *more geometrico,* it is exactly in reference to this critique that Descartes had opposed, whose underlying reasoning and conclusions he rejects. In the *Principles of Cartesian Philosophy* (*more geometrico demonstratae* and not *dispositae*) he engages in an undertaking that at first glance is quite odd: relying on the abbreviated geometry provided by Descartes as an example (and as a kind of curiosity), he takes up the entire doctrine in order to give it a demonstrative form, which it lacks in *Meditations*. Spinoza thus refuses the hierarchy of preferences established by Descartes himself, which privileges the analytical order in the exposé of his system. But Spinoza not only abandons the form in which the system is presented; he takes care to make clear from the beginning that he doesn't even recognize the content of the doctrine as true. The geometric "translation" that Spinoza gives Cartesian philosophy is thus not a way of saying the same thing in another way: it is even then a way of taking a position to distance himself in relation to it.

The *Ethics*, in which Spinoza develops a philosophical content completely different from that of the Cartesian system, is itself *ordine geometrico demonstrata*, that is, argued synthetically, in a progression that goes from cause to effects. If Spinoza adopts this presentation, it is evident that he sees in it something completely other than a formal disposition of proof, such as Descartes would interpret it. This choice suggests that he does not have an (analytic) procedure *more philosophico* that is distinct from the (synthetic) procedure *more geometrico*, an order of investigation distinct from an order of exposition, a *ratio cognoscendi* distinct from a *ratio essendi*. Between ideas, as between other things, there is one single and unique connection, which goes from causes to effects because it is necessary in itself. It is exactly this identity that determines, outside all guarantee of subjectivity (regardless of whether it is provided by Self *(Moi)* or God—it is in the end the same thing), the objectivity of knowledge, that is to say the power[30] [*puissance*] that it has naturally to express the reality of things as they are in themselves and not only what they are for me. One understands, therefore, that the procedure *more geometrico* is the means Spinoza needed to escape the juridical conception of knowledge, which for Descartes still subordinates the exercise of thought to the coordinates of an artifice.

Synthetically determined, the process of knowledge no longer views things such as they are for me: it grasps them such as they are in themselves. It is thus completely liberated from the finalist illusion, which proceeds by a projection from me; it relies on a strictly causal necessity, and this is the form of its objectivity. It is altogether significant, from this point of view, that book I of *Ethics* achieves this through the statement of the principle of causality presented thus: "nothing exists from whose nature an effect does not follow."[31] This statement possesses certain remarkable features. First, it is formulated in an absolutely general fashion, one that does not signify that its universality is abstract. In avoiding the specification of the object to which this principle applies, Spinoza does not want to indicate that he is indifferent to all content and that he intends only the possibility of formal determination but that he avoids all distinction of content: the principle holds for all reality, for *natura naturans* as for *natura naturata,* in which it is exercised identically. But even if the relationship of the cause to its effects takes very different forms in the process of the *causa sui* and its modal sequence, because in the first case this relationship is intrinsic whereas in the second it is extrinsic, it continues in all cases to affirm a single and same necessity, which cannot be subdivided but must on the contrary be understood as identical; the third form of knowledge is precisely this. On the other hand, in Spinoza's statement the principle of causality literally inverts the terms of the traditional principle: from the well known formula "nothing is without cause," which proceeds in an analytical manner from the effect to the cause, he substitutes "no cause is without effect," which proceeds by contrast from cause to effect, synthetically and summing up in a single phrase the genetic conception of knowledge elaborated by Spinoza. *Causa seu ratio, ratio seu causa.*

It is on this precise point that Spinoza breaks absolutely with the Cartesian problematic of method. *The Mediations* restore effects to their causes: they go from the finite to the infinite, for example from the human soul to God, taking things in the inverse order to which they are actually produced, which goes necessarily from causes to effects. We understand from this point of view that knowledge is first determined as a representation, because it reflects the real in thought and from its point of view, conforming with criteria of validity that at the outset are given within it and that reproduce the order of the real by inverting it. For Spinoza, by contrast, an adequate knowledge "explains" its object to the extent that it affirms itself as identical to it, not in the transparency of a conforming representation but in the likeness of the order of an equally necessary reality.

This is real order in which things were produced, and it must also be that of ideas: this is a genetic order that goes from cause to effects, and it is this that precisely expresses the *more geometrico*:

> We have shown that the true idea is simple or composed of simple ideas in the manner that it shows how and why something is or has been made: we have shown equally that its objective effects in the soul correspond to the formal essence of the object. Which is the same thing as what the Ancients said, to know that true science proceeds from cause to effects.[32]

The reference here to Aristotle is particularly important: *vere scire est scire per causas* (Lewis Robinson indicates the following reference: *Second Analytics 1 C2, Metaphysics 983a, Physique 11 c3*). But we must understand that this in no way signifies a return to sources, which would restore an ancient tradition, circumventing the modern Descartes. In fact, Spinoza takes care to distinguish himself immediately from this tradition: "except that as far as I know, they never conceived the soul, as we are doing here, as acting according to fixed laws, a sort of spiritual automaton."[33]

The Ancients (Aristotle) are preferable to the moderns (Descartes) to the extent that they affirmed the necessity of knowledge through causes. But they did not grasp the causal character of the process of thought, which itself proceeds according to its causes, according to a necessary order identical to that of things; they therefore ignored the nature of true causes, and as a consequence they had to present knowledge in a fictive order.

In effect, for the Ancients, the formal cause of an idea is a universal abstract, genre, or type, but this returns us to a capacity to imagine that is within us, from which we "freely" invent fictions, according to laws that are external to knowledge itself. But for Spinoza, and this is what is intended by his theory of the "spiritual automaton," the cause of an idea resides in the power [*puissance*] of the intellect, grasped not as the singular power of an individual subject but as the eternal property of the mode of thought; thus it is thought, infinite attribute of substance, that expresses itself in a manner determined in each idea, which engenders it "adequately."

On this point, Spinoza is in agreement with Descartes against the

Ancients: to think is to proceed by singular operations, which are intuitive or deductive. It is to link ideas in a sequence effectively present to the mind, taking a short cut through universals, that is, through abstract ideas: reasonable beings are pure possibility, they have only a fictive value, and they are the symptom of an essentially inadequate thought.[34] "In so far as we are engaged in an investigation of reality, we will never be permitted to infer something from abstract ideas."[35] "We must, above all, deduce all our ideas from physical things, that is to say, from real beings, progressing as much as possible following the series of causes, from real being to real being, and in a manner that does not detour through abstract things, or universals, neither by deducing something real from them, nor deducing them from something real: in effect both interrupt the real progress of the intellect *(verum progressum intellectus)*."[36] This "progress," the real process of knowledge, proceeds neither from things to ideas nor from ideas to things, but it goes from idea to idea, that is to say it links acts of thought between them, according to a necessary causal order that is the same as the one in which things are linked in reality. *Ordo et connexio rerum, idem ac ordo et connexio causarum, idem ac ordo et connexio idearum.*

The *more geometrico* functions in the framework of a complex philosophical strategy, and the theoretical dispositif to which it corresponds produces a double effect, because it simultaneously plays Aristotle against Descartes and Descartes against Aristotle; Spinoza is not Machiavellian only in his politics. Aristotle against Descartes: he privileges the genetic method, which proceeds synthetically from causes to effects, and thus compels us to an identification of the order of things and that of ideas. Descartes against Aristotle: he discards the abstract conception of knowledge, which is at the same time formal and empirical, for the benefit of thought in action, effectively present in the ideas that express their power [*puissance*]. But we must understand that this critique of abstraction does not lead us, to recall a well-known formula of Cavaillès, from a philosophy of concept to a philosophy of judgment: thought that affirms itself in each idea is not the manifestation of a free subject that reigns over the products of its creation like a king in his kingdom (Self or God: one is nothing more than the image of the other), but it depends itself on the real objective process that relates the singular idea, as a mode of thought, to substance that expresses itself and acts through thought. Neither Aristotle, nor for that matter Descartes: Spinoza.

The movement of thought proceeds from the same necessity as all reality. "Humans think": this axiom expresses, with the material evidence of fact, the absolutely natural character of the process; it must be mastered according to its own laws, which regulate the movement of the "spiritual automaton." Here, we see the point at which Spinoza is close to Hegel: in establishing a necessary relationship between knowledge [savoir] and the process of its production, he permits it to grasp itself as absolute and thus to grasp the absolute. Taken outside this objective development, knowledge is nothing more than the formal representation of a reality for which it can provide only an abstract illusion. But here as well Spinoza already distances himself from Hegel: in making thought an attribute of substance, he constitutes its movement as absolutely objective and delivers it from all reference to a subject, even if it be thought itself. From there, essential causality, which is the basis of all rationality, is defined without teleological presupposition. The most subtle form of this presupposition would be given by thought, the autonomous subject of its own activity, which takes itself as the objective of its realization, but this conception of a thought that returns upon itself, to itself, as a subject, and appropriates all reality in its self realization, is exactly the key to Hegelian idealism. Consequently, the interpretation Hegel proposes of Spinoza begins to vacillate: for Spinoza, thought is not the unkept promise of a premature dialectic, already impossible, but it is already the critique of a perversion of the dialectic, with which Hegel himself is already engaged, in producing the concept of "subjective logic." Here it is Hegel, it seems, who has to answer to Spinoza.

Adequate Idea and Inadequate Idea

In the strategy of knowledge that Spinoza elaborates, the procedure more geometrico thus contains an essential position, and it leads, quite the contrary, to a formal conception of truth, to present truth as a necessary, objectively determined process. But this has the consequence of completely overturning the traditional relationship established by philosophers, by Descartes in particular, between truth and error. One can already read the famous pages where Hegel denounces abstract thoughts "which rigidly oppose the true to the false" in Spinoza's own text: although it is true that here they are written completely differently and produce effects that are inadmissible for the Hegelian spirit.

In axiom 5 of book 1 of *Ethics*, Spinoza affirms the agreement [*conventia*] of the true idea with its object. This proposition, which is not a definition, does not express the intrinsic character of the true idea: it does not constitute an idea starting from its cause but characterizes it only a posteriori through one of its properties as is confirmed by definition 4 in book II, which distinguishes the extrinsic and intrinsic qualities of the true idea. The notion of *conventia*, which relates the idea to an object that is outside it, evidently designates an extrinsic quality. By contrast, the causal definition of the true idea determines it through its *adequatio*; it is this concept, which is essential for Spinoza and which marks its rupture with the traditional conception of knowledge. In effect, by *adequatio* we must think of exactly the opposite of that which reveals itself as *conventia*.

Adequatio is the intrinsic determination of the true idea, that is, that which produces its truth *in the idea*. The assertion that this determination is interior to the idea must be taken very seriously; there is no need to step outside the idea, to go to an exterior, which would be for example its object, to affirm the necessary existence of its content that it effectively "contains," because it discovers reality within it by staying within its own limits. We find ourselves here, apparently at the outer limits of an idealism: the self-sufficiency of the idea eliminates all exterior determination from it and thus all criteria of objectivity in the traditional sense of the term. But an excess of idealism can also border on a materialism or at least produce certain materialist effects.

The essential function of the category of *adequatio* is to break with the conception of knowledge as representation that continues to dominate Cartesianism. To know, in the sense to represent, to re-present, is literally to reproduce, to repeat; the idea is thus nothing more than a double, an image of the thing for which it provides a representation, which exists and subsists outside of it. What is essential within this empiricist system that vulgar materialism has taken into account? It is the presupposition that the idea, the representation of an object, for or in a subject, has its content outside itself, a content that it can consequently only imitate, designate, simulate, indicate, or even, as they say, "reflect." Consequently, the problem of knowledge consists in justifying this relationship of conformity between the idea and the object that it confronts, and this is not possible except through the discovery of a guarantee that confirms the truth, or again the "objectivity" of an extrinsic relationship between the form and content of knowledge.

For example, we know that when Descartes first attempts to establish the truth of ideas on the basis of their sole internal evidence, he discovers the insufficiency of this formal criteria and the need for a superior guarantee of objectivity: this unshakable assurance that resists even the proof of a hyperbolic doubt is given by an unerring and all powerful God, creator of eternal truths, such that it is necessary that our ideas have a content outside us, a content to which they correspond in the exact manner that they cause us to know. This God of truth is also God the master engineer, who adjusts the system of nature and maintains it in an order according to imperial and irrefutable laws: it is he who adapts ideas to things and ensures thus that what we know, we know truly, and outside the risk of any illusion. But this exemplary system of guarantees, incarnated in an all-powerful being who rules over our ideas like a king over his subjects, permits as well the establishment of a strict separation between the order of that which is true, ordained by God, to which we had better submit, and the disorder that exists outside these limits and constitutes the indeterminate, anomalous, and menacing universe of error.

We must say a few words about the theory of error developed by Descartes, because Spinoza made this one of his principal targets. According to this theory, a false idea cannot be ordained by God by reason of his perfect nature that, on the contrary, guarantees all truths. Error is that which God could not create without contradiction. It exists, thus, in the domain of knowledge, that which is strictly attributable to human nature and to the part of a strictly negative free will, which it refers to. Free will is for Descartes paradoxically what makes human nature similar to divine nature, because it is infinite in us just as in God, but the identity that establishes itself here is one of an inverted, perverse, diabolical image. We delude ourselves; this is to some extent the only manner in which we ourselves can be creators, all-powerful in the work that depends on our absolute initiative, but it is a laughable caricature of divine creation, a malign imitation of it, which reproduces negatively, in the traces of a shadow, that which God himself has inscribed for once and for all in reason, in luminous characters. The error is thus attributable to this portion of nothingness that persists within us and is the proper sign of our disgrace. From this an essential consequence arises: if we err, it is because we wish it so. Thus, the best remedy against error is also found in the free will that engenders it; it is enough that we desire to do right by the correct use of our liberty, of our power to judge, and that we submit ourselves to divine decree, in resisting this burden that pulls us downward, by suspending the effects of this negativity for which we alone are responsible and which opposes us to the order of truth. Thus, between a purely positive truth, which expresses the omnipotence of an authentic creator, and a purely negative error, which expresses only the weakness of a creature and his insane efforts to take the place of his master, there is an absolute separation, a clear limit, a distinction that it is not possible to ignore: it returns truth and error each to its proper place and it forbids all communication between them.

But as we have seen, Spinoza refuses to link the act of knowing to the initiative of a subject (God in the case of truth, us in the case of error); he also refuses the strict separation, the opposition that this establishes between truth and error. First, it is certain that, because we make mistakes, we do not make use of our free will, even in a detrimental manner; to the contrary, we shut ourselves off in the unrelenting order of illusion and mistrust, inevitably engendered from the point of view of imagination. Error is a mechanism ruled by the strictest conditions, which are also those of our everyday enslavement. "Inadequate and confused ideas follow one another *with the same necessity* as adequate ideas, otherwise called clear and distinct."[37] When we possess the truth, we no longer accede to the dignity of a creator-subject, not only because all ideas are true in God, and thus outside our initiative, but because even in God they are submitted to necessary laws that chain them to each other, according to an order that is itself also an order of things and from which they cannot escape. Thus, in understanding as in ignorance, the soul reveals itself as nothing but a "spiritual automaton," which functions according to objective determinations, outside all possible intervention (which would be reserved for the initiative of a perfect being), and in the same way above all obligation. True ideas, like false ideas, explain themselves through their causes; thus we see a fundamental commonality appearing between them, which forbids us from separating them into two separate orders and placing them on either side of an already delineated limit, even this one that separates the negative from the positive.

For Spinoza, ideas are not images, passive representations, and they do not reproduce (more or less correctly) realities that would be exterior to them, or at least it is not this that constitutes them as real. This is what he explains in a striking formula, which evidently critiques Descartes: they are not "mute paintings on a canvass," illusive fictions of a reality or model that would persist outside them, which they could at most resemble. Ideas, all ideas, are acts, that is, they always affirm something in themselves, according to a modality that returns to their cause, that is, in the last instance the substance that expresses itself in them in the form of one of their attributes, thought. The soul is a spiritual automaton because it is not subjugated to the free will of a subject whose autonomy would be to all extents and purposes fictive; it is exactly for this reason that ideas are not automatic forms, ones that reproduce, for example, the "copy machine of realities" invented by philosophers who want at all costs to separate the true from the false. There is no subject of knowledge, not even of truth beneath these truths, that prepares its form in advance, because the idea is true in itself—singularly, actively, affirmatively, in the absence of all extrinsic determinations that submit it to an order of things or the decrees of the creator.

Here we find once again the idea of adequation, which fundamentally signifies that the true idea has no relationship except to itself, because this is how it is engendered by substance, according to a sequence of determinations that constitute its form in the attribute of thought, a sequence that finds itself, moreover, identical to all other attributes. The *adequatio* is thus the key to truth, because it expresses this intrinsic relationship of the idea to itself. For example, this is what *Letter* 60 says to Tschirnhaus: "between a true idea and an adequate idea, I recognize no difference but this: the word 'true' relates uniquely to the relationship *(convenientia)* of the idea to its ideat, whereas the word 'adequate' concerns the nature of the idea in itself: there is thus no real difference *(revera)* between these two sorts of ideas, if it is not this extrinsic relationship."[38] In fact, it is the same thing to talk about true ideas and adequate ideas, but if one seeks to explain them, it is something completely different. In contrast to the immediate and literal signification of the word, which contains agreement within the idea of adequation, and thus an exterior adjustment, through the category of *adequatio* Spinoza expresses this necessity or internal causality of the idea that links it to itself, through the intermediary of all other ideas on which it depends in the attribute of thought and which makes thought into a singular affirmation, an act, of the absolutely infinite substance. Just as with things, with all that exists, ideas are subordinated to a causal order that explains them completely.

The function of the idea of adequation is thus, first of all, critique. It permits us to expunge from the causal determination of the idea everything that arises from another order, which for example, according to its ideat, its object, also necessarily exists: "by adequate idea I mean an idea that, insofar as it is considered in itself, without relationship to its object, has all the properties or intrinsic characteristics of a true idea."[39] Between ideas and things, there exists no relationship of correspondence that subordinates one to the other but rather a causal identity that establishes each one of them in the necessity of its order, or of its movement, or better still of its own process. Thus ideas are not formed in a resemblance of objects that they represent and from which they are derived as an origin, in the way that one can find in the idea that which was first given in the thing: "ideas both of the attributes of God and of singular things recognize as efficient causes, not the object of which they are the ideas *(ideats),* i.e. the things perceived, but God himself insofar as he is a thinking thing."[40] But one can no longer say, inversely, that things themselves are created in the image of the idea from which they would have been formed and that they are thus its manifestation, in the fashion that we find in the thing that which is already given in the idea: "the formal being of things which are not modes of thinking does not follow from divine nature because it knew these things first: rather things which are the objects of ideas follow from and are deduced from their own attributes in the same way and with the same necessity that we have shown that ideas follow from the attribute of thought."[41] This affirmation is evidently symmetrical to the preceding one. Things were not "created" by God conforming to a preliminary idea, which they would then express; by the same token, ideas do not arise from things whose representation they provide. Here Spinoza denounces two inverse errors, which are in the end equivalent because they derive from the same proposition: that of the hierarchical subordination of attributes and their affections. But the causal sequence is initiated entirely within the form of each attribute, in a manner that leaves nothing to be desired and that forbids all communication, that is to say all comparison, between the attributes themselves.

Between the idea and its ideat, there is therefore no longer a relation of conformity that leads one to depend on the other, no matter how this simplification is achieved. This is the meaning of the famous passage in *The Treatise on the Emendation of the Intellect*: "one thing is a circle, another thing is the idea of a circle" (§33). Is the result that the idea (which is determined solely within itself, that is, through its connection with the other ideas that constitute the attribute of thought) has lost all "objectivity" in the immediate sense of the term, that is, all relationship with the object of which it is the idea? Not at all, for two essential reasons. The first is that the idea itself is a thing, to the extent that it is causally determined, as are all the affections of the substance. Thus it can be the object of an idea, a very important property that we will return to. On the other hand, because of its position in the order and the connection of the elements that form the entire ensemble of thought, the singular idea is identical to its ideat, insofar as it occupies exactly the same position in the order and connection to its own attribute, no matter what this is. And yet, this order is the same as the preceding one, because all the attributes equally express substance without the privilege of a hierarchy that would imply the subordination of one to the other. It is therefore exactly because it has no communication with the ideat (except through the intermediary of the substance itself in which all forms of attributes that expresses themselves are all the same) that its idea is adequate to it: the idea coincides with the ideat absolutely, in a manner that leaves nothing to be desired. Thus the meaning of axiom 5 of book 1 of *Ethics*, which also affirms the harmony [*convenance*] of the true idea and its object, becomes clear: between the adequate idea and its object there is certainly a correspondence. Nevertheless, the ordinary relationship between these two terms is reversed. The true idea is not adequate to its object because it corresponds to it; one must say, quite the contrary, that it corresponds to it because it is adequate, that is to say determined in itself, in a necessary fashion.

A very important consequence results from this: an idea cannot be more or less adequate, in the way that a representation imitates its model more or less, and can be itself measured by this degree of conformity. The theory of the adequate idea eliminates all normativity from the order of knowledge and simultaneously prevents the return of the finalist illusion that haunts classical theories of knowledge. The idea is totally adequate, exactly to the extent that it is thereby necessary, in the absence of all intervention of free will: this is the key to its objectivity. Spinoza expresses this in a provocative formula: "all ideas are true insofar as they are related to God,"[42] that is, insofar as they are interpreted according to the causal necessity of the process that has engendered them. From this point of view, all ideas are adequate; all ideas are true. That includes inadequate or confused ideas; false ideas are also true in their own way. This is why Spinoza writes, "verum index sui *et falsi.*" There is even in the nature of truth something that makes reference to the possibility of error and explains it. Inversely, Descartes creates an insurmountably binding separation [*séparation en droit*] between truth and error (even if there was not one in fact) that obliges him to look for the specific origin of error by constructing the theory of human free will. For Spinoza, by contrast, the theory of error is immediately included within the theory of truth and helps to constitute it: false ideas are also singular ideas, and in both cases the problem is to understand how they are necessarily produced.

The traditional expression "to distinguish truth from falsehood" thus acquires, in Spinoza's doctrine, a completely novel significance. It does not indicate the ideal limit that traces a prescription or a prohibition between two irreducible orders, which he resorts to enforcing through good will, but it returns rather to the difference between *modes of knowledge.* And yet, by the mode of knowledge, Spinoza intends a certain manner of entering into a relationship with ideas, itself determined practically by a manner of being, that is, by conditions of existence: the ignorant person is also a slave. There are distinct practices of knowledge, which depend on an entire ensemble of material and social determinations. Thus, is it not true that the imagination following a popular expression of the classical age is a "kind of knowledge," a capacity for error, that is, a power to engender certain ideas that are false in themselves? Because "there is nothing positive in ideas whereby they can be said to be false,"[43] that which is false, that is, that which places us in a certain state of illusion, is a determinate relationship to ideas, to all ideas, which causes us to perceive them, we might even say live them, in an inadequate manner, "mutilated and confused."

An idea is thus never false in itself. Does that mean that it is also never true in itself? This is exactly Descartes's thesis: taken in themselves, ideas are nothing but passive representations. They are neither true nor false; truth is a function of judgment, which animates ideas through the intermediary of will. It is that which gives or refuses its consent to representations of the intellect and declares them in conformity with reality or not. From this point of view, if there is an active element in knowledge (as it appears, for example, in the Cartesian theory of attention), this element is essentially subjective, because it depends on the affirmation of a self who proffers judgments and who makes use of his free will, by granting or by refusing the credibility of the ideas that intellect proposes to him. There is nothing like this with Spinoza, who refuses the Cartesian distinction between the intellect and the will. The active character of knowledge does not depend on the initiative of a free subject; rather, it is the idea itself that is active, insofar as it expresses in a singular fashion the infinite causality of substance. As such, it would not be indifferent to its content of truth, in the manner of a passive representation. Considered in God, following the causal sequence that sustains it, the idea is always true, adequate to its conditions. What leads, then, also on occasion to its identification as false?

When Spinoza defines falsehood as a "privation of knowledge,"[44] he does not mean to say that it is something intrinsically negative, thus exterior to the order of knowledge, but to the contrary that it cannot be constituted except in relation to knowledge, for which it is a "mode." The inadequate idea is an incomplete idea, to the extent that we cannot grasp it except by mutilating it. In itself, in God, it is adequate, but by understanding it in a partial manner, we are prevented from perceiving the necessity within it, and it is this contingency, whose real causes are within us, from which the illusion of a free will is derived.

It is necessary here to return to a well-known example: the imagination, which is a form of comportment, a manner of living realized materially and socially in the subjugated existence of the slave, "represents" the sun to us at two hundred paces, but we discover that this perception is false, because reason explains to us that the sun is not a big round ball that shines at our horizon but a star that we are very far away from and that is found at the center of a system of stars, of which we occupy only a part. What distinguishes imaginary representation from true knowledge? It is the point of view from which this knowledge originates, and with it our mode of knowledge. In the case of the imagination, knowledge is subordinated to the point of view of the "free" subject, which situates itself at the center of this system of representations and constitutes this system as if it were autonomous, as an empire within an empire; thus, in this apparently free human universe, the sun appears as a huge object that adorns the scenery of life and finds through its relation to life its place and its use, because what is specific to the imagination is exactly to relate everything to the "self." But if I change my life, and I cease to "represent" reality from my own perspective, that is, according to goals, as if reality were made only for my use, I see things in a completely different way. An absolutely de-centered universe, in its total objectivity, can no longer be dependent on the initiative of a subject, whatever that be, even an all-powerful creator. Things no longer depend on an arbitrary order, but they are related one to another in a necessary causal sequence, in absence of all determination by goals.

To represent reality through imagination and to know it adequately are two entirely different things. And yet, even in an imaginary representation, from the example we have just provided, there must be something adequate, something true. In effect, if we, and the majority of humans, consider reality from an imaginary point of view, it is not because we really want to, through a behavior in which we bear the responsibility of judgment, but because we cannot do otherwise; thus we must take literally the idea that we are slaves to the imagination.

In the life that this creates for us, free will is itself nothing more than a necessary illusion, from which we cannot escape. The imagination ignores causes that actually determine our activity, but it does not do away with them; in this sense, there is something in inadequate knowledge that is not purely subjective and which is itself true in its own way. This is why, when we know reality adequately, when we understand, from the rational point of view of necessity, that the sun is not as we represent it "spontaneously" to ourselves two hundred feet away, nevertheless we do not stop seeing it as it first appeared to us, from the point of view of imagination.[45] Better: we know that it appeared to us necessarily so and that it could not have been otherwise. The sage is not one who decides voluntarily to reform his intellect for once and for all, to eliminate, once and for all, all the false ideas that can be found there, and in this way to suppress from his existence all the effects of the imaginary mode of knowledge. It is the half-wit who believes himself to be delivered from all his passions, as they do not truly belong to him and do not depend on him; on the contrary, the free man knows how to reckon with them, because he has grasped adequately the manner in which they are necessary. *Verum index sui et falsi*: the true takes into account the false as well in its objectivity, exactly to the point where it ceases to appear false in order to demonstrate its own truth.

What is it, then, that is true in the false idea? Let us return to the example of the sun that we first see at two hundred feet. This "idea" is adequate and true within God. It is within us that it is mutilated and confused, because we grasp it incompletely, in the manner in which it presents itself as detached from its cause. In what way is this imaginary representation nevertheless adequate? In what it indicates objectively, and entirely differently from the ideal of the sun that we relate to spontaneously; what it expresses, in fact, is the disposition of our bodies, which predisposes us to perceive the sun in a way that de-natures reality within. Thus the image is false in relation to the object it observes. But this does not signify that it is a purely illusory representation, an idea without an object, which would be enough to refute in order to dismiss it. In effect it is an idea, a true idea if not an idea that is true. As such, it is adequate, and it corresponds to an object that is not the one we immediately attribute to it and that itself

can be found elsewhere than in the place where we have spontaneously located it: not there, where the sun is found objectively, the real
sun, from which we have formed a mutilated and confused image,
but here, where we are, with our bodies that prevent us from having
an exact representation of the sun. The false image of the sun is a
true idea if we relate it to our own corporeal existence. In what way,
then, is it inadequate? Insofar as it is separated from the knowledge
of its object, for which it substitutes another content. Pascal distills
the same reasoning in a striking summary: "Although the opinions of
a people are sound, they are not so as conceived by them, since they
think truth is where it is not."[46]

The freedom of the sage does not consist of suppressing the passions and the effects of servitude but of modifying his relationship to
his passions and to the images that accompany them or elicit them;
in recognizing the necessity that they express themselves in their own
way, he transforms them into joyous passions, into clear images, which
are explained in the totality of their determination. Spinoza's politics
consist specifically of this, because knowledge, which depends first on
modes according to which it is practiced, is also a matter of politics.

This detour is much too short to encompass the real complexity of the Spinozist theory of the imagination, but it permits us to
provide evidence for the completely original character of the truth
that flows from it. Its uniqueness is manifest in two essential points:
the intrinsic determination of the truth in relation to the category of
adequation and the immanent relation between truth and error that
is its consequence. On these two points, it seems obvious that Spinoza
anticipates theses that will also be developed by Hegel.

In effect, Hegel opposes the dogmatic, metaphysical, constricted
conception of truth with a speculative conception that first constitutes
a truth through the relationship of truth to itself:

> Habitually, we name "truth" the agreement of an object with
> our representation. In this case we presuppose an object to which
> our representation must conform. In a philosophical sense, by
> contrast, if expressed in an abstract and general fashion, truth
> signifies the agreement of a content with itself.[47]

From a philosophical point of view, then, we must not understand truth to mean a property, a formal relationship, extrinsic to the idea, envisioned in its relationship with an object that confronts it, but a determination of content itself that affirms itself as true, or not true, in itself. To know something truly is not to form a representation from an exterior and subjective point of view, but it is to develop its own nature, such as it reflects itself in the movement that constitutes it. Here, we are very close to the notion of adequation: we find within it a critical function in the elimination of an abstract problematic of truth, defined by the agreement between a representation and its object, but positively, we also engage ourselves in the analysis of the process of knowledge. In effect, according to Hegel, this content that expresses itself as true is nothing other than thought returning to itself to grasp itself once again in its self-realization. This is why knowledge is an immanent relationship of thought to itself, excluding any attempts to head toward an exterior, in order to reunite with a reality in which existence is determined abstractly, outside itself.

On the other hand, it is well known that the Hegelian conception of truth as an intrinsic determination of thought implies an entirely new relation between truth and error. From the speculative point of view, the false is not a negative that can be nothing but negative and that would be so through its complete exteriority to truth: to the extent that knowledge is inseparable from the process through which it is realized, it develops by returning to itself, as an immanent negativity. In this sense, the truth itself is equally a negative in relation to the falsity that it overcomes in the progress of its self-development. This is why it is no longer possible to maintain dogmatically a rigid separation between the true and the false. Moreover, the dialectic does not permit a positive and negative to be fixed in such an opposition. In falsehood it is the truth itself that "produces" itself, in the form of its negation, which it cannot do except by immediately contradicting this determination, in order to establish itself in a superior relation to itself. As Hegel bluntly states, "One can also know falsely."[48] To know falsely is still to know: truth is always implicated in error and vice versa. Hegel radicalizes this conception to the point of refusing to accept that we might take the false, as one would in a truncated dialectic, as a "moment of truth," which would once again be a way of subordinating the false to the true, by positing it as an intermediary, a means that leads to the truth but would disappear in its result once this was completed. Between truth and falsehood, one must think to the point of unity. The failure of this reciprocal appearance is that the truth cannot be reflected except abstractly, and partially, as a given, a state of fact; it is an idea that is nothing but an idea, which is separated from the movement in which it realizes itself and becomes real.

It seems, then, that on the question of truth Spinoza and Hegel arrive at comparable conclusions. It is true that they are achieved through different approaches and are expressed in disparate terms. But even by the admission of these two authors, what value is a result that is taken out of context from the procedure that establishes it? Moreover, our objective is not to compare these two philosophies in order to distinguish them from each other; this would not be possible except at the cost of an abusive simplification of their content, which would lead to a real distortion of their meaning. Rather it is to place in evidence a phenomenon that is highly disconcerting: Hegel declares himself furthest from Spinozism exactly at the point on which the two doctrines appear to coincide. Is his refutation not able to take stock of this momentary convergence, to refrain from subsequently denouncing its superficial character, in discovering other motifs that allow him to distinguish himself?

Rather, his approach is exactly the opposite: to demonstrate the insufficiency of Spinozist doctrine, Hegel imputes to it a certain number of philosophical positions that are not Spinoza's, that Spinoza has even expressly rejected, because they adopt an abstract conception of knowledge incompatible with the point of view of an immanent rationality. What is strange in this undertaking is that Hegel confronts Spinoza with an argument that strongly resembles one that Spinoza developed against the Cartesians: he has thus replied in advance to the objections raised by Hegel. Therefore, the attitude of Hegel is marked by a formidable, apparently inexplicable misunderstanding: what Hegel has "forgotten" to read in Spinoza is what he was better placed than anyone to recognize in terms of its importance and significance.

Evidently, this cannot be a simple blunder, because Hegel has taken the problem of Spinozism very seriously, to which he has dedicated numerous critiques, and drawn on serious and well-intentioned sources. This is why one must look elsewhere for the reasons for this disregard: it can be found only in Hegel's system itself, which through its own development constrains him to distort the reality of Spinozism. In effect, to better distinguish himself from it, Hegel had to substitute Spinozism with a fictitious doctrine, created for the needs of his cause and eliminating all the historical innovations of Spinoza's system. Everything happens as if to better "surpass" Spinoza, Hegel had to first reduce him and in diminishing him lead him back to positions that were in fact those of Hegel himself. But in this necessity where he found himself minimizing Spinozism in order to refute it, should we not see, on the contrary, the defect that exposes Hegel, an indication of his excessive character, which would be intolerable for Hegel himself?

Here we can better understand why it is not enough to compare these two systems in order to declare an analogy of simple resemblance between them. It is because their relationship is essentially that of a contradictory unity: Hegel opposes himself to Spinoza at the exact moment where their common heritage reveals itself. What Hegel could not support in Spinoza, and what he could not eliminate except at the risk of betrayal, is a system of thought that called his own system into question, in which his philosophical position was itself implicated. This is why there is not simply an external relation between the two systems, whether a relation of independence or of lineage: the philosophical theses on which Hegel and Spinoza are opposed are the basis of a real alternative, whose terms are linked in an immanent fashion. To return to the particular question under study, the fact that demands an explanation is therefore this one: Hegel and Spinoza confront each other to the extent that they lay claim to the same conception of concrete, active, absolute truth.

For Spinoza as for Hegel, truth is an internal determination of thought, which excludes all relation to an exterior object. But, and this is what is really at stake in their conflict, they invoke very different realities under the term *thought*. For Spinoza thought is an attribute, that is, an infinite form in its kind, of substance, which is absolutely infinite. For Hegel, it is spirit, as subject of itself, which identifies itself as such in the process of its becoming-Real, which eventually appears in totality, as totality: the rational development of thought discovers this as absolutely unique, because it absorbs all reality, all content, within thought. It is precisely this exclusive privilege of thought that the philosophy of Spinoza does not allow, because in his philosophy thought is neither the sole expression of substance nor even its best expression: at the most, it is one of the "essences," in which it acts, developing its own causality.

It is thus possible, at the risk of a chronological violence, to talk about the refutation to which Spinoza himself subjects Hegel: what awaits this refutation is the idealistic presence of the dialectic, which bases its universality on the presupposition that thought, by reason of its internal reflexivity, is the form par excellence of the real, of all the real: it is as such that it presents itself as an absolute rational order that gathers, and absorbs, all other orders, in the process of its own totalization. The Hegelian dialectic, which presents itself as a circle of circles, presupposes a relation of hierarchical subordination between all the elements that it reunites, and this subordination is reflected through an ultimate term, from whose point of view the entirety of its progress can be understood, because it has a meaning. But it is exactly this presupposition that is immediately rejected by Spinoza, because he eliminates from his conception of the real, from substance, any idea of a hierarchical subordination of elements: as an attribute of substance, thought is identical to everything and therefore has nothing above it, but the sequence through which it is realized poses, at the same time, its absolute equality with all other forms in which substance is also expressed, and these are infinite in number. By contrast, Hegel thinks of Spirit as subject and as entirely within a perspective of eminence, which constrains and subordinates unto itself all that is produced as real and which would appear therefore as its manifestation. This subordination, which installs a hierarchy of forms within the movement of reason, is the key to Hegelian teleology; it is this teleology that Spinoza eliminates.

This leads us to rather paradoxical question. In establishing a hierarchy of all the forms of its realization, from the point of view of spirit that grasps itself as subject, as all, and as end, is it not Hegel himself who, in a surprising reversal, situates himself within the point of view that he condemns in Spinoza, the point of view of substance? What characterizes this point of view, in effect, is that within it a Whole is proposed, concentrating all reality, in such a way that it cannot subsequently do anything but profit successively from determinations that are less and less real and that exhaust themselves in their series. What appears scandalous to Hegel in this "cycle" is not so much the relationship between the whole and its parts that determines this conception but the order of succession in which they are realized: following Spinoza, it is the Whole that is given first in an absolute beginning. What Hegel proposes is simply to reverse this order, by placing the Whole at the end of the process and by arranging its determinations as moments that progressively lead there. But at the end of this reversal the relationship of immanent integration, which subordinates the components to the whole in a hierarchical order, is integrally maintained; this is principally what constitutes the evolutionism of Hegelianism.

In contrast, Spinoza thinks of the process of knowledge in a nonevolutionary manner as a process without end [fin]: a process of self-determination of thought that permits one to know the real in totality, following a law of absolute causality, but without completely exhausting the determinations within it. A process without end would be completely unthinkable for Hegel. This is why he was not able to recognize it even in the terms through which Spinoza considers it; here his need to interpret this process without end surfaces in the falsified image of a process that begins absolutely. But this distorted image is nevertheless adequate from Hegel's perspective because by providing him a caricature, it repeats the intensive order, the relationship of eminence, and the unity of integration between the whole and its parts, which constitute the presupposition, compelled by its own thought.

It is clear from this that Hegel is literally not able to understand what Spinoza says, because this would mean that he must simultaneously renounce the presuppositions of his own system. This is why, in order to satisfactorily resolve the question he asked Spinoza, it was absolutely necessary for him to absorb Spinoza's point of view into his own, to present Spinoza as a moment in his own doctrine: a point of beginning, a provisional moment, a moment to surpass, a moment already passed, a threat already overcome, because it tossed aside the perspective of an outdated history, which could no longer speak, except to memory, outside all actuality.

This system of defense that Hegel constructed to protect him from Spinoza's truth loses a great deal of its effectiveness once we see within it a representation that does not correspond to the object to which it refers: Spinoza, but from the position that Hegel himself seeks to maintain, and whose frailty he would cruelly divulge. Hegel liked to think of himself as the master of the image he imposed on Spinoza, but it is rather Spinoza himself who offers a mirror in which he projects, without knowing it, his own truth.

⇒ 3 ⇐

The Problem of Attributes

The Ambiguity of the Concept of Attribute

Hegel's objections concerning the question of the relation of the attributes to substance can be situated within and expands on the same perspective as his critique of the procedure *more geometrico*. The preceding discussion bears essentially on the conditions of a real knowledge, and it thus puts into play the position of thought in relation to the real. Yet the intervention of the categories of substance and attribute in the treatment of this problem reveals an essential divergence between Spinoza and Hegel. For Hegel thought and the real are fundamentally united in that they arise from the same process in which the mind, the actual, is its own subject for itself: beyond the unilateral presentation of the real as substance, there is *also* its apprehension as subject, that is, as a totality in movement. In contrast, when Spinoza presents thought not even as substance but as an attribute of substance, he concedes once again that he falls short of a truly rational knowledge, for which his system can provide only an imperfect and incomplete sketch.

In this displacement—from thought as substance that has become subject to thought as an attribute of substance—what is at stake is first the status of thought. In positing thought "outside" of substance and in a certain way dependent on it, Spinoza, according to Hegel, removes it from its position of preeminence at the same time as he contests its universal vocation. In this sense Spinoza remains outside the idealist perspective because he denies thought the character of substance (which Descartes, in contrast, granted). In effect, it seems indeed that between substance, which is absolutely infinite, and its attributes, which are "infinite *only* in their kind,"[1] there is a hierarchical difference analogous to that which separates the whole from its parts. If thought is therefore an attribute, which the Spinozist system asserts incontestably, and if the attributes occupy a subordinate position in relation to substance, which grants them diminished or incomplete functions, then thought is no longer this absolute process that affirms its necessity through its realization. It is rather only an aspect or a moment in this process, which does not contain all its conditions within itself and whose development, if we consider it within itself, is contingent to the extent that it depends on an exterior cause. This is how Hegel talks of attributes, "that is to say terms that do not have a particular existence as being in and for themselves, but that exist only as sublated, as moments."[2] But are the attributes parts of substance for Spinoza? And, following Hegel's interpretation, is the relationship of dependence that links them to substance a hierarchical relationship between elements that are essentially unequal? The entire question rests here.

It must be understood that in this argument, by undertaking a critical analysis of the nature of attributes in general, Hegel circumvents a difficulty that is central for him, which specifically concerns one of Spinoza's attributes, Thought, to which he extends these initial objections. It is not surprising, then, that he repeats the same arguments regarding the attributes that were brought to bear against Spinoza's method: here again, what Hegel reproaches Spinoza for is the formalism and abstraction that, for Hegel, characterizes his entire system. In effect the attributes, as defined by Spinoza, are for Hegel abstract essences, points of view *about* substance that remain external to it and thus only "represent" it in an incomplete manner, outside all possibility of a concrete development:

> Spinoza's definition of the absolute is followed by his definition of the attribute, and this is determined as the manner in which intellect comprehends the essence of substance. Apart from the fact that intellect, in accordance with its nature, is postulated as posterior to attribute—for Spinoza defines it as mode—attribute, determination as determination of the absolute, is thus made *dependent on an other*, namely, intellect, which appears as external and immediate over against substance.[3]

At issue here is of course the definition Spinoza gives the attribute at the beginning of book I of *Ethics*: "By the attribute, I mean that which the intellect perceives of the substance as constituting its essence."[4] Apparently, Hegel follows this definition to the letter: if the attribute is that which the intellect perceives of the substance, it thus follows that it does not exist by itself outside the intellect that perceives it and in which it would appear as a representation, that is, an image or an idea of substance, external to it, and by this fact it is necessarily incomplete. So the gap that separates the attribute from substance becomes apparent: it is nothing but a point of view in which substance is reflected, but not within itself in the particular movement of its internal reflection because, according to Hegel, the Spinozist substance is essentially immobile. Instead, it must be said that substance is reflected outside itself, in the intellect that perceives within it *one* irreducible essence, which represents the totality of substance through an act of mutilation, by reducing it to just one of its aspects or moments.

Hegel's objection is apparently very strong, because it brings to light a formidable contradiction in Spinoza's own statement: the attribute "expresses" the substance, and it is in a certain way identical to it, it participates in its own infinity, it constitutes its own essence. One could say, once again, that it is substantial, and nevertheless it does not present substance in its intimate nature, but does substance have only one nature? As a foundation, the Spinozist substance is for Hegel an abyss, a nothingness of determinations, but such as it would appear, as it presents itself outside itself, for an intellect that comprehends it.

But what is this intellect that perceives substance and on which, then, the nature of the attribute is found to depend? Whether it is a finite or infinite intellect—recall that Spinoza's definition does not entertain this distinction—it is a mode, that is to say an affection of substance, through the intermediary of one of its attributes, which in this case is thought. It is thus that the circle clearly appears in which his abstract mode of reasoning encloses the Spinozist system: in the "order" of the system, the attribute, as an essence of substance precedes the mode which is one of its ulterior determinations, and nevertheless in his definition the consideration of one mode, that of intellect, intervenes. Better still, this definition makes the nature of the attribute depend on the existence of this mode, without which it would be not only incomprehensible but even impossible.

For Hegel, the Spinozist system is essentially abstract because it wants to think the absolute in a beginning, as a beginning: the determination of the absolute is thus restored to a regressive order of the manifestation of substance outside itself (because it has nothing in itself), first in its attributes and then in its modes. But, by virtue of its formal character, this order is reversed the instant it unfolds: to the extent that the mode succeeds the attribute, the mode depends on the attribute. Nevertheless, Spinoza thinks of, or better defines, the attribute through the mode and thus as a mode; with the result, at the very least, that the distinction between the attribute and the mode becomes incomprehensible.

But this incoherence is not attributable to faulty reasoning. It has a meaning; it expresses the very limit of Spinozist thinking that, following the premises, the "principles" that it gives itself, cannot avoid falling into such difficulties. The absolute self-sufficiency of substance, its instantaneous unity given in a foundation that absorbs all reality into itself but from which nothing can escape, except appearances or "ways of being," gives its ontological guarantee to the system but at the same time prevents it from developing; it is necessary, then, in its development, to call into question these premises: the "passage" from substance to attributes is a formal and arbitrary process by which substance destroys or exhausts itself, dispersing its profound unity in a multiplicity of attributes, which do not "understand / comprise" [*comprennent*] it except through ignorance of its true nature. The incoherence, the weakness of the Spinozist notion of the attribute, expresses the necessary or rather the inevitable exteriority of substance to itself, which can be grasped in its essence only if this essence is opposed to it as a determination, taking hold of it from outside, which must therefore be inadequate to it. But this inadequacy is only the fault of the substance itself: as a form that is universal and empty, it is incapable of returning to itself to grasp itself in itself as true. This is why the inconsistency of the Spinozist system, such as it appears in its definition of attributes, unfolds "logically" from these premises, of which it is the necessary consequence. The vicious circle, in which Spinoza turns, is also his truth: it is the condition of possibility of his discourse and the manifest symptom of his failure.

Because he reasons abstractly, Spinoza can determine the absolute only by decomposing it, in "passing" from the point of view of coherence that is given to it immediately through an analysis of its elements, the "essences" that constitute it. Once one abandons the foundation in order to approach what it founds, by envisaging its successive determinations, the attributes and then the modes, one sees its unity is undone or even disappears and it is a multiplicity, a diversity that takes its place. Indeed, not only are the attributes external to the substance (and thus manifest the exteriority of the substance to itself, which is incapable of assembling itself effectively in an intrinsic movement), but they are also external to each other, as aspects or points of view, irreducible essences that can be posited only alongside one another, and enumerated, without the possibility of establishing a true community between them. And this is indeed an unequivocal affirmation of Spinoza that the attributes, which do not act on one another and which are not linked by a reciprocal relation of communication, are fundamentally independent.

In this separation of attributes, Hegel sees exactly the symptom of their powerlessness to equate themselves with the absolute, which they partially "represent." Thus, the immediate and empty unity of the substance scatters in a multiplicity of attributes that express it in incomplete forms, and these cannot be grasped together, comprised in an effective whole, but are assembled, juxtaposed, added one to another, like pieces abstracted and arbitrarily held in a totality.

But—and here Hegel's critique reaches its crucial point—not only do the attributes exist as separate entities, each posed itself, in the solitude of its abstraction, they are also opposed to each other. Being only points of view of substance whose content they share and which they cause to appear in a mutilated fashion, they are in a way confronted with one another, as concurrent forms, whereby each exists in the absence of all the others and in opposition to them.

Here a new argument is emerging, one that takes as pretext the well-known thesis *omnis determinatio est negatio*: the attributes determine substance negatively, that is, in a privative manner. Thus what gives form to an attribute is what is missing from all the others; this is why it is irreducible to them.

We will consider this argument on its own terms later on. For the moment we retain only one consequence from it. We have seen that by positioning the attributes as following substance as its abstract determinations, the Spinozist system finds itself inevitably caught up in a regressive movement. In part, but in part only—because, let us recall, the root of Spinoza's error is found in his point of departure, from which he could only deviate—to know a unique substance absolutely, he then retraces his steps and thus rediscovers Cartesian dualism. In his *Lectures on the History of Philosophy*, this is how Hegel presents what he calls the Spinozist idealism, by reducing it to his principal inspiration:

> Spinoza's philosophy is the objectification *(Objektivierung)* of that of Descartes, in the form of absolute truth. The elemental thought of Spinoza's idealism is this. What is true is quite simply the one substance, whose attributes are thought and extension (nature); and only this absolute unity is true, and the real *(wirklich, die Wirklichkeit)*, it alone is God. It is, as with Descartes, the unity of thought and being, or what constitutes in itself the principle of its existence. For Descartes, substance, the Idea, has quite assuredly being itself in its concept; but it is only being as abstract being, not being as real being *(reales Sein)*, or as extension, but corporealities, something other than substance, not one of its modes. In the same manner, the I, that which thinks, is for itself also an autonomous being. This autonomy of two extremes is overcome in Spinozism and it arises from these moments of absolutely singular being. We see that, what is being expressed here, is the grasping of Being as Unity of opposites.[5]

At first glance this text illuminates what separates Spinoza from Descartes: what the latter poses as autonomous substances, thought and extension (which Hegel assimilates into "nature," that is, the "real"), are reunited, reconciled by Spinoza through the absolute unity of substance, which is also "the unity of opposites." But we know that for Hegel this is an abstract unity, that is, a false unity that decomposes in the process of its self-determination, exactly in these same oppositions that it has therefore only provisionally reunited, by "surpassing" their opposition. In the way that Spinoza represents them, these oppositions, which are nothing more than oppositions, can be surpassed only in an illusory fashion; rather, they are simply transposed. This is why at the foundation of the Spinozist system we rediscover a Cartesian dualism, albeit in a modified form.

Hegel's commentary on the definition of attributes in the same chapter in *Lectures* has exactly this meaning:

What comes second after substance is the attributes: these belong to it. "By attribute, I understand what the intellect perceives of substance as constituting its essence," and for Spinoza, this alone is true. This is a major determination: the attribute is at the same time a determination and a totality. Substance has only two attributes, Thought and Extension. The intellect grasps them as the essence of substance; the essence is nothing more than substance, but it is only the essence from the perspective of the intellect. This perspective is external to substance; it can be envisaged in two ways, as extension and as thought. Each is the totality, the entire content of substance, but only under one form; this is why the two sides are in themselves identical and infinite. This is true perfection. In the attribute, the intellect grasps the entire substance; but how substance passes into attributes, is not explained.[6]

If the entire content of the substance is found in each attribute, it is exactly to the extent that substance is itself devoid of all content. The attribute is only a form, which can certainly be autonomous and infinite; it remains no less deprived of all real movement and thus of a concrete unity. The attributes are essences that confront one another, that are opposed to each other, and their extrinsic relationship reveals the powerlessness of substance, that is to say the powerlessness of the absolute, posed as immediate, to determine itself through itself.

But what is above all characteristic in these two preceding texts is an extraordinary omission. Spinoza affirms that substance expresses itself in an infinity of attributes, of which we perceive only two, thought and extension. Yet when Hegel characterizes the nature of attributes, he acts as if there are only the two attributes we perceive: "it (substance) has only two, Thought and Extension." This restriction has extremely important consequences, because it permits Hegel to establish a filial relationship between Spinoza and Descartes; it is also what authorizes him to present the unity of attributes within substance as a unity of opposites.

Let's return to the definition Spinoza gives the attributes: they are "what the intellect perceives of the substance as constituting its essence."[7] We have already remarked that Spinoza does not clarify what the intellect is here, that perceives substance: is it an infinite intellect that perceives all its essences or a finite one that perceives only two? Why does this distinction not appear in the general definition of the attributes? In any case, it is clear that Hegel does not take any notice of this imprecision, or rather this lack of precision, and that he interprets the definition of attributes in a very particular sense, a restrictive one: for him the intellect that "constitutes" the attributes by perceiving substance is the finite intellect that apprehends the attributes only under those two forms of thought and extension.

Guéroult has emphasized the Kantian inspiration for Hegel's interpretation of Spinoza; it is really this implicit reference to Kant that justifies the accusation of formalism leveled against Spinoza. The attributes are not just the "essences" of substance; they are its forms and, at the limit, its phenomena. The attribute is substance such as it would appear to an intellect that decomposes it according to the very conditions of its perception, that is, that determines it by limiting it. In this sense, for Hegel the infinity of attributes, which express their identity with substance, is an infinity without content: it is the infinity of a form that, in itself, as form, is a finite form, in the limitation that constitutes it and from the point of view of the intellect that "perceives" it. Thus everything is connected: the powerlessness of Spinoza to think concretely about the absolute results from the fact that he has situated himself from the start within the point of view of the finite intellect, which because of its own nature is incapable of grasping the infinite other than by decomposing it, that is, by reducing it to abstract essences. Note that underlying this entire argument, the Kantian distinction between reason (devoted to the unconditioned) and intellect (which does not determine its object except under conditions) presents itself. What Hegel did not see, did not want to read in the definition of attributes given by Spinoza, is precisely the anticipatory refusal of such a distinction. This refusal is expressed by the fact that the notion of understanding figures in this definition in an absolutely general manner, without which there would be room for some difference—whatever there may be—between several forms of understanding.

From there it is evident that Hegel does not explain Spinoza's text but rather proposes an interpretation of it. Through this interpretation he rediscovers Descartes in Spinoza: the intellect that serves to determine the nature of attributes is a finite intellect that perceives only two attributes; the unity of substance decomposes itself, comes apart, in the distinction between thought and extension that reestablishes within it an unacknowledged duality. In this sense, Hegel can say that Spinozism is a failed attempt to surpass the limits of Cartesianism: even if they treat the same problem in a different way, both rest on the same premises, that of the relationship between two distinct entities, between which the conditions of an agreement must be established. Because Spinoza has maintained the unity of substance from the outset, which is therefore a unity without content, it follows that thought and extension—in which this unity subsequently decomposes—are formed in opposition to each other, as opposites that must be reconciled, and do not exist except in a formal sense.

We will see that this interpretation completely misses what Spinoza effectively argues in his demonstrations. Because according to Spinoza, thought and extension do not confront each other as terms in an opposition that must then be overcome; this is exactly what the thesis of their irreducibility signifies, which excludes all relations between them, even a relation of opposition. But if we return to literal interpretation of this system, we perceive that this independence of attributes (which are nonetheless identical within the substance whose essences they constitute) is comprehensible only through the fact that the substance expresses itself not in one, two, nor for that matter any number of attributes but in their infinity, which forbids the establishment of relationship between them term by term, whatever form it may take. But to understand this is to situate oneself in a form of reasoning that has nothing to do with the one that Hegel attributes to Spinoza.

The Reality of Attributes

Through his critique of Cartesianism, Spinoza invalidates, in advance, a Kantian type of problematic of knowledge, posed in terms of the relationship of subject and object or form and content. It is this that Hegel (who nonetheless declines commentary on this problematic and pretends to surpass it) has absolutely ignored; this oversight governs his entire interpretation of Spinozism. What should astound us here is that at the point of an essential convergence between Hegel's philosophy and Spinoza's, Hegel, on the contrary, discovers a motif of divergence. This inversion can be explained in only one of two ways. Either Hegel develops irrefutable arguments that allow him to establish that a Spinozist critique of the classical conception of truth is insufficient, and by this event, falls into the same errors as the classical conception, from which (as Hegel asserts) it remains inseparable. Or this Spinozist critique is intolerable for Hegel because, still more radical than his own, it highlights the limits and reveals the complicity that continues to link the Hegelian system to previous conceptions, which Hegel claims he disarms by resolving all the contradictions within them. We will see that it is this latter explanation that should be adopted.

Let us return to the problem of attributes. The latter, according to Hegel, are "determinations," "forms" through which substance is reflected in the point of view of intellect. In a way, substance is content without form, immediately given in its absolute indetermination, in the manner of the empty Being of the Eleatics: it subsequently externalizes itself in these forms without content, which reflect it in the manner of Kantian categories. But this schema betrays Spinoza's doctrine on at least one point: if for Spinoza the attributes are forms or kinds of being, or natures, or even essences, they are certainly not forms in opposition to a content, any more than they are predicates in opposition to a subject, or abstract categories in opposition to a concrete reality that would remain outside them. Or else we could just as well say they are themselves contents that stand for a form, substance, because the latter "consists" of them and comprehends them as "constituting" its essence. What this signifies, quite simply, is that the terms *form* and *content* are altogether inappropriate to characterize the relation that links attributes to substance.

If the attributes are "what the intellect perceives of the substance," they are not at all thereby dependent on the point of view of intellect, where they would exist as reflected forms, nor, even more, the point of view of a finite intellect, opposed to an infinite reason. Here we must take seriously the fact that Spinoza uses the word *perceive (percipere)* in his definition of attributes: the intellect *perceives* the attributes as constituting the essence of substance. If we refer to the explanation of definition 3 at the beginning of book II of the *Ethics,* we note that this term has a very precise meaning: concerning the idea that is a "concept of the mind," Spinoza writes, "I say concept rather than perception, because the word perception seems to indicate that the mind is passive with respect to the object, whereas concept expresses more of an action of the mind." This clarification can be redirected and applied to the definition of attributes: Spinoza does not say that these are what intellect "conceives" of substance precisely because this would imply an activity of intellect in relation to its "object," on which it would impose a modification, for example in giving it a form, by "informing" it. The attribute is what the intellect "perceives" of the substance because in the relation that is established here there is, on the contrary, a passivity of intellect in relation to substance, which it accepts such as it is, in the essences that constitutes it, that is to say in its attributes.

The term *intellect,* as it appears in the definition of attributes, cannot therefore be interpreted in a Kantian sense. Even if it were a matter of our own singular intellect, the finite intellect, the objection that Spinoza directed against Bacon remains valid: "He supposes, that the human intellect, as well as the errors that one must impute to the senses, is fallible by virtue of its singular nature and the ideas that belong to it, and not the universe: *just as it would be with a curved mirror,* which in its reflection, mixes its own characteristics with those of the things themselves."[8]

Yet Hegel's interpretation of the role of intellect in the definition of attributes follows this direction exactly: the intellect that reflects substance in the form of its attributes is very much a kind of deforming, or informing mirror, which impresses its own mark on the images that it produces, in such a way that it is the mirror that produces the image that is seen rather than the object that reflects itself within it. But for Spinoza, if intellect is a mirror—which is also questionable because ideas are not images—it is certainly not a kind of active mirror that intervenes in reality, decomposing it to reconstruct it according to its own measure. At least in the case that concerns us, it must be a perfectly objective mirror, which "perceives" substance, such as it is, in the essences that actually constitute it. The definition that Spinoza gives the attributes clearly excludes any creativity on the part of intellect.

A remark is necessary here, which does not become completely clear except in what follows. We have just shown that the relation of perception that links the intellect to substance in the definition of attributes implies passivity rather than activity. But if one examines it a little more closely, this idea of passivity also proves to be somewhat troubling. Doesn't this signify that the attributes, as faithful images that are content to reproduce a model, are passive representations, corresponding exactly to the objects they enable us to see, that is, that they are, to repeat a well-known expression, "mute paintings on a canvas"? Thus, what we would have gained on one hand, by ceasing to consider the attributes as forms engendered by intellect, we would have evidently lost on the other, by reducing them to ideas that passively reflect an external reality. To overcome this new difficulty, it must be added that attributes are neither "active" representations nor "passive" representations, images, nor even ideas of the intellect or in the intellect; the attributes are not in the intellect, as forms through which the latter would apprehend them, objectively or not, a content given in substance, but they are in substance itself, whose essences they constitute. It is clear that this precision is enough to rid the definition of attributes of any notion of passivity: the attributes are active insofar as it is substance that expresses itself in them, in all of its essences.

Yet to renounce the consideration that attributes are ideas of the intellect is, at the same time, to call into question another aspect of Hegel's proposed interpretation. In order to present the abstract nature of attributes, Hegel separates the attributes from substance, by presenting their relationship as a relationship of succession: *first* substance, *then* the attributes. Thus the identity of attributes and substance, however clearly asserted by Spinoza, becomes altogether problematic: outside of substance and subsequent to it, the attributes are really nothing but the forms through which intellect reflects substance, by dissociating them from the foundation to which they refer. But this idea of an anteriority of substance in relation to its attributes, which establishes a hierarchical relation between them, is totally contrary to the letter of Spinoza's doctrine.

Here, barring irrefutable proof to the contrary, we must take up the argument of such commentators as Deleuze and Guéroult, who, following Robinson, have emphasized the "genetic" and not "hypothetical" character of the first propositions of the *Ethics,* which result in the demonstration of the existence of God, that is, of the unique substance that comprises an infinity of attributes. This is the generally accepted idea that Spinoza's *Ethics* "begins" with God: Hegel takes up this idea again in his own way, by holding it against Spinoza that he "begins," as if he were Chinese, with the absolute. But if it is altogether doubtful that the Spinozist system is constructed on the foundation of an absolute beginning, an attentive reading of the beginning of the *Ethics* shows that this beginning could not really be God, that is, an absolutely infinite unique substance; of the latter, first of all, we have only a nominal definition (definition 6), and we must wait until proposition 11 to discover that this definition corresponds to a real, actually unique being. What has happened in the interval?

If we interpret the first ten propositions of *Ethics* in the sense of a general ontology or a formal combinatorial, in order to turn them into a statement that only concerns possibilities[9] (which amounts to denying them all real meaning), we might reply that nothing really happens in them at all. They have only a preparatory value, they serve as a methodological precondition to an actual discourse on substance that will only come later, at the moment when the existence of the latter is effectively established, which puts an end to any consideration of pure essences without taking any position on their existence.

We should note immediately that this interpretation coincides with Hegel's on an essential point: it turns the discourse about substance into a kind of absolute beginning. This is why, as long as it is not a question of substance itself—personified in some way, that is to say of God—one might say Spinoza's demonstrations have nothing more than an introductory function. If truth be told, they say nothing, because their object is "being in general," envisaged outside the conditions of its existence. What reappears here is the formalist conception of attributes, explained in terms of a dualism of essence and existence, which Spinoza nevertheless explicitly rejects: "the existence of the attributes differs in no way from their essence."[10]

Doesn't such a reading call into question the necessity of reasoning using the method established in *more geometrico,* in a truly causal, synthetic progression? According to Spinoza, true discourse is also and at the same time actual, which excludes any undertaking of an

investigation of the possible and also any submission to the precondition of a beginning, or an introduction. We must again take up the
totality of propositions that precede the demonstration of the existence of God to determine their status.

Guéroult presents these propositions according to the following
division:[11]

- "The propositions 1 through 8 carry out the deduction of
  constitutive elements of the divine essence, namely, substance
  with a single attribute."
- "The second section, (prop. 9 through 15) concerns the construction of God through his simple elements, substances with
  a single attribute . . . and conferring on him the recognized
  characteristics of each of them."

We will see that certain of these formulations arouse serious objections, and they cannot be maintained. However, even if they present
an inaccurate discourse, which deviates on at least one point from the
letter of the system, they allow a very important aspect of Spinoza's
demonstration to be highlighted, an aspect that has never before appeared so clearly.

Indeed, to return to the terms of the question posed earlier, if
we follow the essentials of Guéroult's analysis, even if it also appears
inadmissible on certain points, we realize that something indeed occurs in the propositions that open book I of *Ethics*. And this event is
situated precisely at the intersection of propositions 8 and 9, at the
moment when one "passes" from *substantia unuis attributi* (let us set
aside for now the translation of this expression because it poses a
problem) to absolutely infinite substance, which possesses all the attributes and necessarily exists, in such a way that no other substance
can be conceived. Thus, to return to Guéroult's expression, the substance is itself "constructed" through the elements that compose it,
that is to say the attributes, themselves, insofar as they constitute
substance (because the attributes are "substantial," even if they are
not, strictly speaking, substances). Substance appears then, in its real
process, and the discourse of this objective genesis does not express an
empty knowledge, which could be reduced to the formal precondition
of a combinatorial that combines diverse elements into a whole, but

it actively expresses the effective movement of its object, in a certain sense, in its concrete history.

The essential merit of this analysis is that it gives the notion of *causa sui* its full significance. If God is a "cause of himself," this is not in the sense that Hegel interprets this: as an immediate gift of the absolute in the gesture of an original foundation, which exhausts itself at the same time as it communicates its entirety in a single stroke, in the irreducibility of an inalienable presence that could therefore be determined only from outside. But the *causa sui* is nothing other than the process within which substance engenders itself through the "essences" that constitute it, on which its existence is established; this movement succeeds at the moment when it produces substance, as the product of its activity, as the result of its own determination. From this point of view, the Spinozist substance has nothing to do with the Being of the Eleatics. In its immanent life—although Hegel never ceases to speak of the "dead substance"—it is a movement toward self, affirmation of self, exactly the opposite of an unreal content that must seek its forms outside itself. Here, again we find ourselves "very close" to Hegel, even though he remains completely blind to this proximity.

It is this movement that expresses the definition of God that must be understood genetically and causally: "By God, I understand an absolutely infinite being, that is to say a substance consisting of an infinity of attributes where each one expresses an infinite and eternal essence."[12] This definition is synthetic or geometric because it determines its object necessarily by producing it: if he is *causa sui,* he is not without cause, God is on the contrary absolutely determined by himself; the attributes are precisely the forms of this determination. On the basis of such a definition, one can deduce in a way that is also necessary all the properties of this object: "When I define God as the perfectly sovereign being, this definition does not express an efficient cause (I mean actually an efficient cause that is as much internal as external). I would not be able to deduce from this all the properties of God. It is quite the opposite when I define God as the absolute infinite being (see *E* ID6)."[13]

Thus, engendered in its attributes, which are its internal efficient cause, substance is also cause of itself; it is clear from then on that the substance is not an immediate absolute, because it must be deduced, even if from itself.

We thus find the relation between substance and its attributes to be profoundly modified. First it is no longer possible to affirm the exteriority of the attributes in relation to substance: the attributes are in substance as elements or moments through which it constitutes itself. On the other hand, if we absolutely insist on the need to establish an order of succession between substance and attributes, it is no longer at all certain that substance should be placed *before* the attributes, but it is they rather that precede it, as conditions of its self-production, because they maintain an essentially causal role in the process of its constitution. This explains a frequently observed anomaly: the *Ethics* does not "begin" with God, but it ends there, or at least it arrives there, after a whole series of demonstrations, a difficulty that interpreters traditionally circumvent by emptying of all content all the propositions that do *not yet* concern the unique and really existing substance, in order to turn them into nothing more than the formal preconditions of a discourse that really begins after them.

However, we shall see, it is no longer satisfactory to talk of an "anteriority" of attributes in relation to substance. This is why we shall be content for the moment to insist on another aspect of the argument, which is essential and which concerns the identity of the attributes and substance. If one admits this identity, it is no longer possible to think this inequality between substance and attributes that presupposes a relation of chronological succession as well as one of a hierarchical subordination. There is no more or less being or reality in substance than in its attributes, but there is exactly *as much* in each, or at least that is what one could say if this reality could be measured quantitatively. The attributes are not less than substance; for example, they are not essences that, taken in themselves, lack existence, but substance is exactly what they are. In the *Principles of Cartesian Philosophy* Spinoza has already written,

> When he (Descartes) says: "it is a greater thing to create or preserve substance than its attributes," surely he cannot understand by attributes that which is formally contained in substance, and differs from substance itself only by reason. For then it would be the same thing to create a substance and to create its attributes.[14]

But God, a substance that comprises all the attributes, "creates" neither substance nor the attributes, which is something Descartes can scarcely "understand."

Letter 9 to Simon de Vries, if read correctly, establishes that *attribute* and *substance* are different names for the same thing, in the same way that the names *Israel* and *Jacob* designate the same being. It is true that this letter has more often been read the wrong way, as a confirmation of the formalist interpretation of attributes—as if it were the attributes themselves that were different *names* for the identical and unique *thing* that would be the substance. The persistence of this error[15] can be explained in only one way: in his letter, Spinoza talks of *two* names for the same thing, and the examples he uses develop this hypothesis. Everything unfolds as if the view of his readers remains fixated on this number, which in itself has absolutely no significance. The opportunity is thus ready-made to repeat a common fantasy in metaphysics, for which Hegel has already provided us a good example: "two" seems only to indicate one thing, the duality of thought and extension, following the Cartesian division of substances; this is what leads us to consider the attributes, identified for once and for all as two attributes that our finite intellect perceives, as names, that is, as forms external to a content that they designate in an extrinsic manner. But on this point Spinoza is perfectly clear: the attributes are essences, hence realities. Thus they are absolutely not names in themselves, that is, designations of substance by an intermediary, a means by which substance would decompose itself abstractly into a multiplicity of perspectives or appearances.

To grasp this real identity that links attributes and substance, it is enough to bring together two texts, whose cross-referencing eliminates all equivocation:

> By attribute I mean every thing that is conceived in itself and through itself, so that its conception does not involve the concept of any other thing.[16]

> By substance I understand that which is conceived in itself and through itself, such that the concept does not involve the concept of any other thing.[17]

Attribute and substance arise from one and the same definition, which bears on an identical reality: the fact is here immediately legible. Spinoza could have just as easily written, "By *substance* and *attribute* I understand one and the same thing."

And again, "By attributes of God, one must understand that which expresses *(exprimit)* the essence of the Divine substance, that is to say that which belongs *(pertinet)* to substance: it is this, I say, which the attributes themselves must involve *(involvere)*."[18]

Exprimit: the attributes express the substance. Clearly this does not mean that the attributes represent the substance in the form of a predicate, a property or a name; rather, this means that they constitute it, in what one might call its concrete being. *Pertinet*: the attributes are contained in the substance and, equally, it is contained in them. They are in no way external and arbitrary manifestations, dependent on the free will of an intellect that would reflect substance according to its own categories; note that the definition we are commenting on here no longer makes any reference to the intellect. *Involvere*: attributes and substance are inseparable to the extent that they cannot be conceived without one another, outside one another, and this reciprocal dependence expresses nothing other than the fact of their real unity.

One remark to conclude. Perhaps the equivocations that have accumulated around the interpretation of the initial definition of attributes (*E* ID4) could have been avoided if Spinoza had written this definition in a slightly different way: "by attribute I understand that which constitutes the essence of substance, and it is thus that the intellect perceives it (such as it is)," a formulation that eliminates any kind of dependence of the attributes on the intellect. After all, admitting the rigorous character of Spinoza's text does not necessarily signify one must follow its meaning literally, nor turn it into an object of adoration, by treating it like a receptacle in which great mysteries lie sleeping, which one must only contemplate at a distance, taking care not to wake them. One must explain the *Ethics* by the *Ethics,* just as Spinoza has elsewhere explained scripture by scripture, that is, to determine the system of material constraints that organize the text and that permit it to actually fulfill its objectives; from there, it should be possible eventually to identify its lacunae.

The Diversity of Attributes

The attributes are thus identical to substance, and likewise substance is the same thing as its attributes; it is only from the point of view of intellect that a distinction between substance and attribute can be established, which means that this distinction has no real character but is only a distinction made by reason.

However, care must be taken not to interpret the relation between substance and attributes in the sense of a formal reciprocity. If there is, incontestably, an identity between them, this identity is not an empty and abstract equality, without which one could no longer understand what the role of the notion of attribute is in the necessary economy of the demonstration, and one might be tempted purely and simply to suppress it. In this sense, apparently, Spinoza asserts that "nothing exists in nature if not substances and their affections as it is evident by axioms 1 and definition 3 and 5."[19] And again, "Outside of substance and accidents, nothing exists in reality, or externally to the intellect. All that exists, is either conceived through itself or through something else, and its concept either involves or does not involve the concept of another thing."[20] In the real, that is to say outside the intellect (and we are referred back to the point of departure, it seems), if the attributes have no real existence, if they do not detach themselves from substance except from the point of view *(perspectu)* of the intellect, are they not, then, beings of reason, intellectual fictions external to all content, that is, pure forms of representation?

Let us recall that what exists exclusively for the intellect are not the attributes themselves (which are certainly not "in" the intellect) but their distinction in agreement with [*leurs distinction d'avec*] substance. But a new argument must be added here: the existence of the attributes in substance, which is the key to their identity, is not an indifferent unity, which would be the result of a simple formal equality, it is a concrete identity, which is an identity in difference. This is why the attributes are necessary to the determination of substance, whose internal causality they express and realize. But how does substance pass into attributes, or attributes into substance? This is what must now be understood.

Let us return to the division of book I of the *Ethics* proposed by

Guéroult. The first eight propositions have as an object the *substantia unius attributi,* which permits the elimination of the concept of a substrata that is immobile, undifferentiated, and thus in itself unknowable. Thus, it is established from the beginning that substance exists only in its attributes, which are in themselves substantive. But the additional consequence of this reasoning is that there are as many substances as attributes; as Guéroult remarks, in this initial development substance is written in the plural, as in proposition 5, which demonstrates an essential point for all that follows (two substances cannot be distinguished except by their attributes).

In propositions 9 through 15, we pass from plural to singular: from *substantia unius attributi,* infinite "only" in its kind, to a substance that comprises an infinity of attributes that can be said to be absolutely infinite. It comprises all the attributes because it cannot lack a single one. This "passage" is summarized in *Letter 36* to Hudde as follows: "if we suppose but one single indeterminate and perfectly exclusive being exists by its own sufficiency, *then it is necessary as well* to accord existence to an absolute indeterminate and perfect being: it is this being that I shall call God." Thus we are led, as if by the hand, from the idea of attributes to that of a substance: if we first know the perfection of attributes, we must also know that it cannot be understood outside of the absolute perfection of God, who contains them all. In fact, if we confine ourselves to the attributes, each considered on its own, we would naturally be led to think about them negatively and oppose them to each other, by grasping the specific nature of each one through what is lacking in all the others. But the infinity of attributes can be grasped positively only if we restore it to an absolutely infinite, divine nature, in which they coexist without opposition. This is why the attributes cannot exist outside of God, but they are necessarily in him, where they affirm themselves identically as infinite essences in their kind, in a mode of determination that excludes all negativity. Inversely, substance is nothing other than the unity of its attributes that it gathers within its absolute existence.

This reasoning has already given pause to the first readers of the *Ethics,* as attested in *Letter* 8 of Simon de Vries to Spinoza: "if I were to say that each substance has only one attribute and I have an idea of two attributes, I could quite reasonably conclude that there are two different substances, since where you have two different attributes you have two different substances. On this point once again, we request that you give us a clearer explanation." But the problem here is actually unsolvable, to the extent that it poses the diversity of attributes from a point of view that is, in the first place, numerical. For Simon de Vries, "one" attribute is an expression that has no meaning except in relation to a series, "one, two, three, . . . an infinity of attributes." This presentation is characteristic, primarily because in this infinite series, in designating the multiplicity of attributes, it privileges a particular number, which is coincidentally the number two. But this choice reveals immediately that the question here is envisaged exclusively from the point of view of finite intellect, which only knows precisely two attributes, thought and extension; as we have already indicated, it is entirely significant, on the contrary, that this point of view never enters into Spinoza's reasoning, which uses the notion of intellect in general.

On the other hand, the breakdown of attributes according to a numerical succession has as a consequence that the "passage" from substances that are infinite only in their kind to an absolutely infinite substance appears as a gradual and continuous progression: everything occurs as if the attributes were added to each other in substance, which would itself be composed through an infinite summation. But to the contrary, it is highly significant that Spinoza presents the process in which substance engenders itself through its attributes in an entirely different manner: substance actualizes itself in a clean break, which passes without intermediary from one level to another, in such a way that the relationship between the infinite only in its kind and the absolutely infinite first presents itself as a true contradiction, which is resolved suddenly, by force, beyond any attempt at reconciliation.

Once again, let us take up the reasoning from its beginning: substance is first thought of in the real diversity of its attributes, as indicated in propositions 2 ("two substances with different attributes have nothing in common with each other") and 5 ("in nature there cannot be two or more substances of the same nature or attribute"). Next, substance is thought of in its absolute unity, inasmuch as it gathers all the attributes within it, by positing itself as identical to them. Here we have to deal with a genuine reversal of perspectives; how should it be interpreted?

One might be tempted to understand this reasoning as reasoning through the absurd: it is in this sense that the formalist interpretation proceeds, which we have already critiqued. We might then say, in the first instance, Spinoza suggests the possibility of real and distinct substances, each determined by an attribute, in order to be able subsequently to refute this claim, in discovering after the fact, through an artifice of presentation, the absolute unity of the substance that coincides with its unicity. Considered this way, his reasoning is reduced to a certain way of using proofs; it loses its synthetic character and its objective meaning. This is why, following the exigencies of the procedure *more geometrico* (which as we have shown are not simply formal), this interpretation must be rejected.

It is necessary, then, to grant both aspects of the argument equal weight: considered from the point of view of the diversity (or infinity) of its attributes, substance is neither a fiction nor the representation of a pure possibility, which could not be constructed except by an enumeration toward the infinite, because such an enumeration has no sense except from the point of view of the imagination. But it is the same content, an identical reality that presents itself as diversity and then as unity. Yet this content cannot be presented in the conciliatory and harmonious progression of an achieved order, which would risk the repercussions of the aporia of immediate foundation denounced by Hegel. On the contrary, it must present itself in a contrasting movement that simultaneously reveals these extreme aspects and demonstrates in the same instance their solidarity, their community, that is to say their inseparability. Thus, these two aspects are not sequential but simultaneous.

The true meaning of the distinction between substance and attributes, as it is established by the intellect, appears thus; it is this distinction that permits the apprehension of the substance, such as it is, the complex reality of its nature. That is, it permits us to think its unity to the limit, absolutely; it is because it comprises the infinity of attributes that substance is absolutely infinite. The unity of substance is thus not an arithmetic unity; it does not designate the existence of an individual irreducible to all others by the simplicity of its nature. Substance is not a being, and this is the fundamental condition of its unicity: it is everything that exists and that can be understood, which thus has its cause only in itself. Moreover this plenitude of being, this absolute affirmation of self, which constitutes substance, cannot be an empty form of the One, that would be nothing but the One, that would not be, if we can say this, anything except a One: it is this infinitely diverse reality that comprises all its attributes and that expresses itself in their infinity. This reality is not that of a Being that would already enclose this totality, by virtue of an initial gift, but it is first that of an irresistible movement, through which the attributes pass and unify themselves in a substance that appropriates them.

There is only one substance, but it comprises an infinity of attributes; its unity is incomprehensible outside this infinite diversity, which constitutes it intrinsically. The result is that substance has multiplicity within itself and not outside itself, and from this fact, multiplicity ceases to be numerical, which Spinoza expresses exactly by saying it is infinite; in effect for him, infinity is not a number to the extent that it cannot be represented by the imagination. We are here poles apart, we can see, from the project of a "philosophical calculus" of the mechanical enumeration of parts that formally constitute a being, to which Hegel would like to reduce *more geometrico*.

The result, which Hegel ignored, is that the identity of substance and attributes is not formal and abstract but real and concrete. This identity develops in a double relation: that which binds substance to its attributes, without which it would be an empty being, and through which because of this we could recognize only a minimum of reality, and not the maximum that pertains to it; and that which binds the attributes to substance, outside which they would exist negatively, as opposites.

Imitating the style of Hegelian discourse, we could say that the relationship between the substance and the attributes is identity, having become that in which the absolute affirms itself as actual. And this process is that of the *causa sui* or, if you will, the return of substance to itself.

The Constitution of Substance in Its Attributes

Up until now we have spoken about self-production or a self-constitution of substance *within* its attributes. We must now specify that this has nothing to do with a genesis of substance *through* its attributes, and eliminate the ambivalence still contained in Guéroult's commentary, which we have followed for the most part until now.

In effect, if all the attributes together belong to substance, constituting its being (*E* IP10S), they do not coexist within it as parts that would adjust to each other to finally compose the total system. If this were so, the attributes would define themselves in relation to one another through their reciprocal lack; they could no longer be conceived each in itself, because they would be limited in their own nature by something else. Moreover, an attribute, such as extension, could only be limited by itself, which is absurd because it is infinite in its kind: "even though Extension denies itself Thought, this is not an imperfection in it; but if on the other hand it was deprived of a specific extension, there would be an imperfection; as would actually happen if it were determinate being, or if it were deprived of duration or location."[21]

To think the infinite, whether it be in the attribute (in a kind) or in substance (absolutely), is to exclude any notion of divisibility; substance is entirely complete in each of its attributes (because it is identical to them), just as, moreover, all extension is in each drop of water or all thought is in each idea. We have said previously that for Spinoza, the infinite is not a number; this is why it evades all division. Indivisible substance is not the sum of all its attributes.

This obliges us to return to one of our previous assertions. We have said that substance does not have the simplicity of a being, given immediately in an irreducible presence excluding from itself all determinate content, but has the complex reality of an absolute movement that comprises all its determinations. However, this complexity of substance that expresses itself in the *internal* diversity of its attributes is not, as a consequence, endowed with a composite character. This is why it must be said that substance is simple, just as much as it is complex, in this very precise sense that it is not divisible into parts: "this being is simple and not composed of parts. For in respect of their nature and our knowledge of them component parts would have to be prior to that which they compose. In the case of that which is eternal by its own nature, this cannot be so."[22]

This specification is extremely important, because it excludes all mechanistic presentations of movement in which substance produces itself; the process of *causa sui,* immanent in substance, is not a temporal genesis, which would operate in a succession of distinct operations, through elements that are already present, whose combination would produce substance as a result or outcome. The relation of substance to its attributes is not one of a whole to its parts, or of a complex totality to the simple elements that constitute it.

From this point of view, certain of the formulations used by Guéroult to present the "genesis" of the substance are unacceptable, and the use of texts on which he relies is undoubtedly improper. For example,

> Undoubtedly, Spinoza conforms, in this case, to the prescriptions which he has set forth in the *Emendation of the Intellect:* to arrive at the most simple ideas *(idea simplicissimae)* to reconstruct with them, the complex idea which is constituted therein according to its internal implications. Consequently, when it concerns God, one will discover first the *"prima elementa totius naturae,"* in order to know the simple substances with a single attribute, which are *origo et fons naturae,* in order to constitute from them "a total, singular and infinite being," outside of which nothing is given, and which, at the same time, is itself, *origo et fons naturae.* This reconstruction, which operates according to the norm of the true given idea, leads to the genetic definition of God.[23]

The term that is problematic is that of *reconstruction,* which here interprets the procedure of *more geometrico* in a very particular sense.

Let us note first of all that to transform the procedure *more geometrico* into a construction or reconstruction of the complex from the simple is to reduce it to a method, that is, finally, to an artifice of exposition, which subordinates the necessary progression of reasoning to the model of an order, in this case one that proceeds from the parts to a whole, or from the simple to the complex, and we are thus scarcely removed from Descartes. But what Spinoza wanted to think via the *more geometrico* is not another method, a new order of exposition, but precisely something other than a method, which would submit the presentation of truth to the precondition of an order, according to a schema of a necessarily abstract reflection. It is thus that we encounter difficulties when reason is simply formal, for example, asking ourselves whether substance comes before the attributes, or the attributes before substance, or else if the attributes are more or less "simple" than substance. From a synthetic point of view these questions are in the strict sense meaningless.

On the other hand, the idea of a construction of substance presupposes that it would not only be constituted but, moreover, composed of elements that would be its attributes. This presupposition is particularly evident in the translation Guéroult gives the expression *substantia unius attributi*,[24] which he renders as "substance having one single attribute." But this notion forms the basis of his whole explanation of the entire beginning of *Ethics*, because he uses it to designate the simple element through which substance is "constructed." This translation is impossible, not only because it substitutes *unicus* for *unus* but also for a fundamental reason: it treats the unity that constitutes each attribute as a number, that is, as a term in a series in which all the attributes figure as elements or as moments of an infinite progression, of which the substance is the final expression, or the result.

Such a conception is absolutely foreign to Spinozism, as Guéroult has himself masterfully explained: "the enumeration (of attributes) has not been completed because it has never begun, for the good reason that there is no numeration."[25] One does not progress through the attributes, which would appear one by one from then on, to substance by means of a progression to the infinite:

> The axiom invoked at the end of the scholium of proposition 10 from part I (. . . the more a being possesses a reality or being, the more it possesses attributes . . .), follows from the idea that we have of one absolutely infinite being, and not from the fact, that there are or there might be beings possessing three, four, or more attributes.[26]

Between the *substantia unius attributi* and the absolutely infinite substance that possesses all the attributes, there is *nothing*, no intermediary that would subordinate this passage to rules of a mechanical composition. This is why it is preferable to present this passage as a reversal, or as the development of a contradiction, which itself identifies in substance its absolute unity and the infinite multiplicity of its essences.

If the attributes were added to each other or were arranged to-gether to engender substance, they would cease to be irreducible, and it is their identity with substance, that is, their substantial character, which would, because of this, be compromised. Then the attributes would no longer be essences that were infinite in their own kind and thus not able to be limited by anything but would be degrees of reality, necessarily unequal, and positioned in relation to one another within the framework of a progressive hierarchy that would integrate them all together into the absolute. But Spinoza is just as far removed from this Leibnizian conception of order as he is from that of Descartes.

A very important consequence results from this. We have just seen that the attributes, even if they are in reality distinct, exactly because they are in reality distinct, are not like beings that could be enumer-ated, even in a perspective tending toward the infinite, because this would act to reduce their distinction to a modal distinction, that is, in a certain way, to think about the infinite from a finite point of view. But what is true about the attributes is a fortiori true of substance that contains them all: one can no more count substance any more than one can count its attributes, at least if one renounces the point of view of imagination. This is why the thesis of its *unicity* is so difficult to comprehend: it makes no reference at all, in effect, to the existence of a unique being, a substance that would exist as a single specimen, to the exclusion of other possibilities:

> Nothing can be called one or single unless some other thing has first been conceived, in relation to it, as having the same defini-tion (so to speak) as the first. But since the existence of God is his essence itself, and since we can form no universal idea of his essence, it is certain that he who calls God one or single shows either that he does not have a true idea of him, or that he speaks of him improperly.[27]

This is why, if Spinoza writes "that God is unique, that is to say that in Nature there is only one substance *(non nisi unam substantiam dari)* and that it is absolutely infinite,"[28] one must certainly understand that this notion *non nisi una,* strictly negative, has no causal signification

whatsoever and cannot thus arise in the definition of divine nature: absolute substance is unique, in fact, but this is nothing but a consequence, not even of its own reality but of our power to imagine, which creates a fiction, not simply of two, three, or any other number of substances but more generally of substances existing in a determinate number, among which "one" is never the first. To say there is a single substance is to speak from the imagination that can only consider the absolute negatively, from nothingness, that is, from the part of the possible, which it envelops. By himself, God is not "one," any more than he is two, or three, or beautiful or ugly. Contrary to a tenacious tradition, it must be said that Spinoza was no more profoundly a monist than a dualist, or whatever other number one wanted to assign this fiction, a number best at most for those who are ignorant or slaves.

The Order and Connection of "Things"

The attributes are not "less" than substance. Nor are some "less" than others: this is what is expressed in the thesis of their reciprocal irreducibility. The attributes are incomparable, and this is why they are identical in the substance that necessarily possesses all of them, which it could not do if one introduced any inequality between them. No form of being is superior to another; therefore there is no reason why one would belong to God in preference to another or to the exclusion of another. It is thus that God is at the same time, and in an identical fashion, a "thinking thing" and an "extended thing,"[29] but as well all the other things that we cannot comprehend by reason of the limits of our intellect. On this point we must return to the book of Deleuze, which gives a definitive critique of the notion of *eminence* and shows that this is completely foreign to Spinozism. Eminence is in a certain sense the classical concept of "supersession." But Spinoza always reasons formally (*formaliter*), that is, not to the exclusion of all content but outside of any perspective of eminence (*eminenter*), because this reintroduces into knowledge the presupposition of the possibility that it is a fiction. In contrast, the imagination proceeds by simple transpositions, or amplifications; this is the example of the triangle, which if it could talk would say that God is *eminently* triangular (see *Letter 56* to Hugo Boxel). God is not in reality at the summit, or the end of a hierarchy of progressive forms, whose properties he would gather together by "superseding" them.

This is why Spinoza is not content to resolve the question posed by Cartesian dualism: he reverses the problematic completely. In Hegel's interpretation of Spinozism everything happens as if substance expresses itself principally in two attributes whose absolute unity it constitutes, these same attributes that we perceive, and to which Descartes attributed the status of independent substances. Then, all other attributes appear in relation to these as possibilities, pure fictions, and they cannot be conceived rigorously except through this model of two "real" attributes that we actually know. But it is exactly such a conception that the synthetic reasoning followed by Spinoza renders impossible; following this reasoning, each attribute must be "conceived through itself," that is, in its own infinity, which confers a substantial nature upon it, and not through its relationship with another attribute, whatever that may be. To understand the nature of attributes is precisely to rule out considering them term by term in order to compare them.

When Spinoza says that attributes are "infinite only in their kind," an expression we have already encountered often, this does not mean that their infinity is in some way limited and incomplete. On the contrary, this kind of conception characterizes the point of view of the imagination. In the *First Dialogue* that follows chapter 2 of the *Short Treatise*, it is Desire that declares, "I see that thinking substance has nothing in common with extended substance and that the one limits the other."[30] This phrase brings together three assertions that are actually interdependent: (1) the irreducibility of attributes is presented as the separation between substances, (2) these substances exist in relation to one another in a relationship of limitation, and (3) this opposition is a relation of two terms that is thought on the basis of the distinction between thought and extension. But these three assertions and the logic that links them are undone by reason, because reason considers things from the point of view of their necessity: (1) the attributes are identical within substance that includes all of them, (2) they are therefore not opposed to each other in a necessarily unequal relationship, and (3) their nature cannot be grasped outside the fact that they are an infinity, which prohibits us from engaging them in an exercise of enumeration.

The key to the new reasoning that Spinoza introduces into philosophy is the thesis of the identity of the attributes in substance, in which they are unified at the same time as they remain really distinct. This unity is expressed in a well-known proposition: "the order and the connection of ideas are the same as the order and connections of things."[31] This proposition is often interpreted as if it forms a relationship of agreement between everything that depends on thought and on extension. Such an interpretation is inadmissible. In effect, if in this statement the word *ideas* truly designates the modes of the attribute of thought, the word *things (res)* absolutely does not, in a restrictive way, designate the modes of the attribute of extension but the modes of all the attributes, whatever they are, *including thought itself*: ideas are just as much "things" as some other affection of substance, whatever it may be. The proposition thus signifies that everything that is included in an attribute, that is, in any form of being, whatever it is, is identical to that which is included in all the other attributes, exactly in the same manner that it is identical to itself. In returning to itself without escaping its own order, thought discovers everything that is contained in substance, inasmuch as it expresses itself in the infinity of all its attributes; we already have guided the theory of the *adequatio* toward this conclusion. But this can be said of all the attributes, which are identical to all the others, not in a relation of comparison, correspondence, agreement, or homology, which would imply their exterior reciprocity, but in their intrinsic nature, which unifies them immediately in substance that constitutes them and that they constitute.

From this point on, there is no place to propose an identity between two, three, four, or infinite series or attributes, whose order and connection would be seen to match. We must understand, which is impossible if one maintains the point of view of imagination, that this is *one and the same order, one and the same connection,* which is realized in all attributes and constitutes them identically in their being: substance is nothing other than this unique necessity, which expresses itself all at once in an infinity of forms. There is thus no mystery to what one finds in every type of being, that which belongs equally by definition to all the others: for this there is no need for the intervention of a prior formula or harmony. We see then how laughable it is to present the Spinozist "monism" as a supersession of Cartesian dualism: the mode of thought put to work by Spinoza produces its effects on a completely different terrain, where these old questions of philosophy are simply invalid.

Another consequence results from this displacement of problems. It is not simply that the attributes do not limit each other in a relationship between terms that would be necessarily a relationship of subordination; our intellect is itself limited by the fact that it apprehends only two attributes of substance. By grasping only one, following its own order and its own connection, it would comprehend substance such as it is in its absolute necessity, that is, in the causal chain that constitutes its being. To know the nature of an attribute, in its intrinsic infinity, is at the same time to know the nature of all the others. This is why Spinoza says even though we perceive only two attributes we are nevertheless not *deprived* of the knowledge of all the others, to the extent that we understand that they exist necessarily according to an order and connection, which are the same ones that we know. Thus even within the limits prescribed to a finite intellect, we can know everything, that is, think about the absolute within the form of necessity.

All this comes together in the theoretical *dispositif* developed by Spinoza: the infinity of attributes, conceived independently of any numerical series, is the condition through which we escape all traditional dilemmas of philosophy. From the point of view of the absolute, there is no longer a confrontation between unequal and incompatible kinds of being, thus there is no longer the necessity to justify their coexistence or their accord through the compromise of an external, evidently arbitrary and irrational guarantee: the causality of substance is at the same time the condition for and the object of an absolute knowledge, which poses only intrinsically necessary relations, and whose immanent development discovers its forms in itself, outside of any intervention of a free will, whether this was placed under the responsibility of a finite subject or an infinite subject.

Hegel's Error Regarding the Attributes

To take the measure of the road we have traveled, let us return now to one of Hegel's texts devoted to the question of attributes:

> Spinoza further determines attribute as infinite, and infinite, too, in the sense of an infinite plurality. However in what follows only two appear, thought and extension, and it is not shown by

what necessity the infinite plurality reduces itself to opposition, that, namely, of thought and extension. These two attributes are therefore adopted empirically. Thought and being represent the absolute in a determination; the absolute itself is their absolute unity and they themselves are only unessential forms; the order of things is the same as that of figurate conceptions or thoughts, and the One absolute is contemplated only by external reflection, by a mode, under these two determinations, once as a totality of conceptions, and again as a totality of things and their mutations. Just as it is this external reflection which makes that distinction, so too does it lead the difference back into absolute identity and therein submerges it. But this entire movement proceeds outside the absolute. True, the absolute is itself also thought, and so far this movement is only in the absolute; but as remarked, it is in the absolute only as unity with extension, and therefore not as this movement which is essentially also the moment of opposition.[32]

Of interest in this passage, and this is why it must be cited it in its entirety, is that it solidly exposes a certain number of assertions that, applied to their declared object—Spinoza's philosophy—prove themselves equally erroneous. From this point on it is likely that the contempt Hegel directs toward Spinoza's philosophy depends on the "logic" that has engendered these errors, "logic" that is altogether external to the letter and the spirit of Spinozism.

First of all, Hegel reduces the attributes to external forms of reflection that have lost all real integrity with substance from which they apparently emerge: there is from this point on no rational justification for the movement by which substance "passes" into its attributes. This interpretation presupposes, as we have demonstrated sufficiently, that the relationship of substance to its attributes is a hierarchical and chronological relationship: substance, which thus presents itself as an immediate foundation, exists before its attributes and is greater than them. But the concept of attribute, as Spinoza himself has established, specifically excludes the possibility of such a subordination, which makes no sense, except from the perspective of eminence.

Next, for Hegel, the thesis in which substance expresses itself in an infinity of attributes has no real significance; this is why he recalls it only as a point of information, as a simply formal consideration. In fact, if we limit ourselves to content, the unity of the substance remains reflected through the relationship between two attributes, which are thought and extension. But this content cannot be rationally justified; it is only recognized empirically. Hegel writes elsewhere, "Spinoza places substance at the summit of his system and defines it as the unity of thought and extension, without demonstrating how he arrives at this difference and the reduction of this to a substantial unity."[33]

Hegel's error consists here of proposing the real distinction between attributes as a relationship that proceeds term by term, incarnated in the difference between two attributes placed side by side. From such a perspective it is inevitable that this distinction would appear arbitrary and that it would be simply juxtaposed to the unity of the substance, which is given elsewhere. But we have seen in Spinoza's demonstration that the existence of an infinity of attributes enabled us to overcome this difficulty at the outset: the reciprocal irreducibility of attributes is thus perfectly coherent with their identity in substance, whose nature they express in every possible way and outside all empirical restrictions.

As a consequence, the identity of order that intrinsically constitutes substance is transformed by Hegel into a formal correspondence between two exterior series, the order of things (extensions) and the order of representations (thoughts). Between these two ensembles, it is not possible to have anything but an arbitrary and exterior community, in the manner of an agreement decreed by God, in a Cartesian philosophy, between nature and reason. But in Spinoza's system taken literally, the fact that this identity of order never leads to identity between two separate orders, and this entire problematic of the agreement between thought and being, which presupposes their separation, is dismissed from the start.

On the other hand, the separation of thought from the real, which is according to Hegel the condition of their subsequent reunion in the absolute, devalorizes thought. Even if he places it in an equal relationship to extension, this reasoning puts thought in an inferior relationship to the absolute exactly to the extent that he does not return thought to the absolute except through the intermediary of its relationship to extension. "It is not in the absolute, except as a unity with extension," which signifies that it cannot, by itself, through its own movement, equate itself to the absolute. Hegel repeats, "True, substance is the absolute unity of thought and being or extension; therefore it contains thought itself, but only in its unity with extension, that is, not as separating itself from extension, hence in general not as a determinative and formative activity, nor as a movement which returns into and begins from itself."[34]

Thought cannot realize in itself its relationship to the absolute, because it must pass through extension to discover itself as the moment of a unity that is actualized only in substance. But we have said enough not to have to insist again that, for Spinoza, the infinite diversity of the attributes implies that they are at the same time irreducible to and equal within substance. Thus the difference between thought and extension, or any relationship between any attributes whatsoever, does not have their subordination to substance as a consequence (as with that which is divided compared to that which is united), but on the contrary, it identifies them within substance absolutely. This is as true for thought as it is for any other attribute in general.

Finally, the distinction between attributes, reflected through the distinction between thought and extension, is interpreted by Hegel as a relationship of opposition; the coexistence of these external forms is also their confrontation, because they represent one substance concurrently by dividing it. By this act, the unity of the substance is itself only a resolution, the supersession of this conflict, the reunion in the absolute of terms that, in themselves, are separated and antagonistic: it is a unity of opposites, a unity that is necessarily abstract, that formally and by means of the intellect reconstitutes a totality that was beforehand artificially decomposed in its elements. We will see that this transposition of Spinoza's system into terms that are evidently not his own, a transposition that implicitly introduces notions of opposition and contradiction, the dialectic in the Hegelian sense, is at the very foundation of the divergence that separates the two philosophies.

It is in developing this question for itself that we will manage to shed light on the reasons, that is to say the stakes, of this entire discussion. Because it is not enough for us to establish that Hegel was "mistaken" in his reading of Spinoza and that he completely missed the real significance of Spinoza's system. We must also first understand why, defying the evidence, he wanted with all his might to make this philosophy say exactly the opposite of what it establishes, in a manner that leaves no room for equivocation. As if his discourse were at this point so intolerable that it would be necessary—even though it is impossible to eliminate it by simple refutation—to suppress it completely by substituting it with the fiction of an inverse and laughable discourse.

We find that this final debate turns entirely around a single phrase and its interpretation: *omnis determinatio est negatio.*

⇒ 4 ⇐

Omnis Determinatio Est Negatio

AS HEGEL SAID IN HIS *Lectures on the History of Philosophy*, Spinoza had a rather grandiose phrase. We will return it to its context and discover that what it says does not have a lot to do with what Hegel finds there, which is, rather, an abyss of meaning. We can even ask ourselves whether this phrase—which he translates as "die Bestimmheit ist Negation" *(Logic)* or further, "alle Bestimmheit ist Negation" *(Lectures)*—was not written by Hegel himself, insofar as a statement belongs to the one who makes use of it. In any case, the use he makes of it has precisely the precondition that he has taken it out of its context and that he takes it absolutely, as an almost magical formula within which the entire framework of Spinozism, with its contradictions, its promises and its failures, can be found as a kind of summary.

Here, we should not be led astray by the cult of the literal. What Hegel read in Spinoza—and all authentic reading is in its own way violent, or it is nothing but the mildness of a paraphrase—matters just as much as what he actually said, or rather, what counts, is the reaction of these two discourses upon each other, because it offers an invaluable insight for each them. From this point of view, whether the famous phrase is Spinoza's or Hegel's, it is the best of symptoms for analyzing the relationship between these two philosophies.

We cannot solve the problem by proposing an interpretation of this phrase that attributes it to Hegel's imagination, emphasizing its fictitious character in order to dismiss it. Again, we must know what logic leads Hegel to attribute this phrase to Spinoza, to make it the principal marker and motif of their divergence.

The Negativism of Spinoza

Let us begin by clarifying the meaning of this phrase, such as Hegel understands it. The meaning is fundamentally double and corresponds to the place Hegel grants Spinoza in the history of philosophy, which is that of a precursor. In the phrase, something "grandiose" announces itself; Hegel himself uses this expression, which takes only the form of a premonition, separate from the means that would allow it to be realized. This is why it presents two aspects at the same time. On one hand, it cannot be understood except in relation to this essential truth, which already takes shape within it; on the other hand, it does not exist except through the failure that prevents its promise from being kept. And what characterizes it, therefore, is its incompleteness. It thus represents a truth in movement, stuck in the middle of a route that it should travel. This is why it can be considered either from the point of view of the task that it has completed or from the point of view of task that remains to be done in order to complete its goal.

Let us first look at this phrase in a positive light, extracting its positive content. This consists of the link that is established between determination and negation; that which is determined carries a negation within itself, and it is this negation that causes it to exist as something determinate. In addition, negation is not only a lack, because through its intermediation something positive can be posed: negation is in a certain sense a product of existence, which implies that it would have a constitutive function. In this case, as Hegel explains in the addition to paragraph 91 of the *Encyclopedia,* reality cannot be comprised in its solitary relation to a fully positive and foundational being, which would not be so, except by remaining indifferent and exterior to all effective reality: how could such a being, indeterminate in itself, also be a principle of determination? This reasoning strongly resembles the argument that Plato, in the *Sophist,* already used against the Eleates, to arrive from a different point of departure at a conclusion that was quite close to Hegel's: to hold a rational discourse on that which exists, it is necessary to accord nonbeing, thus the negative, some kind of reality.

Following this first aspect we see that Spinozist philosophy, whose "immobility" Hegel never ceases to denounce, begins to move a little: admitting a principle of effective negativity, at least at the level of that which has a determined existence, it no longer holds to its initial position, that is, to the affirmation of a being that is absolutely and completely positive, which comprises everything within it and in which all reality disappears. Besides empty and dead substance, it recognizes a world of determinations, which do not exist except through their own negativity. But is this not already the work of the negative, even if it reveals itself in an incomplete form that does not yet master the necessity of the concept?

It must be immediately noted that Hegel does not discover this sort of promise in the phrase he attributes to Spinoza because he reads it in the opposite sense. *Omnis negatio est determinatio*: in all negation there is something of determination, that is, something that is positioned and that acts, that produces effects and makes something exist. Put another way, in all negation there is also something positive: it is a means, an intermediary, a mediation that leads toward something else, which puts a stop to the tyranny of an empty and formal identity and reveals that there is no effective content except through the alteration of this identity, through this movement, this passage that exceeds the immediate presence to self of the positive that is nothing but positive and that realizes it in another, through the path of the negative.

However, and here is the downside of the formula, which would appear if you read it in the correct sense, exactly as Spinoza would have written it, whereby this internal link of positive to negative would not appear except in an unsatisfactory and insufficient form, but the formula is not truly understood. Because he has remained within the point of view of intellect (in the Hegelian sense), Spinoza continues to separate the positive and the negative, which for him belong to two separate orders. From the side of the absolute, which is immediately given outside all determination, there is nothing except the positive of a being for which nothing lacks and which cannot become more than it already is in this originary presence. This is why the negative, even if its intervention is recognized as necessary, should be cast outside it: it would appear only where the determinations produce themselves, that is, in the sphere of that which is finite and is by nature exterior to infinite substance.

Thus the phrase *omnis determinatio est negatio* takes on an entirely new meaning, which is precisely a negative, or restrictive, meaning: all determination is negative, that is, it is only something negative, and is nothing but negative. The reality, the existence of the finite does not think of itself in any way except through difference, through subtraction, through a relationship to the absolute of substance. For Spinoza, as Hegel interprets him, determination is a regressive movement, not the return to itself of that which is, however, but its decomposition, its degradation, its fall from grace. The determined is that which cannot grasp itself except through a shortcoming, according to its own shortcoming, a lack of being, the negativity that determines it: it is the ineffective that holds itself at a distance from substance and is powerless to represent it, except in an inverse image.

Hegel says, again, that Spinoza conceived negation in a manner that is only abstract, as a principle of independent alteration of the positivity he located once and for all in the absolute. Abstract negation is negation envisaged restrictively, as a failing, insofar as it is only negative. For Spinoza, the negative is opposed to the positive, and it cannot be reconciled with it but remains forever irreducible to it. Thus, between the positive, which is nothing but positive—and which is itself an abstraction because it carries this restriction within it; it is the specific contradiction of Spinozism that cannot escape introducing negativity into its substance [*sa substance*]—and the negative, which is nothing but negative, no passage can be established that would effectively provide the movement of the concept and would permit us to understand the intrinsic rationality within it. By the fact that the absolute is an immediate, there is nothing outside it; or rather outside it, there is nothing but "beings," which can only be measured negatively, arising from nothing, from the shortcoming of substance that intimately composes them and is the cause of their falseness.

We rediscover here an objection that we know well: the Spinozist substance has eliminated from its own order, like a foreign body, all determination, and this is exactly the condition of its absolute identity to itself. Thus it can have extrinsic relations only to that which is not it. This is true foremost for the attributes or the genres that are determinations of the substance and already belong to the finite world. One understands consequently that they cannot be apprehended except by an intellect, that is to say a mode, that confers on them this abstract and finite existence, foreign to the plenitude of substance. This is true subsequently, and a fortiori, of the modes themselves, or what Hegel calls the individuals, which, not having their principle of existence within themselves, are truly nothing in themselves, if not appearances soon condemned to disappear, which is for them the best way to manifest their limited reality.

In addition, the philosophy of Spinoza, in contradiction with his proclaimed affirmation of the plenitude of the positive, is at its basis a negativism, as with all oriental thought:

> In a similar manner, in the oriental conception of emanation the absolute is the light, which illumines itself. Only it not only illumines itself but also emanates. Its emanations are distancing *(Entfernungen)* from its undimmed clarity; the successive productions are less perfect than the preceding ones from which they arise. The process of emanation is taken only as a happening, the becoming only as a progressive loss. Thus being increasingly obscures itself and night, the negative, is the final term of the series, which does not first return into the primal light.[1]

An astounding reversal! Because not a single common measure can be established between the positive and the negative, and they remain absolutely exterior to each other, being in its primal light is fated, soon to be subsumed by the shadow, which will take its place entirely and will devour it in the nothingness that is no less absolute, where it destroys itself. Here is another text in which Hegel describes this fall, in a compelling manner:

> Substance as it is intuitively understood by Spinoza, immediately, without prior dialectical mediation, insofar as it is the universal negative power [*puissance*], is as it were only this dark, shapeless abyss that engulfs within all determinate content, as being originating from nothingness, and produces nothing that would have a positive consistency in itself.[2]

"It is the universal negative power": to the extent that the universality of substance is empty and as such fated to immobility and to death, it can be invested only by this inverse power that corrupts it, that defeats it and that at the same time declares its profound truth: nothingness.

We see thus where the presentation of the absolute as pure positive leads: to the triumph of the negative that is really its end. Thus the stakes of the debate appear clearly: in acknowledging a constitutive function of the negative and in creating the conditions of its alliance, of its unity with the positive, it is necessary above all for Hegel to defend the positive against itself, to prevent its degradation, which is inevitable if it submits to the temptation to be sufficient unto itself in the empty, abstract plenitude of its immediate being. In relation to how they first appeared, these positions are exactly the inverse: laying claim to the positive without division, Spinoza has in effect chosen the negative, or at least resigned himself to it. Whereas Hegel, in according his share of reality to the negative, makes it into the instrument or the auxiliary of the positive, whose triumph he unwittingly ensures: the ruse of reason. This signifies that in the negative, providing it were considered in a rational manner, there is something that tends toward the positive, and it is this that necessarily escapes an abstract understanding [*entendement*], for which positive and negative, definitively exterior to each other, are also irreconcilably opposed.

This rational grasp of the negative is what expresses itself in the idea of absolute negativity. We cannot understand this idea without leaving the sphere of abstract reflection, which represents things in their immediate relation to themselves; if we consider them in their movement, we see that they are not themselves except by the intermediary of the other that they reflect into itself [*en soi*]. But this passage is negation, negation of immediate being, but it is also already negation of the negation, or rather negation of the negative itself, to the extent that it discovers in its concept that which it is in itself and for itself.

What we currently designate by the expression "negation of the negation" is thus the infinite rationality of the process in which all reality brings itself into being. But the natural tendency is to interpret this rationality in terms of an abstract reflection. It thus becomes a relationship between two terms, which are two distinct and successive negations. This is the formal scheme of the triad, which too often sums up the presentation of Hegelianism and which Hegel himself expressly rejected: first a being, given in its immediate presence, and subsequently its negation, that is, the recognition of the other that defeats this immediacy, and finally a new negation, which "adds" itself to the preceding one, if we may say, or takes it as an object and invalidates it, reintegrating the initial being in its identity, augmented by all it has become, by all it has "learned" in the succession of these episodes.

But what Hegel wanted to think in relation to the negation of the negation is something completely different, which cannot be reduced in such a way to the mechanical apportionment of a temporal series. In the preceding schema, the negation of the negation results from the combination of two separate operations, in which the adjustment corrects the effects in producing a kind of equilibrium, but these two operations are themselves identical, equivalent; the entire efficacy of the process comes from their repetition. One finds, "following a well-known grammatical rule," as Hegel says himself, that the result of this operation is positive, but this positivity is only observed, it is not rationally demonstrated, and there is nothing about it that justifies its necessity. Moreover, even admitting that two negations "produce" an affirmation, to the extent that they succeed, is not to say that the operation always progresses to completion, that a second negation will arise to correct the first one; the return to itself of the positive is from this moment on no longer guaranteed.

Additionally, the negation of the negation, in the Hegelian dialectic, does not allow itself to be led to the combination of two negations. Rather, it consists of an intrinsically coherent and necessary process, in which the same negation develops all its effects, from beginning to end. In the first instance, this negation discovers itself as finite negation, that is, it is abstractly determined, in the most common sense of the negative, as an act of opposition that installs the other opposite to and outside the same. This treatment of the negative as exteriorization is exactly the one Hegel imputes to Spinoza. But in a second instance—which succeeds the preceding one in a manner that is not simply chronological but logical—this negation grasps itself and understands itself as infinite within itself. It thus appears that it has no other object *finally* except self, or in other words, taken absolutely, it is the negation of self as negation. The negation of the negation is thus for Hegel not the superposition of two negations that annul themselves by combining with each other—moreover, it is not apparent how this adjustment would be able to constitute a becoming—but rather the unique and immanent movement of a negation that extends to its limit, that returns to itself, and thus produces determinate effects.

Absolute negation is thus negation that contradicts something, contradicts itself within this thing as negation, and resolves itself in bringing this thing into being. It is the negation that is no longer only negation but that, going further, discovers within itself the path that leads to the positive. Thus, as we have just indicated, the negative appears as an intermediary: its immediate appearance is returned, subordinated to the interests of the positive, whose arrival it anticipates. This is why the expression "negation of the negative" would be preferable to designate the entirety of this process, because it properly indicates the intrinsic liaison of these moments, and also because, in the confrontation that operates here between the positive and the negative, it is the positive that sets the stakes and must carry it along, whereas the negative is inexorably subordinated, as a means it uses for its own ends. We will return later to this point, because it is essential.

As regards this conception of the negative that has been developed, the insufficiencies of Spinozism are evident for Hegel: "Spinoza remains within negation as determinateness or quality; he does not attain a cognition of negation as absolute, that is, self-negating, negation; thus his substance does not itself contain the absolute form, and knowledge of it is not an immanent knowledge."[3]

By virtue of the abstract mode of reflection he has fixated on, Spinozism is an arrested thought, incapable of grasping the negative in the movement that carries it irresistibly beyond itself toward the positive: "he remains within" immediate negation, grasped restrictively as a negative that is nothing but negative, and "he does not attain" the resolution of this negativity in the effective and the rational, that is, in the concept. This is what explains the descent into the negative where, finally, his whole system ends up; having posed from the outset the absolute as identity immediate to itself, he cannot think of it except in exterior abstract determinations, which are its negation and only the negation. It is in this way that the progression of this negative, far from conjuring the appearance of negativity by bringing into being a positive, does nothing except reinforce this negativity, in a progressive degradation of the absolute, culminating in its complete disappearance. The weakness of Spinozism comes from what he was unable to find in the intellect as an effective weapon against the negative, and in particular this absolute weapon that is infinite negativity, or negation of the negation, because this belongs to rational thought, to the extent that it does not allow itself to be reduced to the determinations of intellect, and it guarantees within it concrete development, immanent life.

Hegel again declares that Spinoza's reasoning engages in irrec-
oncilable or unsolvable oppositions because he has not achieved the
rational process of contradiction:

> The intellect has determinations that do not contradict each other.
> The negation of the negation is a contradiction; it is thus an af-
> firmation and however it is also negation in general. The intellect
> cannot support this contradiction; and yet the contradiction is
> its rationale. This point is a shortcoming in Spinoza, and this is
> his lack.[4]

For Spinoza, to determine a being, no matter what it is, would be to
determine it in a finite manner: the determination is reflected by intellect only as a limit, that is to say, as we have seen, as a relationship of
exteriority. This is why a being is always determined by another being,
whose negation it constitutes. Thus thought as attribute—that is, determination of substance—is posed as an "op-position" [un op-posé] in
the limitation that separates it from another attribute, extension. These
two terms do not contain the conditions of their unity within themselves, which must therefore be reflected outside them, in substance
where they are indistinct, indifferent. Thus, from the absolute to its
determinations, and from these determinations to the absolute itself,
no rational progression can be established at all, because it is a question of irreducible terms, which unite exclusively negative relations.

The rational thinking of the contradiction affirms, by contrast,
a unity of opposites, which it is not content to associate with or to
reunite in a mechanical equilibrium but whose intimate liaison it reveals at the same time as it achieves it. The contradiction (Widerspruch)
distinguishes itself from the opposition (Gegensatz) in that it is not a
fixed relation between distinct and antagonistic terms but the irresistible movement that discovers in each of these elements the truth of
the other and thus produces them as moments of a unique process in
which they appear as inseparable.

According to Hegel, the Spinozist substance is nothing but a unity
of opposites because it resolves in one stroke, without real necessity,
the exterior antagonism of its determinations; the Hegelian concept
is a unity of contraries because its development is also returned to

itself, which poses an identity by linking the same and the other and thus recognizes them as interdependent. Having established that for Spinoza the absolute is given from the beginning in the totality of what it is, it is not able to engage in this movement, to appropriate its own contradiction for itself, to resolve it by becoming itself, but it must endure the inevitable antagonisms that cause it to abandon its laughable pretension of being a being immediately identical to itself.

This is why the conception of the determination as negation, grasped in a manner that does not yet understand the movement of absolute negativity through which the negation turns against itself and becomes the auxiliary of the positive, also represents the limit of Spinozist thought: it makes clearly visible what he lacks in order to succeed in his project of thinking the absolute. This is what justifies the very particular type of reading of Spinoza's philosophy that Hegel undertakes, a reading through its failings: on every level of the text, Hegel rediscovers this same necessity of thinking contradiction to its limit, that is, of thinking of it in light of its necessary resolution, and each time he attests as well to the same powerlessness of Spinoza to achieve this objective, a powerlessness whose best indicator is the absence in his system of the concept of negation of negation.

A Powerless Dialectic

Two examples will enable us to better characterize this very singular approach that consists of taking a philosophy on the basis of its failures in order to realize its own tendencies; it concerns Hegel's commentary on definitions 1 and 6 of book I of *Ethics*.

The first definition has as its object the *causa sui,* this primordial notion that implies a reflexivity of substance, and sets in motion the transformation through which it becomes subject: "If Spinoza had developed more closely what is contained in the *causa sui,* its substance would not have been Immobile *(das Starre)*."[5] What then is contained in this notion, and how has this content been able to pass unnoticed?

Hegel first explained this definition in a text published in Jena in 1802:

> Spinoza began his *Ethics* with the following declaration: "by cause
> of itself, I understand that whose essence involves in itself exis-

tence, or that whose essence cannot be conceived except as existence." But the concept of essence or of nature cannot be posed
unless one makes an abstraction of existence; one excludes the
other; the one is not determinable except in opposition to the other; if one connects the two and one posits them as one, then their
liaison contains a contradiction, and both are negated together.[6]

Here Hegel discovers a positive reference in Spinozism because he interprets it immediately in a dialectical sense: the necessary unity posed
in the *causa sui* between essence and existence is rational insofar as it is
the unity of a contradiction, whose solution it constitutes. Although
it seems that, later, Hegel began to suspect Spinoza of not being able
to go beyond thinking of intellect [*entendement*], for the moment he
discovers support in Spinoza, in his own effort to justify the "negative
side,"[7] which comprises all authentic philosophy and which is the
effective condition of its rationality. Thus Spinoza is, one might say,
on the right side of reason, because he ensures its triumph over the
oppositions that hinder the intellect, and thus he hastens

> the transformation of the rational into reflection and the knowl-
> edge of the absolute into a finite knowledge. But the fundamental
> form that leads this transformation from one end to the other
> consists of establishing the opposite of Spinoza's first definition
> as a principle, explaining a *causa sui* as that in which the essence
> simultaneously envelops existence, and affirms as fundamental
> principle that thought *(das Gedachte)*, simply because it is thought,
> does not simultaneously involve being *(ein Sien)*. This separation
> of the rational in which thought and being are one into opposing
> terms of thought and being, this absolute attachment to this op-
> position, this understanding raised to the absolute [*l'entendement
> érigé en absolu*] constitutes the foundation that this dogmatic skepti-
> cism repeats without respite and which he applies everywhere.[8]

In order that Spinoza's philosophy escapes the condemnation thus
leveled against abstract reflection, and even in order that this philosophy might condemn it still further, we must proceed with a double
transposition: restoring the relationship that establishes the definition

between essence and existence with regard to that of thought to being and identifying this relation as a contradiction, and the defined object, the *causa sui,* as the resolution of this contradiction. It is clearly apparent that the "authentically rational" character of Spinoza's philosophy cannot be recognized except under the conditions of its falsification. But what remains of this rationality if, returning to its literal interpretation, one abandons the transpositions that salvage it?

In truth, the commentary on this same definition that Hegel proposes later in his *Lectures on the History of Philosophy* distances us still further from the text:

> The unity of existence and universal thought *(die Einheit des Gedankens und der Existenz)* is asserted from the very first, and this unity will forever be the question at issue. *Causa sui* is a noteworthy expression. The effect is opposed to the cause. The cause of itself is the cause, which produces an effect, separates an "other," but what it drives out *[faire sortir]* is itself. In this displacement *[mise en dehors]* it also does away with the difference: the position of self as an other is the loss and at the same time the negation of this loss. It is a purely speculative concept. We imagine that the cause produces an effect and that the effect is something other than the cause. On the contrary, the exteriorization of the cause *(das Herausgehen der Ursache)* is here immediately surpassed, the cause of itself produces nothing but itself: this is a fundamental concept in all speculation. It is the infinite cause in which the cause is identical to the effect. If Spinoza had further developed what lies in the *causa sui,* his substance would not have been Immobile.[9]

This time, it is a new contradiction that Hegel discovers in the *causa sui*: the contradiction of cause and effect. This contradiction, which carries within it the causality of the substance—because the cause cannot be thought except in relation to its effects through which it exteriorizes itself—is immediately overcome, in the identity of substance to itself, which forges the unity of opposites, cause and effect. But this "dialectic" is immediately arrested, because instead of making his system coincide with the development of this contradiction, Spinoza has at once presented this contradiction as resolved by immediately positing the identity of substance to itself. It is a beautiful example of a philosophy that, as if "shot from a pistol,"[10] straight away exhausts all the potency of its content and subsequently has nothing more to say—nothing more that could be true, that could be understood. To develop the content of *causa sui* more precisely could signify only one thing: to keep its contradiction open for as long as is necessary for its maturation, in order that its solution contains all intermediaries necessary to its realization, instead of closing it off right away, under the impetus of this theoretical impatience that "demands the impossible: to achieve the objective without the means [to do so]."[11]

From the first lines of *Ethics*, Hegel thus discovers the mark of insufficiency that is characteristic of Spinozism: the contradiction, present implicitly, is nevertheless deprived of its rational clarification in an orderly and progressive argument.

In the sixth definition, where the object is God, Hegel discovers the same broken promise of rationality. In his commentary in the *Lectures*, he is interested above all in the explanation that accompanies these definitions, which bears on the difference between the two infinites, absolute infinity and infinity only in its kind. This is the explanation as formulated by Spinoza:

> I say "absolutely infinite" and not "infinite in its kind." For if a thing is only infinite in its kind one may deny that it has infinite attributes. But if a thing is absolutely infinite, whatever expresses its essence and does not involve any negation belongs to its essence.[12]

If this text holds Hegel's attention, it is because the concept of negation figures here on its own terms; here, therefore, we must find evidence of the Spinozist interpretation of this concept.

That which is absolute only in its own kind, that is to say the attribute, is therefore that which we can deny an infinity of things. Hegel interprets this specific feature in the following manner: the attribute is that whose nature envelops a negation, and as long as this is the case, it is a determination of substance, an exterior determination, only negative. This infinite is, he continues, the "bad infinite," the infinite of the imagination, which is represented only by a passage to a limit "and thus following the infinite"; it is opposed to the infinite of thought, or the absolutely infinite, which locates itself outside all negativity but which is pure affirmation of itself, or equally the infinite in act, that is, the infinite conceived as actual and not only representative of a possible. And Hegel concludes this summary by exclaiming, "Entirely correct, but this could have been better expressed as: it is the negation of the negation!"[13] If we take the relationship of the attributes as a contradiction—and we have seen actually that to develop the notion of attribute, Hegel retains only two attributes, thought and extension, which he places facing each other—God is this contradiction, resolved, to the extent that he is at the same time absolute affirmation of self and absolute negation, that is, the overcoming of all specific negations that constitute the specific essence of each attribute. In this way once again movement toward the rational is initiated, which is entirely characteristic of Spinoza's approach, such as Hegel understands him, even if this movement is immediately halted, and the fertile contradiction is immediately fixed in a sterile and abstract opposition.

The misuse of this interpretation proposed by Hegel rests evidently on something said nowhere by Spinoza, that the essence, which constitutes each attribute, "envelopes a negation"—without which evidently this essence can no longer be "conceived by itself." On the other hand, because Spinoza writes that the absolutely infinite contains in its essence "all that expresses an essence and *does not envelop a single negation*," this expression designates the attributes themselves, insofar as they are all in the substance that expresses itself in them, in a completely affirmative manner; to introduce the attribute of negativity into essence, it is necessary to detach it from the substance in which it exists, to try to understand it in an abstract manner through the difference that separates it from all the others. It is thus necessary to refrain from conceiving it in relation to itself—and yet it does not exist as such except in substance—in order to conceive it in its relationship to other essences, which it negates and which negate it. But it is absolutely necessary that Hegel thus reverses the true nature of the attributes—and we have seen how, in retaining only two of them and placing them in a relation of opposition—in order to identify an infinity of attributes, from that which is "infinite only in its own kind," with the infinity of the imagination or the bad infinite, such as Spinoza characterizes it elsewhere, in his *Letter* 12 to Louis Meyer. That which is infinite in its own kind is thus not less or otherwise infinite than that which is absolutely infinite, because it is not infinite except within itself.

This is why we cannot say, as Hegel does, that the idea of the negation of the negation is lacking in Spinoza's philosophy and that it is the cause of its imperfection and incompletion. As Spinoza says himself, the word *imperfection* signifies "a thing that lacks something that nevertheless pertains to its nature."[14] But the idea of "negation of the negation" and the very particular conception of the contradiction that is associated with it, is exactly the one that Spinoza's reasoning definitively excludes. Likewise, the commentaries of Hegel, which we have just reproduced, are more than just erroneous, or incongruous, to the extent that they forcefully apply to Spinoza's demonstration exactly the type of argumentation it has eliminated from the beginning, as Hegel himself remarks elsewhere. Nevertheless, this incongruity is not unwarranted, precisely because it puts in evidence, *a contrario*, an essential characteristic of Spinozist philosophy, its *resistance* to a certain form of argument that it is useless to compare it with, because it constitutes a refutation of it in advance: this is the Hegelian dialectic.

The Finite and the Infinite

Let us return now to the formula *omnis determinatio est negatio* and see what it means for Spinoza himself. It appears in *Letter* 50 to Jelles, which we have already referenced to explain that God, as Spinoza understands him, can only improperly be characterized as a unique being. Literally, what is written there is *determinatio negatio est,* and it takes it the form of an incidental assertion. In his commentary on *Ethics,*[15] Robinson goes so far as to assume that this phrase is not the work of Spinoza, from the letter written originally in Dutch, but that it must have been added, in the form of a clarification, in the Latin version. Without taking this extreme position, we see right away the disparity between this inscription, as it appears in the Latin text of the letter of Spinoza, and what Hegel concludes from it. From an incident that refers to a very particular context, which we will revisit, he has created a general proposition, which takes on a universal significance, by the addition of a little word that changes everything and confounds many things: *omnis.*

Rather, in *Letter* 50 to Jelles, Spinoza does not address the problem of determination in general; he takes it up in relation to a very particular case, which is that of the figure. It is necessary to return to the passage in its context:

> With regard to the statement that the figure is only a negation and not anything positive, it is obvious that pure matter, considered in an indefinite manner (without limitation), can have no figure and that the figure exists only in finite and determinate bodies. For he who claims to have perceived a figure indicates nothing other than the fact that he conceives a determinate thing and the manner in which it is determinate. This determination therefore does not pertain to the thing according to its being *(juxta suum esse),* but on the contrary it is its nonbeing *(ejus non esse).* This is why because the figure is nothing but a determination—and the determination is a negation—it could not, as has been said, be anything but a negation.[16]

This text allows no equivocation, provided that one understands it integrally. Its "object" is the figure, which is a very particular reality to the extent that it is neither an idea nor a thing but *a limit*; in this sense, it is not a real physical being but only a being of reason, and this is why its content is negative. Thus, "to perceive a figure" is not at all to "perceive" a thing, such as it is, but it is to "conceive" it as determined, that is, insofar as it is limited by another thing; the figure expresses nothing other than this reciprocal limitation, which exists between "finite and determinate bodies" and represents them not according to their own being but according to what they are not.

In anticipation, let us relate this definition to what Spinoza says in another letter where he treats the same problem in other terms:

> Concerning the whole and the parts: I consider things as parts of a certain whole, in so far as each of them adapts to the others, so that they are all harmonious and concordant with each other, as far as possible; but in so far as these things oppose each other, each of them thus forms in our mind, a separate idea, and must be considered not as a part, but as a whole.[17]

To perceive a figure is to conceive a thing insofar as it is limited by another, which opposes itself to it; it is thus to consider it as a whole and to distinguish it from other things that do not belong to this configuration. But if one takes another point of view, in which by contrast it adapts itself or agrees with things that appear here to act on it from outside, it presents itself as a part in relation to a whole, which proceeds itself from another determination. What follows then is that the representation of the figure does not depend on the thing that limits it but on the point of view of the intellect, which carves it out of the infinite series of singular things, considering it as a whole. On the other hand, and we will see that this idea is very important to Spinoza, the notion of totality insofar as it depends on such a determination does not represent the positive existence of a being, which affirms itself once and for all in an apprehended individuality, but it carries within it the idea of a limitation and, through its intermediary, a negation. The hint of a distinction emerges here, which is scandalous for Hegel, between substance and subject. Substance is that which cannot be subject, to the extent that being absolute, thus indeterminate, it cannot be determined as a whole; inversely, the subject is that which, according to its own limitation, cannot be substance.

What causes a problem here is the notion of determination. It is evident that the way it operates in *Letter 50* to Jelles, it does not apply to any type of reality whatsoever. It obviously does not concern the attributes, which are themselves unlimited and whose essence contains no negation at all; we have explained well enough that they do not limit themselves in relation to one another, which is the consequence of their own infinity, and the condition of their substantial character; on the other hand, it would be absurd that they would limit themselves and be limited within themselves. But could the notion of determination, as it is defined here, all the same be applied to the modes, for example the mode of extension, whose existence, on the contrary, implies a limitation? This does not appear likely either.

In effect, "finite and determined" bodies are not determined in this sense, that is, negatively, except if an intellect conceives of them from the point of view of their reciprocal limitation, independently of the effective order of nature, within which they agree with each other, as the parts of a whole. Thus the sequence of modes presents itself as a discontinuous succession, whose terms are separated by the fact that they negate each other, by opposing each other. But is this representation adequate? It is without a doubt not, to the extent that it does not know its objects according to their cause: the infinite substance that expresses itself within them in an absolutely continuous manner. By positing the finite outside the infinite, as the negative in relation to a positive, this representation considers it from the abstract point of view of imagination, which separates that which is intimately united, and which interprets all totality as if it were constituted in itself, through the relationship of its parts.

To determine extension through the figure, as Descartes has done, is to understand it negatively, reducing it to a reciprocal, indifferent, and incomplete relation of limitation, to an abstract order in which movement can intervene only from the exterior:

> In the case of the Cartesian extension, conceived as an inert mass, it is not only difficult but totally impossible to deduce from it the existence of the body. Matter at rest, in effect, will persevere in its rest in so far as it is at rest; it will not be put in motion except by a more forceful exterior cause; this is why I did not hesitate to say long ago that the Cartesian principles of nature are useless if not to say absurd.[18]

It is also to understand it completely from the point of view of the finite, from which its infinity cannot be grasped without contradiction, as the *Letter* 12 to Louis Meyer clearly indicates:

> Therefore, it is nonsense, bordering on madness, to think that extended substance is composed of parts, that is, bodies that are really distinct from one another. It is as if someone were attempting through the addition and accumulation of a multitude of circles to produce a square, a triangle, or some other object of a radically different essence than that of a circle.[19]

The manner in which the imagination thus proceeds is evident here: to understand extension, it delineates it or divides it, and it tries then to reconstitute it, to engender it, through the elements thus obtained. But this "genesis" can be nothing but fictive: it expresses nothing more than the powerlessness of the imagination to represent the infinite except by dividing it, in a strictly negative manner, thus inadequate to its essence. And yet the quantitative, taken as it is in itself, as it is conceived by the intellect, appears by contrast as indivisible, that is, irreducible to discrete parts, which are only its negation and through which it cannot be understood positively.

In a comment in book I of *Logic* dedicated to the "concept of quantity in Spinoza,"[20] this is what Hegel designates as the notion of *pure quantity,* relying on the scholium of proposition 15 (*Ethics* I):

> If we pay attention to the quantity as it is in the imagination, which is the most frequent and the easiest case, we will find it to be finite, divisible and composed of parts: if by contrast, we pay attention to it as it is in the intellect, and conceive it in terms of substance, which is more difficult, then, as we have already demonstrated sufficiently, we will find it infinite, unique and indivisible.[21]

To determine quantity in relating it to an exterior cause is to deny its infinity, which prevents us from understanding its positive essence.

It is in this connection that Spinoza introduces a distinction between what Hegel calls the bad infinite and the rational infinite, but this distinction has nothing to do with that of the infinite in its kind and the absolute infinite. The bad infinite corresponds to the attitude of the imagination, which pretends to understand all things by delineating them, that is, by denying their essence, in a necessarily inadequate understanding. But this distortion applies equally to substance and its affections:

> Because there are numerous things that we cannot grasp except by intellect and in no way through imagination, such as substance or eternity, one relies truly on the unreason of the imagination if one attempts to explain such concepts with the aid of notions such as time and measure, which are nothing but aids to imagination. *Even the modes of substance cannot be correctly understood if one confuses them with these beings of reason or aids of the imagination.* When we act in this confused fashion, in effect, we separate them from substance and the manner in which they flow from eternity, neglecting thereby that very thing without which they cannot be understood.[22]

To understand finite modes adequately requires conceiving them not in terms of their finitude, that is, their reciprocal limitation (cf. *E* ID2), but in terms of the infinity on which they are dependent and which they must comprise within their own concept, if it is true that "knowledge of the effect depends on the knowledge of the cause *and envelops it*" (*E* IAx4). By contrast, for the imagination finitude is an insurmountable given in itself, and it represents it as it is, outside all reference to the infinite, by strictly finite means, that is, as Spinoza says, by measure and by number; the imagination transposes this fixation on the finite to the infinite, which it attempts to analyze with the aid of the same instruments, in vain.

To understand this relationship of implication or envelopment that links the finite and the infinite to an adequate understanding, Spinoza borrows an example from geometry that we must emphasize, because Hegel comes back to it repeatedly, in the chapter of *Lectures on the History of Philosophy* (a commentary on the sixth definition of book I of *Ethics*) and in book I of *Logic* (a historical remark on mathematical infinity that is found at the end of the chapter on quantum).

In order to give the discussion a little clarity, let us beginning by taking up the geometric example Spinoza provides:

> All the inequalities of space *(inegalitates spatii)* lying between two circles, AB and CD, and all the variations that must subsume matter delimited in this space exceed every number. And this conclusion is not reached because of the excessive size of the intervening space: actually, no matter how small the portion of this space that we take, the inequalities of this small portion exceed any number. Nor is this conclusion reached, as occurs in other cases, because we know neither minimum nor maximum; actually, in our example we have both one and the other: the maximum is AB and the minimum is CD; our conclusion is only reached because the nature of the intervening space between the two circles can support no other conclusion. This is why, if someone wanted to determine this variation by a certain number *(certo aliquo numero determinare)* it would be necessary at the same time to arrive at a circle that was not a circle.[23]

In this text "intervening space" between the two nonconcentric circles designates the ensemble of distances, comprised between AB and CD, that separate the two circumferences. The "inequalities of this space" is the ensemble of differences between these unequal distances or their variation. This ensemble is not reducible to any number, because it consists of a continuous variation, which is a consequence of the circularity of figures ADA and BCB. But this "uncertainty" does not come from the intervening space between the two circles, being "of too large a magnitude," that is, an unlimited magnitude; on the contrary, it is limited by the two circumferences, which form the extremes of its variation. Additionally, if one takes only a part of this space, for example going between AB and CD, like the hands of a clock, the same uncertainty persists; moreover, it appears in this case that the sum of unequal distances contained within this half space, although not representable by any number, is half of the sum of inequalities of the total space contained between the two circumferences, an ensemble that itself is not reducible to any number; *Letter 81 to Tschirnhaus* adds this precision.

The difficulties that this example illustrates are only difficulties for the imagination, which wants to represent everything by numbers and which in the present case seeks to analyze magnitude by a number, which leads to unsolvable paradoxes. But mathematicians, who perceive things clearly and distinctly, don't allow themselves to be constrained by these paradoxes:

> In effect, beyond the fact that they found many things that cannot be explained by any number, which makes the powerlessness of numbers to determine everything evident enough, they also have many things which cannot be equated *(adaequari)* to any number but which exceed all possible numbers. And yet, they do not conclude that these things are superior to all numbers in consideration of the multitude of their parts but that in consideration of the particular nature of the thing it cannot without manifest contradiction support the number *(numerum pati)*.[24]

There are limited magnitudes that cannot be enumerated, because the movement that constitutes them is absolutely continuous, and thus indivisible. It is the imagination that sees a contradiction, and stops itself there, whereas for the intellect the notion of continuity is perfectly clear and distinct.

Let us see how Hegel interprets this same example, first according to the passage of the *Logic* that was written by Hegel himself (that of *Lectures* was reconstructed from notes of students):

> We know that the mathematical example with which he illustrates the true infinite is a space between two unequal circles that are not concentric, one of which lies inside the other without touching it. It seems that he thought highly of this figure and of the concept it was used to illustrate, making it the motto of his *Ethics*. "Mathematicians conclude," he says, "that the inequalities possible in such a space are infinite, not because of the infinite multitude of parts, for its magnitude is fixed and limited and I can assume larger and smaller such spaces, but because the nature of the thing surpasses every determinateness *(weil die Natur des Sache jede Bestimmheit übertrifft)*." It is evident that Spinoza rejects this conception of the infinite that represents it as a multitude or as a series that is not completed, and he points out that here, in the space of his example, the infinite is not beyond but actually present and complete *(gegenwärtig und vollständig)*. [This space is an infinite space "because the nature of the thing surpasses *(übersteigt)* every determinateness," because the determination of magnitude contained in it is at the same time not a quantum. This infinite series Spinoza calls the infinite of the imagination; on the other hand, the infinite as a relation to self he calls the infinite of thought, or *infinitum actu*. It is, namely, *actu,* it is actually infinite because it is complete and present within itself *(vollendet und gegenwärtig).*][25]

In the second edition of *Logic* the passage between square brackets is modified in the following manner:

> This space is something that is limited but also something infinite "because the nature of the thing surpasses all determination," because the determination of magnitude that is contained there is also not representable as a quantum, or, following Kant's expression, which has already been cited, a synthesis cannot be

completed and lead to a discrete quantum. How, in general, the opposition of continuous and discrete quantum leads to the infinite must be clarified in a later note. This infinity of a series Spinoza calls the infinite of imagination; by contrast, infinity as a relation to itself (as he calls it) is the infinite of thought or *infinitum actu*. It is strictly speaking *actu*, it is actually infinite, because it is complete and present within itself.[26]

Here finally is how the same example is presented and interpreted in the *Lectures on the History of Philosophy*:

Spinoza also introduces some geometric examples here as clarification of the concept of infinity; in his posthumous works, for example, he provides a figure as image of this infinity (even before his *Ethics*). He sets out two circles, one lying within the other without being concentric. The surface between the two cannot be deduced, it cannot be expressed in a determinate relation, it is not commensurable. If I want to determine it, I must proceed to the infinite—an infinite series. This is the "beyond" *(das Hinaus)*, which is always defective, affected with negation, and yet this bad infinite is complete *(fertig)*, circumscribed—affirmative, present in this surface. The affirmative is thus negation of the negation, *duplex negatio affirmativa*, following the well-known grammatical rule. The space between the two circles is actual, it is a circumscribed space, entirely and not just on one side, and yet the determination of the space cannot be sufficiently indicated by a number. The determinate does not create the space itself, and nevertheless it is present. Or again, a line, a bounded line, consists of an infinity of multiple points, and nevertheless it is present and it is determined. The infinite must be represented as actually present. The concept of cause in itself is thus true actuality. As soon as the cause has an other just opposed to it, the effect of finitude is present, but in this case this other is at the same time surpassed, and it becomes once more [the cause] itself.[27]

In reading these texts we can first ask ourselves whether they are an accurate representation of Spinoza's passage, which we reproduced at the beginning, insofar as they are a liberal interpretation of it. This concern is supported by the fact that Hegel, each time, refers back to a "*Letter* XXIX of Spinoza." But in all the editions of Spinoza's correspondence, this number corresponds to a letter to Oldenberg, which talks about something completely different. Rather, it is clear that it is the *Letter* 12 to Louis Meyer, which is at issue here, but it is referenced at the price of a certain displacement of its actual content.

First, Hegel's version of the example is not the same as the one provided in Spinoza's text: in each case, the same figure is used with very different meanings, as Guéroult has argued.[28] As we have seen, Spinoza considers the variation of distances contained between the two circumferences and remarks that it is continuous. In this case, it cannot be determined by a number. In *Logic* and in *Lessons*, Hegel talks only about the space between the two circumferences, which is constituted through an infinity of unequal distances and which is nevertheless "complete and present" because it is comprised within fixed limits. If we interpret the example this way, we can evidently no longer find what rationale exists to present nonconcentric circles; the same reasoning would work if all distances between the circumferences were equal. Hegel thus neglects something, which is on the contrary essential to Spinoza's reasoning: it is the idea of a variation contained between a minimum and a maximum, thus a determinate progression, which nevertheless cannot be represented by a number.

But this is not the most important modification made to Spinoza's text. It is all the more characteristic that Hegel introduces, injects in this text, the notion of the infinite in act, which does not figure there expressly as we can easily affirm, returning to the text reproduced earlier. It is true that the letter this text is extracted from is known as the letter on the infinite (Spinoza himself uses this expression, in his *Letter* 81 to Tschirnhaus) and begins as follows: "You ask me what I think about the Infinite, which I will do willingly." How does the geometric example find a place in the context of this discussion on the infinite?

To overcome these difficulties predicated on the current use of the notion of the infinite, the use by the imagination, it is enough, says Spinoza, to respect a certain number of distinctions. There is that which is infinite by its nature (and conceives itself in itself as infinite) and that which is infinite by the power [*force*] of its cause (and not by its own essence); there is that which is infinite because it is without limits and that which is infinite because it is not numerically determinable. We have been preoccupied here with two successive distinctions, discussed with no regard for the precise context that they share; in his commentary on the letter on the infinite, Guéroult relates them to the enumeration of four successive cases, which seem excessive in relation to Spinoza's text. These two distinctions relate to substance (which is conceived through itself) and its affections (which cannot be conceived through themselves) and to reason (which knows things adequately, such as they are) and the imagination (which represents things in an inadequate manner). The traditional paradoxes of the infinite arise from the fact that these distinctions are not respected; on the contrary, it suffices to reestablish them, in order that all contradictions be not resolved but rather eradicated, because they arose only from terms in which a problem had been badly posed.

The geometric example introduced by Spinoza relates to one of these distinctions: it presents that which is infinite, because it cannot be determined by a number, even though it is contained within certain limits. One must remember that it is the imagination that is compelled to determine a continuous progression by a number contained between a minimum and a maximum: to achieve this, it attempts to divide the variation into parts and to reconstitute it according to these elements. But the progression, being continuous, cannot be divided in this manner. This is why it appears that it cannot be determined numerically. To follow this reasoning more closely, it is thus the imagination that discovers an infinity here, in a quantum that cannot be equated with any number and that it determines therefore through a passage to the limit, as exceeding all numbers, thus as unlimited. In what way is this representation inadequate? In the sense that it ignores the essential fact that its object is limited, because it is contained between a minimum and a maximum. It is thus also finite in the exact meaning that Spinoza gives to this notion ("is called finite in its own kind which can be limited by another of the same nature," E ID2). It seems thus that the error of imagination consists of taking as infinite, in its attempt to determine it numerically, a thing that is in itself, we might say, finite.

But things are not this simple, nor this cut and dried. In order to escape the penchant of the imagination, it is not enough to reestablish a neat separation between the infinite in a strict sense, that is, unlimited, and the finite, that is, the limited. Such a separation, taken literally, is also the act of the imagination: it neglects the essential character of the finite, which cannot be explained through itself, which does not exist outside the infinite that produces it and whose concept it necessarily envelops. From this point of view, the geometric example also applies to another case singled out by Spinoza: the case of that which is infinite by the power [*force*] of its cause and that which is proper to all modes, whether they are infinite or finite. The variation of distances contained between the two nonconcentric circles is also infinite, not in itself, because it is limited, but as an affection [*affection*] of a substance that expresses itself in it as the cause in its effect [*la cause dans son effet*].

Here, apparently, we rediscover Hegel, because despite all the liberties he takes with Spinoza's text, he has drawn certain essential tendencies from it. On one hand, in effect, Hegel has understood that what is at stake in this example is a certain aspect of the problem of causality, represented by the relation between substance and its affections. On the other hand, he designates this relationship by the notion of the infinite in act *(infinitum actu)* in a manner that seems pertinent. This notion appears in Spinoza in the paragraph that precedes the one setting out the geometric example: those, he says, who ignore the true nature of things because they have confused it with beings of reason, through which the imagination attempts to represent it (by knowing the number, measure, and time), "will deny [*neiront*] the infinite in act" *(infinitum actu negarunt)*. What is an infinite in act? It is an infinite that is not given in an unlimited series, thus in a virtual or potential manner, but all at once; it is that which is present in a limited reality, such as a variation contained between a minimum and maximum, in an "actualized and present" manner, to return to the words of Hegel. This notion, borrowed from the vocabulary of the scholastics, indicates that the position adopted by Spinoza on this question is as far from Descartes's as it is from Leibniz's.[29] For Descartes, who proceeds analytically through evidence of finite reason, the infinite in act is incomprehensible because it cannot be constructed intuitively; for Leibniz, who resolves the problem of continuity through the method of infinitesimal calculus, there is only one infinite power [*puissance*], expressed as *eminenter sed non formaliter*, thus always outside of an assignable limit. Spinoza's affirmation of the existence of an infinite in act and of its rationality is extremely important, to the extent that it expresses the effective presence of the infinite in the finite, through the intermediary of the act through which it is actually produced: this presence cannot be denied [*niée*] except by those who reduce the nature of things to a numerical criteria, which leads them to ignore the infinity within this nature, or misrepresent it in the idea of an unlimited series, which excludes the possibility of an infinite in act.

If we adopt this explanation, the other infidelity Hegel commits in his consideration of Spinoza's text also appears to be justifiable. In effect, if the notion of the infinite in act correctly designates this immanent presence of the cause in its effects (cf. *E* IP18, "God is the immanent but not the transitive cause, of all things"), all the specificities of the geometric example as set out by Spinoza seem superfluous. Any finite mode, no matter which (e.g., the surface contained between two circumferences, whether they are concentric or not, or again, to return to the example proposed by Hegel, the infinity of points contained in the segment of a line), expresses an infinity that it envelops formally *(formaliter sed non eminenter)* as its cause. Here we are returned to the point of departure: why does Spinoza expressly introduce in his example the idea of a variation contained between a minimum and maximum, a variation that depends on the fact that the two circles are nonconcentric?

In his geometric example, if Spinoza had wanted only to represent the idea of a finite quantum that nevertheless contains an infinity of parts and exceeds any assignable number, he would not have needed this precision, but this simplification would have at the same time led to the inevitable reduction of this infinite to an extensive relationship between the two elements, a relationship envisioned negatively, thus in a manner inadequate to the very nature [*nature même*] of the thing. He would have thus returned to the point of view of imagination, which, on the contrary, he seeks to distinguish himself from. But for the intellect, which grasps things as they are, according to their own causality, it is a question of an entirely different infinity that must be understood affirmatively, in the proper meaning of absolute affirmation of its nature, whatever it is. This would appear exactly in a variation that is continuous but limited—it can therefore be considered outside all determinations of magnitude (this is what indicates the precision accorded to *Letter* 81 to Tschirnhaus)—which proceeds intensively, decidedly not according to an abstract relation and determined negatively or numerically between two extrinsic parts, but rather through the power [*puissance*] of the cause, which acts within it simultaneously and which is substance in person, in the form of its extended attribute. This difference between two infinities, extensive and intensive, is strongly emphasized by Deleuze.[30]

Intensive infinity directly expresses an immanent and nontransitive relation, which links substance to its affections and which is known only through the intellect. From this understanding something very important can also be concluded: infinity, as it can be understood in the modes, is no different from infinity that constitutes substance; rather, it is formally the same thing. This is why the distinctions prescribed in *Letter* 12 to Louis Meyer cannot be reduced to an instance of enumeration, where each time a different form of the infinite would be presented, as if one could have several kinds of infinity. Because, whether it is expressed as *causa sui* in substance, in its capacity as *natura naturans,* or it manifests itself in the inexhaustible series of finite modes as *natura naturata,* whether it is conceived adequately, that is positively, through intellect, or represented inadequately, that is to say negatively through the imagination, it is always the same infinite that acts necessarily.

Here we must take seriously the idea that the infinity of substance passes intensively, in all its modes, *without dividing itself:* all extension is indivisibly in a drop of water, as all thought is present in each act of thought and necessarily determines it. And this is why "if one part of matter was annihilated, the whole of Extension would vanish at the same time,"[31] and similarly for ideas, which are "part" of thought. Thus, the inalterable continuity that constitutes all modal reality, whatever the limits in which one envisions them, whatever the scale at which one considers them, expresses the absolute, that is to say the unity of substance: it is the knowledge of this infinite in act that constitutes "the intellectual love of God," or knowledge of the third kind.

As we will come to see, this knowledge is affirmative: it does not proceed in a regressive manner of modes toward substance, which would thus be thrown back to the infinite, their limit, but it proceeds from substance to its affections, that is, from cause toward its effects, synthetically in an absolutely necessary and continuous progression, which excludes all possible recourse to negativity. Therefore, one cannot say, as Hegel does, that it is a negation that is surpassed, or overcome, and is constituted in this way, but it is that whose concept excludes all negation, all internal negativity.

If we apply literally, here, the principle crafted by Hegel, *omnis determinatio est negatio*, we should add that adequate knowledge of things according to their own nature also excludes, by virtue of this fact, all determination, which is evidently absurd. In the example we have just discussed, we have dealt exactly with an infinite that cannot be determined by any number but is in itself actually determined, because it is finite. It therefore appears necessary, according to the concept of determination, to introduce a distinction as well: to determine something negatively is to represent it abstractly according to its limits, in separating it from God that acts within it and attempting to adapt it to formal norms, pure beings of reason, forged by the imagination (e.g., to grasp it in terms of a certain part of the durée that is assigned to it). We relate it, then, to that which it is not, to its possible disappearance, and we present it as contingent. To determine something positively is by contrast to perceive it in its singular physical reality, according to the immanent necessity that engenders it within substance, according to a law of causality that is the same one through which substance produces itself, because it is substance that produces itself in its affections; it is also to envisage it from the point of view of eternity, insofar it is itself eternal, that is, insofar as it cannot be destroyed, other than by an exterior cause (*E* IIIP4).

All this discussion, which leads us into a consideration of apparently extraneous details, but which it was not possible to condense, thus returns to a fundamental principle that characterizes the entire philosophy of Spinoza: there are not two separate orders of reality, two "worlds," one infinite, the other finite, in which forms would function of necessity, according to distinct laws of causality. Nor is Spinoza's objective to discover a harmonious relation between these two orders, realized through a gradual series of intermediaries, which would permit the passage from one to the other in a successive movement: this is the "order" imagined by Hegel, which goes from substance to attributes then from attributes to modes, in a progressive determination of the absolute, that is, by denying it [*niant*] in the relative. For Spinoza, it is a single and same order, not at all the abstract order of the imagination but the concrete, physically real order of substance, which expresses itself simultaneously and identically as absolute and as relative, which is understood in a contradictory manner through the intellect and through the imagination. This is why the relation of substance to its affections cannot be exhausted through the simple opposition of the indeterminate and determinate, the positive and negative, as Hegel interprets it, in the terms of a paradoxically abstract logic.

Determination

The rational point of view of the intellect is essentially affirmative: not simply in that all negativity must be attributed to the point of view of the imagination, which is incapable of understanding the substance as it is in itself, but as well insofar as substance acts through its modes, because it expresses itself at the same time in the infinite and in the finite. The interpretation Hegel proposes is thus untenable: the negativism of Spinozism, an inevitable consequence of the empty thought of the absolute, is a fiction, literally incompatible with the system. But is the contrary interpretation more satisfying? Can we say, as Deleuze does, "Spinoza's philosophy is a philosophy of pure affirmation?"[32] Does this "positivism," for which the preceding negativism would be nothing more than the inverse or the reverse, not revert finally to the same thing? We find at least an indicator of this collusion in the fact that these two opposing presentations of Spinozism agree equally in emphasizing its nondialectical character, which one interprets as a symptom of the inferiority and the failure of this philosophy and which for this other is a testimony, by contrast, to its excellence.

Let's go back a little. The formula Hegel puts forward, *omnis determinatio est negatio,* is without a doubt inadequate to the letter of Spinozism. Does this signify that we should substitute it with another formulation: *omnis determinatio est affirmatio?* The meaning of this new statement is clear: determination does not simply have the restrictive value of a degradation of that which is in itself substantial, in a simple movement of exteriorization, passing without return from the same to the other. Rather it is the act through which substance expresses all its causal power [*puissance*]: "all that we conceive to be the power [*pouvoir*] of God necessarily exists"[33] because in God, which is the cause of himself and of all things, essence and power [*puissance*] are one and the same thing. Thus the necessity of modes is neither inferior to nor different from that of the substance; it is precisely the same thing. However, if we remain there, one of Hegel's objections acquires a new force: is not the identity here *affirmed,* deprived of all actual content, plunging everything into this indistinct night where all the cows are gray? To reply to this question, it is necessary to return to the notion of determination, which Hegel uses abundantly in his commentary on Spinoza, and see exactly what it signifies for Spinoza himself.

Analysts have remarked that Spinoza uses the term *determinatio* in many very different ways. On one hand, he uses it to express the idea of a limitation, which is itself attached to that of finitude: *Letter* 50 to Jarig Jelles talks of a "finite and determined" body. Understood this way, the notion of determination envelops a negation without possible contestation, and it applies itself to things, which are "limited by another thing of the same nature."[34] In this sense, substance, which is above all entirely unlimited, is also indeterminate: "since determination denotes nothing positive, but only a privation in the nature of existence which is conceived as determinate, it follows that that which by definition affirms existence cannot be conceived of as determined."[35] It is true of substance and its attributes, whose notion carries no imperfection at all, and which cannot be said to be determined, in the sense that they are not limited by something of the same nature.

Notwithstanding, we must be very careful here: the notion of indetermination should be taken here in an absolutely positive manner. And yet the inclination of words leads us on the contrary to an inverse meaning, in designating an absolutely positive reality through a negative or limiting term. But following Spinoza the words, taken in on their own, do not express the reality that they intend to represent but the point of view of the imagination, which substitutes this reality with its fictions. In particular, this corroborates the entire vocabulary we use to define the absolute:

> As words form part of the imagination, that is to say that we conceive of many fictions, following words, which are composed confusedly in the memory by virtue of some disposition of the

body, there can be no doubt that words no less imagination, can be the cause of many and grave errors, as long as we make no great effort to guard against them. Add to this that they are formed to our liking and in accordance with the understanding of the mob [*la foule*]: thus they are nothing but the signs of things such as they are in the imagination and not such as they are in the intellect. This appears clearly from the fact that, for all things that are only in the intellect and are not found in the imagination, men have frequently imposed negative names, such as: incorporeal, infinite, etc., and that we express in a very negative manner even things which are, in reality, positive, and inversely: thus incarnate, independent, infinite, immortal, etc. without a doubt because we imagine much more easily their opposites; this is why these appeared largely to the first humans and usurped positive names. We affirm and we negate many things because these affirmations and negations conform to the nature of the words and not to the nature of things; so well that, if we do not pay attention to this, we would take easily for true something that was false.[36]

Those who in the Hegelian fashion would like to interpret the indeterminacy of the Spinozist substance in the sense of the negation of a negation (determination = limitation: indetermination = suppression of this limitation) would thus be in favor of these charges; he would fall into a purely verbal speculation. It is true that, on the question of the nature of language, Hegel and Spinoza also have divergent positions: Hegel would not admit that the disposition of words, submitted to purely corporeal laws, would be thus placed outside the rational order of thought.

In Spinoza's case, therefore, things are perfectly clear: the notion of indetermination is in itself, *invito vocabulo,* positive. But does this signify that the notion of determination, which apparently constitutes its opposite, is itself necessarily negative? Is this opposition not attributable exactly to the imagination that thinks about these words and does not see things such as they are?

Actually, Spinoza does not use the term *determinatio* only in the sense of a limitation, whose implications are negative. This appears in the seventh definition of book I of *Ethics*: "this thing is called free which exists according to the sole necessity of its nature and is determined *(determinatur)* to act by itself alone; (it is called) by contrast, necessary, or rather constrained, if it is determined *(determinatur)* by another thing to exist and to produce an effect according to a certain and determined *(determinata)* reason." From the point of view that concerns us, this phrase carries a very important clue, in applying the idea of a determination equally to the reality of substance as to that of the modes: the freedom that pertains to the *causa sui* is not the indifferent and arbitrary activity of a being that is not determined to act according to any cause, in the manner of this incomprehensible God, whose initiatives support the entire edifice of Cartesian philosophy. God is no less determined to act than the things that depend on him; we could even say that he is all the more so to the extent that he reunites all perfections within himself. Indeterminate substance is therefore not free from all determination, but quite the contrary, it is determined by a cause or necessary reason that is its own nature.

All this becomes perfectly clear if we recall that the action of free will that engenders itself *(natura naturans)* differs in no way from the causal action that initiates itself within things that do not have their cause in themselves *(natura naturanta)*. But they are one and the same act: God produces himself nowhere other than in his affections. If no determinations at all were given in God, it is the existence of things and his own specific existence that would be called into question.

We must repeat that God is a cause for singular things not solely insofar as they exist but additionally insofar as they produce effects themselves, which signifies that they are totally determined within God: "a thing that is determined to produce some effect has thus necessarily been determined by God: and that which is not determined by God cannot determine itself to produce an effect."[37] The sequence of finite determinations, which unfold towards the infinite, is thus itself completely determined in God, and this is why he admits no contingency within himself, that is, no indetermination.

The result is that, associated with the idea of a causality that is identical to God and within all that depends on him, the notion of determination has an essentially positive usage, because to produce an effect cannot in any way be a sign of imperfection: "that by which things are said to be determined to produce a certain effect must necessarily be something positive (as is obvious)."[38]

Does this mean that the notion of determination, as it functions in the Spinozist system, is ambiguous, because it refers to a multiplicity of usages, which are for that matter contradictory? Is it not entirely characteristic, on the contrary, that Spinoza uses the same term to designate the infinite causality that exerts itself on behalf of substance and the finite causality executed in the modes, indicating in this way that it does not involve two independent phenomena? Thus, if the notion of determination can be understood simultaneously in a positive and negative sense, it is because this notion does away with the traditional opposition of positive and negative. And here we are, once again, very close to Hegel, but following a different path than the one Hegel has taken: if the function of the concept of determination in Spinoza obliterates the traditional opposition of positive and negative, it is not because it has "surpassed" it or because it has "resolved" it as a rational contradiction, but quite simply because it ignores it. In this movement, a "dialectic" appears that is without a doubt not that of Hegel: is this reason enough to say that it generally does not involve a dialectic?

The Infinite Modes

Following some of the preceding formulas, we might think that the relationship between substance and its affections reproduces the one that it also has with its attributes: both here and there, in a horizontal sense and in a vertical sense, so to speak, the same kind of unity is found, which integrates a diversity by conferring its rationality on it. Does this not mean that this unity is the formal unity of a procedure that reduces all reality to the same, confusedly, by ignoring, by effacing its effective articulations? To respond to this objection, we must clarify the passage of the absolute into the relative, through which substance accomplishes its own exteriorization, or its determination.

The most singular aspect of this passage is represented by the surprising theory of infinite modes that appears in propositions 21, 22, and 23 and the scholium of proposition 28 of book I of *Ethics*, which explains very concisely how the infinite acts within the finite. Even the fact that there are infinite modes demonstrates very well that the infinite does not belong exclusively to substance and to its attributes, the modes, that is to say individuals, by contrast remaining enclosed in their finitude, thus marked in a strictly negative fashion as Hegel appears to believe. We have just seen that there are not two orders of reality, one substantial and infinite and the other modal and finite, but a single and same, continuous and indivisible reality, determined by a law of unique causality, in which the finite and the infinite are indissolubly linked; the infinite modes are in a certain way the place where this unity is forged, where the transformation takes place, or, in other words, the determination of the infinite in the finite.

In effect the infinite modes define themselves in the first instance by their function of transition: they present themselves as intermediaries that ensure a kind of reconciliation between infinite substance and finite modes. This is what is apparently indicated in the scholium of proposition 28: "some things must have been produced by God immediately, namely those that follow necessarily from his absolute nature and others, *through the intermediary of these primary things,* which could nevertheless neither be nor be conceived without God" (*E* I).[39] This appearance is reinforced additionally by the split that Spinoza undertakes within the interior of infinite modes themselves, by proposing a distinction between the immediate infinite mode, which proceeds from the absolute nature of each attribute and expresses it immediately (*E* IP21), and the mediate infinite mode, which flows from attributes insofar as they are already modified (*E* IP22). This internal division appears to conform to the function that is assigned to infinite modes in the economy of the entire system: to provide the means for a gradual passage, a kind of continuous evolution that leads from the absolute to the relative. We should note as well that this is the moment, par excellence, where the Spinozist system presents itself as a formal construction, which multiplies abstract notions to resolve the difficulties that arise from the development of its own reasoning, but are these notions, which without a doubt deserve to be explained more clearly than they are in book I of *Ethics,* as abstract as they seem? Do they actually conform to the function according to which we have just defined them?

Because if we maintain this determination, which renders the infinite mode as nothing more nor less than an artificial procedure to effect a transition from the substance to its affections, in the manner of a middle term in a formal argument, we see the reappearance of an idea that we thought we had avoided, of a hierarchy of beings, which reduces Spinozism to a variation of Neoplatonism, thus confirming the regressive interpretation of the passage from the absolute to relative proposed by Hegel, through which the infinite dilutes itself, exhausted in the finite, until it disappears altogether. Spinoza writes elsewhere, *omnia quamvis diversis gradibus animata tamen sunt,*[40] "all things no matter what are nevertheless animate *in different degrees.*" Is this not indicative of an essentially process-oriented [*processif*] character of the relative that, on the contrary, advances or retreats from a maximum toward a minimum of being by passing in a continuous manner through all intermediary stages, a passage that exactly encapsulates the infinite modes, with their transitory function? But if we accept such an interpretation, we are led as well to reintroduce an "Aristotelianism without Aristotle" in the Spinozist system, following this curious expression of Guéroult,[41] and also the idea of an internal immanent finality,[42] that is, a Kantism without Kant, and also a metaphysics of totality, that is to say a Hegelianism without Hegel. The door is thus opened wide enough, as we see, for every connection, every confusion, every alteration, which purely and simply do away with the singular efficacy of Spinozist reasoning. We will see that such interpretations must be absolutely rejected. To demonstrate this, it is necessary to return to the theory of mediate infinite modes, because they serve exactly to eliminate such conceptions.

As we have already indicated, the notion of infinite modes, as it appears in *Ethics,* is extremely enigmatic. This is what compelled one of Spinoza's correspondents to demand clarification from him, to give this notion a content: "I should like to have some examples of things immediately produced by God and of those things produced by the mediation of some infinite modification; it seems to me that thought and extension are of the first kind; in the second the intellect in thought, motion in extension etc."[43] This is a flagrant error, likening the infinite immediate modes to attributes themselves, but it confirms the difficulty of the problem that needs to be resolved. Spinoza responds in his commentaries, with the dryness of an official report, "Here are the examples that you have demanded of me: those of the first kind, are in the order of thought, absolute infinite intellect; in the order of extension, movement and rest; for the second kind, it is the figure of the entire universe *(facies totius universi)* which remains always the same, even as it varies according to an infinity of modes; on this point see the scholium of lemma VII which comes before proposition 4 part II."[44] We will leave aside the inconsistency here that interests every commentator: although he gives examples of the infinite immediate mode in relation to two attributes, thought and extension, Spinoza gives only one of the infinite mediate mode, the *facies totius universi*, which expressly concerns extension. To characterize these notions, we will restrict ourselves to the case of extension, that is, to the strict problem of the physical, because it should hold for all the others.

In this exact case, the relationship between the absolute and the relative expresses itself through the following distinctions:

extension	substantial attribute
movement and rest	infinite immediate mode
facies totius universi	infinite mediate mode
singular body (individual)	finite mode

Do these distinctions lead to the representation of a hierarchy of forms, integrating all of reality in substance, which, even itself, would be an absolute and ultimate form, placed above and following all others and imposing its determination on them? This would evidently return to the point of view of the imagination.

What does Spinoza want to say in making movement and rest into the infinite immediate mode of extension? Nothing other than this: the substantial reality of extension expresses itself absolutely in movement and rest, that is to say in a certain relation *(certa ratione)* of movement and rest. This idea itself can be taken to mean several things: extension cannot be grasped outside this relation of movement and rest that animates it, and it is clear that what is rejected here is the Cartesian conception of an inert extension, defined exclusively by geometric properties, by expansion [*en extension*], and one to which movement must be added from outside, in the form of a determinate quantity of movement that must be conserved identically to its initial impulsion. But Spinoza also wants to say that all that produces itself in extension is explained by the relationship between movement and rest, which constitutes a kind of fundamental law within it. This is what a passage from the *Short Treatise* (II chap. 19) explains very clearly:

"If . . . we consider extension alone, we perceive nothing other than Movement and Rest in it, from which we find all the effects that result there from; and these two modes of body are such that it is impossible for any other thing to change them except only themselves."

From this point where movement and rest are no longer considered distinct modes, *Ethics* takes up this concept: following lemma II of proposition 13 (book II), "all bodies agree in certain respects," that is, they have common properties insofar as they envelop the concept of the same attribute: extension, which expresses itself immediately in the relationship of movement and rest. Thus we find demonstrated, generatively, the universality of these laws of nature and the possibility of knowing them. If all that exists within extension is explained by movement and rest, it is because extension produces it; in producing itself in this manner, a certain relationship of movement and rest, it acts and affirms itself in this relationship, which represents it absolutely, that is, without intermediary and without restriction. The laws of nature, which express this relationship of movement and rest, are irreducible insofar as they derived immediately from substance, which serves as the basis for study of all natural phenomena.

We can then ask ourselves in what way this ratio, in which the attribute expresses itself immediately, is modal; isn't the attribute itself, considered in its internal causality, in its immanent relation to itself? But the answer to this question comes from itself: the ratio is necessarily modal in that it is exactly a ratio, that is, in that it is determined by a certain relation *(certa ratione),* which obliges us to distinguish it from unlimited and indeterminate substance. What creates a problem, then, is the possibility for the indeterminate to express itself absolutely, immediately, in a determination, which is, it is true, infinite and thus unassignable [*inassignable*]. It is not clear that Spinozist concepts allow us to resolve this difficulty, but they do allow us to confront it; it appears therefore that in the logic of the system, determination is not a deprivation, a negation of the indeterminate, and this is why all determination is not necessarily and exclusively finite. *Omnis determinatio non est negatio.*

Let us see for the moment what there is within the mediate infinite mode: *facies totius universi,* that is, corporeal nature taken in its entirety. It must be said that this notion is ambiguous, because according to the texts, Spinoza gives it very different and even inverse presentations: sometimes he defines it genetically following its cause, which like it is necessarily infinite, and sometimes he constitutes it, or rather he constructs it from the elements that it assembles, that is, finite determinations that it "totalizes." Which of these two movements is adequate to the nature of the mediate infinite mode?

If we follow propositions 22 and 23 of book I of *Ethics,* the mediate infinite mode follows necessarily from an attribute insofar as this is modified by a modification that exists necessarily through the nature of this attribute: in this sense the figure of the universe, considered in its entirety, is this infinite determination that follows from the attribute of extension, insofar as it is already modified by the modification that necessarily follows its nature, that is, a certain ratio of movement and rest. This signifies that from extension, taken absolutely, a certain number of laws of motion follow and that these laws apply to corporeal nature taken in its entirety, from which they carve up after a fashion the global figure. *Facies totius universi* is thus that which deduces itself from substance itself through the intermediary of extension and the laws of nature that express it immediately, that is, the ensemble of corporeal phenomena, insofar as they are subjected to the laws of movement and rest.

But the deduction, which proceeds here from the infinite to the infinite, stops precisely at this point, as proposition 28 makes clear, which explains how finite modes are determined themselves, precisely not from the infinite but in their own internal sequence of steps.

> All singular things, that is, all things that are finite, and which have a determinate existence, cannot exist nor be determined to produce an effect if they are not determined to exist and to produce this effect through an other cause, which is itself also finite and which has a determined existence: and in turn nor can this cause exist nor be determined to produce an effect if it is not determined to exist and produce an effect through another which is also itself finite, and which has a determined existence, and so on to infinity.

This proposition, stated here in an absolutely general manner, will be taken up again in book II of *Ethics,* in the case of modes of thought

(*E* IIP9), then in the case of modes of extension (*E* IIP13LemIII). It immediately sets forth the definition of finite modes, provided at the beginning of book I of *Ethics*: "One calls finite in its kind the thing that can be limited by another of the same nature" (*E* ID2). But here it is established in another manner, through a demonstration that proceeds by elimination: finite singular things cannot be produced either by the absolute nature of an attribute of God or by this attribute insofar as it is itself affected by an infinite modification, and this is why they must proceed from a finite mode, which is their cause and which itself depends on another finite mode, and so on until infinity. We thus see that a kind of break between the infinite and the finite appears here: from the infinite, one cannot deduce anything but the infinite, and the finite cannot itself be deduced from anything but the finite. Thus the idea of a procession of beings that advance or retreat gradually, from the absolute towards the relative passing through all the intermediary stages, disappears. This signifies that between nature taken in its entirety and singular things that fill its figure from their determined existence, there is no continuous passage, but on the contrary a separation. Is this not the rational postulate of the unity of nature that is therefore called into question?

It first appears that the separation occurs here between infinite essences and finite beings. This distinction appears at the end of *Treatise on the Emendation of the Intellect,* where Spinoza distinguishes in the order of nature "the series of singular changing things" and "the series of fixed and eternal things" (§100). The first escapes human consciousness, because of the multitude of infinite circumstances that compose it. Let us recall the fictitious dialogue that, in the appendix of book I of *Ethics,* contrasts the partisans of finalism with those who seek to see things such as they are, in their immanent necessity: a man is dead from the drop of a stone that has fallen from a roof on his head; why has the stone fallen? Because the wind blew at the moment that he was passing. Why did the wind blow at that moment? Because he got up the day before, as the sea began to foment, and the man was invited by friends, et cetera. We see here the reappearance of the infinite regression, which, following proposition 28 of book I, binds all finite determinations together. By definition, this sequence [*enchainement*] cannot be exhausted through knowledge, and this is why the Confusionists take hold of it as an argument and find in it the confirmation of a hidden intention, which gives its meaning to an entire series of events, a meaning that is irreducible to all strictly causal determinations, which do not succeed in exhausting the sequence but require the intervention of final causes. The imagination projects these ends, precisely at the end of an enumeration of finite determinations, which it encloses ideally by totalizing them: it is precisely this conception that eliminates the Spinozist notion of the actual infinite, by disallowing the construction of the infinite through the finite.

To avoid giving a platform to the illusions of imagination, which installs itself in this place that is opened up by the regression to the infinite, this *et cetera* that is the veritable passageway of ignorance, we must renounce the ambition of an exhaustive knowledge of particular things, that is, their global linkages, which is by definition inaccessible: the infinite cannot be apprehended through the finite, in a movement of totalization, or else it loses its intrinsic necessity in order to become a pure possible, that is, a formal fiction. We must thus limit ourselves to the knowledge of things that are "fixed and eternal" and their laws, insofar as they "govern the existence and ordering of singular things";[45] according to these laws, singular things are intelligible, sufficiently at least that the temptation to interpret them in terms of imaginary ends can be abandoned.

We ask ourselves next what these fixed and eternal things are, which Spinoza says again, despite their singularity, are a kind of universal. Let us maintain above all for the moment that it is not possible (without falling into incorrigible error) to grasp the entirety of corporeal nature in terms of finite modes, which it connects to each other, even if these determine each other infinitely through a necessary series. On the contrary, we must seek to understand and master this finite order in terms of essential determinations, possibly the infinite modes that render it intelligible. This signifies that it is not possible to proceed from the finite to the infinite as the imagination does, but it is necessary to go in the other direction, following the real causal order, from the infinite to the finite. Is this exigency compatible with the separation we just established between things that are infinite and things that are finite?

In addition, how can Spinoza present corporeal nature, considered in its entirety through the bodies that constitute it, in terms of an infinite progression, as he does elsewhere in the scholium of lemma VII of proposition 13 (*E* II)? To understand the meaning of this text, we must take it up from its beginning, the abridged natural philosophy that Spinoza proposes in an annex to this proposition, with a view to extracting guidelines to the nature and composition of the human body. In the first instance, these laws of movement are applied to "the most simple bodies" *(entia simplicissima),* a notion we will return to; then, the same laws are applied to composite bodies, that is, to individuals, who are formed from a union of the body; they should therefore be complicated; finally, in the scholium we are discussing, Spinoza develops this amplification to its final conclusion, the nature of the body taken in its entirety, insofar as it is itself a union of bodies, determined by constant laws, from which it cannot extricate itself except by an "extraordinary concourse of God," that is, a miracle, whose necessity could not be demonstrated. The representation of nature, thus unveiled, is obtained through a passage to the limit: "and, if we thus continue to infinity, we shall readily conceive all of nature as a single individual, whose parts, that is to say the constituent bodies, vary in infinite ways *(modis infinitis)* without any change in the individual as a whole."

Spinoza wants to say here that corporeal nature, consisting entirely of an inexhaustible variety of determinations, nevertheless conserves an identical form, in this sense that it remains subordinated to unchanging laws, which exclude all extraordinary intervention and for that matter all finality. And it is already this universal determination *(facies totius universi)* which he makes reference to in his *Letter 64* to Schuller.

But numerous commentators have searched this passage for confirmation of a vitalist, organicist interpretation of the Spinozist system: it is exactly on this point that Guéroult himself talks about an "Aristotle-ism without Aristotle." Let us acknowledge that there is a real difficulty here in Spinoza's text: in giving the infinite mediate mode a generative definition (where we started out), he excluded the possibility of composing it through finite modes by totalizing them, but to the extent that this same infinite mediate mode appears here as a term of infinite progression, which integrates single things in a unity that is at once individual and total, this exigency is, it seems, reversed. The positive effects of this reversal jump before our eyes: to the extent that the infinite mediate mode situates itself at the encounter of two inverse movements, of which one is part of the infinite and the other finite, it is exactly the privileged place of their junction. But then negative effects emerge as well: at the same time that this reconciliation is achieved, the universal principle of determinism, which abandons all finalist illusions, is, if not annihilated, at least greatly attenuated in its application; and then, with the idea of an internal logic of everything, realized in nature considered as a single individual, an immanent finality of this whole reappears, more dangerous still than that of a finality that presumes the recourse to a transcendence.

Let us return to the scholium of lemma VII.[46] In passing from the most simple bodies, which are not individuals (because he refuses all corpuscular philosophy) to composite bodies, then, at the limit, to all of nature considered as the ensemble of all bodies, and itself taken as a Whole, Spinoza gives the impression of constructing a totality from the elements that compose it in reality, in a progressive development. But this impression is mistaken because such a construction is evidently impossible. In its apparent movement, this construction follows the sequence of finite modes to its end, which is presented in proposition 28: it gives a real content to "and so *ad infinitum,*" which ends this proposition. But this ending is really impossible at the level of finite modes themselves because it is not possible to make an inference from the finite to the infinite, as we have shown.

This is not all: not only can this progression not be ended; it never really begins, either. This results from the very particular character of these "pure and simple bodies" from which the common order of nature is explained in the abstract Physics [*l'abrégé de physique*].[47] In effect, these are not primitive material elements, which culminate in an analysis of corporeal nature or the body. Spinoza rejects atoms, which are absolutely simple bodies, or indivisible parts of extension, because "it is just as absurd to assert that corporeal substance is composed of bodies or parts as to suppose that a body is composed of surfaces and the surfaces of lines, and finally, the lines of points."[48] Here we find the same reasoning by which it is impossible to construct the infinite from the finite, to engender it in the movement of an infinite progression.

Nature is thus comprised of nothing but composite bodies, or individuals, because every finite mode is determined by an infinite sequence of causes, which signifies that all finite determination is also infinite, at the same time through the infinite power [*puissance*] of its immanent cause, which is substance itself, and through the infinite multiplicity of its transitive causes. This is expressed for example in axiom 4 of book II of *Ethics*: "we feel that a body is affected in many ways," which appears in the demonstration of proposition 51 of book III: "the human body is affected by exterior bodies in a great many ways." But he applies this property to all "bodies" and at the limit to all "things." The formula *certa et determinata ratione,* which in Spinozist discourse identifies all that exists in the form of finitude, is not reduced, then, to the idea of a unique and elementary determination and which, as such, could be isolated, but to a complex determination, which itself comprises an infinity of determinations:

> If there were something in Nature having no interrelation with other things, and if it were also granted its objective essence (which must agree entirely with its formal essence), then this idea likewise would have no interrelation with other ideas; that is, we could make no inference regarding it. On the other hand, those things that do have an interrelation with other things—as is the case with everything that exists in Nature—will be intelligible and their objective essences will also have that same interrelation, that is, other ideas will be deduced from them, and these in turn will be interrelated with other ideas.[49]

As with the sequence of all "things," the sequence of ideas is interminable. As we have previously demonstrated, for Spinoza there are no ideas that are first or last: they are always already there, there would always already be ideas, contained in an order of infinite causes that link them interminably one to another and prevents them from ever being self-sufficient. The adequate idea is not a simple idea, an intellectual atom, which could be presented in an elementary and isolated intuition; finite reason cannot "know" except through the infinity that acts within it, and thus it knows absolutely without formal limitation. This must also be said of all finite things, which exist *in* themselves, according to their own essence, but not strictly *through* themselves, as if their existence could be deduced from their essence.

This is why, as surprising as this may seem, it must be said that the "most simple bodies" are not bodies that are actually simple, to the extent that all that is real is also irreducible to isolated elements; nothing exists except complex things. Following Spinoza's definition, the most simple bodies are "those which are distinguished from one other solely by motion and rest, quickness and slowness,"[50] that is, that these are bodies we can consider exclusively only in terms of this aspect and to the exclusion of all others. The most simple bodies are thus abstractions, beings of reason, which allow us to construct a discourse on reality but do not exist in themselves in such a form that allows them to be isolated. In this sense, M. Guéroult is justified in distinguishing an abstract physics of most simple bodies and a concrete physics of composite bodies, which take for their object effectively existing individuals.[51] Thus in the *Treatise on the Emendation of the Intellect,* which we have already discussed, the definition takes on its full meaning, in which the knowledge of singular things depends on things that are fixed and eternal:

> Likewise these fixed and eternal things—despite their singularity—will nevertheless be for us—thanks to their presence everywhere and to their very great power [*puissance*]—as sorts of universals, that is to say as a genera of definitions of fixed and mutable things, and as proximate causes of all things (§101).[52]

The most simple bodies do not *exist* in nature, and yet they allow us to understand it, to the extent that they establish the *essential* properties within it; they are not elementary determinations through which its complex reality can be reconstituted, nor are they ideal forms that incarnate themselves in the real by imposing a model of intelligibility upon it; rather, they exist in nature as infinitely powerful, universal genres, which permit us to grasp what there is within it, that is, in the inexhaustible diversity of its forms, of the eternal.

The sequence of transitive causes, *ordo et connexio rerum,* is thus irreducible to a specific form or a specific principle, whatever that might be; totally determined to the extent that it is also interminable, it is the realization of the infinite in the finite, in a series without beginning or end, a totality that is not totalizable, an ensemble that cannot be understood through its elements or deduced through its global form.

This is why the representation of corporeal nature as an Individual or as a Whole must have a very limited significance. It is itself an abstraction: what it considers is the unity of nature insofar as this itself is absolutely determined by constant laws, from which nothing can separate it. But, just as with the notion "the most simple bodies," for which it is a kind of mirror image, we must be careful to incarnate it in an actually existent singular reality. Nature is certainly not, taken in itself, a Whole, even if it is on one hand unique and on the other an ensemble of determinations subordinated to constant principles.

When Spinoza writes, "Nature in its totality is a single Individual, whose parts, that is all the constituent bodies, vary in infinite ways, without changing the individual as a whole,"[53] he absolutely did not intend to say that it conserves itself in a self-identical manner as an arrested form, inalterable, immobile, in the manner of the Forms of the Platonists, because it is its infinity that would thus become problematic. On the contrary, he rejects such a conception, just as Epicurus did when he wrote in his *Letter to Herodote*: "thus the Whole *(to pan)* has always been the same as it is now and it will always be thus. Because it has nothing which it can change into, since there exists nothing outside of it which can enter into it and transform it" (§39). This "whole," which constitutes nature, is the ensemble of all that exists, outside of which nothing can be thought: one understands that it would be in itself inalterable, to the extent that it is irreducible to whatever else would be, other than its own sequence of events [*enchainement*], it is perfectly sufficient unto itself, and it defines for itself alone all that belongs to its reality. But this "totality," which is that of an exclusive and unlimited ensemble, does not allow itself to be reduced to a system of ordered determinations, converging in the constitution of a unique and unified being, in the manner of the Universe of the Stoics. One can apply to Spinoza an analysis formulated by Deleuze apropos Epicureanism:

> Nature as a production of the diverse can only be an infinite sum, that is, a sum that does not totalize its own elements. There is no

combination capable of encompassing all the elements of Nature at once; there is no unique world or total universe. *Physis* is not a determination of the One, of Being, or of the Whole. Nature is not collective but rather distributive; the laws of nature (*foedera naturae* as opposed to the so-called *foedera fati*) distribute parts, which cannot be totalized.[54]

Let us be clear, in order that this connection makes sense; Spinoza does not rule out all possibility of grasping or understanding the elements of nature all at once, in their intensive infinity, because it is this possibility on the contrary that expresses the point of view of eternity, or the third type [*genre*] of knowledge. What he rules out is that this knowledge can be created through a combination, in a law of convergent series, that totalizes the finite through a sort of internal logic of its progression: Spinoza disagrees with Leibniz as much as the Epicureans disagree with Stoicism.

To say that nature is always the same does not signify, then, that it is organized by a formal principle that constitutes it as a totality, but that it expresses itself completely through the sequence of its own determinations, to the exclusion of all external interventions, which would reintroduce the bias of finality. It is this same idea that Spinoza takes up in the introduction to book III of *Ethics*:

> In Nature nothing happens which can be attributed to its defectiveness, for Nature is always the same, and its force and power to act is everywhere one and the same. Which means that *(hoc est)* the laws and rules of Nature according to which all things happen and change from one form to another, are everywhere and always the same, and thus consequently, there can only be one single and same way *(ratio)* of understanding the nature of things such as they are, that is to say the universal laws of Nature.

Here Spinoza makes myth-makers (who claim to place human nature outside the common order of Nature) responsible "for conceiving man as an kingdom within an kingdom," for making the human individual into a free subject who could, through his extraordinary comportment and through the initiative of his choices, modify natural necessity, either to improve it or to corrupt it. But for Spinoza, who prepares himself to "consider human actions and appetites just as if it were an investigation into lines, plans or bodies" (ibid.), there is no specificity of the human subject that would permit him to escape the natural order or even to attempt to do so.

But we must go farther still: there is not a subject at all, whatever it might be, that could oppose itself to nature in order to impose on it the shape of its own intentions. God who, following an important proposition of book I of *Ethics,* is "the immanent but not the transitive cause of things" (*E* IP18), does not himself intervene in reality as an external agent who would subordinate it to his wishes, his ends; through his strictly causal action, he expresses the necessity of his essence in all his affections, in a manner that is completely determined and of course conforms to this essence, and can neither limit nor compromise it. Miracles exist only in the troubled mind of those who want to believe in them because their bodies dispose them to do so and for those who discover in this illusion the promise of freedom:

> They believe that God does not act as long as nature acts according to habitual order; and by contrast, that the power of nature and natural causes are inactive when God acts. This holds for those who have no reason but to adore God and to attribute everything to his power and his volition as much as those suspend natural causes of things and imagine external causes for the order of nature; and the power of God never appears more admirable than when one imagines the power of nature in some way as subjugated by God.[55]

But the problem is not to admire divine power [*puissance*] and to submit oneself to it in adoration, as Descartes himself encourages us to do by placing God in nature like a king in his kingdom; it is to know this power [*puissance*], that is, to understand its internal laws, which leads to the intellectual love of God, the only form of freedom that the sage aspires to.

This is why to explain nature according to the necessity of a sequence [*enchainements*] presumes that we renounce its subordination to the initiative of a subject, whatever that might be, even if this subject were to be placed, integrally within nature itself, and to impose on it the definitive form of a Whole [*Tout*]. We will return to this question, but we can indicate immediately that these illusions of an internal finality are no less dangerous than those of an external finality; they are rather the same thing, which are projected and concentrated from an illusory exterior of an independent subject, within the immanent disposition of a form that grants itself its own ends:

> And since those who do not understand the nature of things are incapable of affirming anything about them, but only imagine them and take imagination for understanding, they thus are firmly convinced that there is an order in things, ignorant as they are of the nature of things and of their own nature. When things are arranged in a fashion that being presented to our senses permits us to understand them easily, we say that they are well ordered; if the contrary, we say they are badly ordered, or confused. And since things that we can readily imagine are more agreeable than others, humans thus prefer order to confusion, as if order was something in Nature outside of the imagination.[56]

In nature itself there is neither order nor disorder; these are notions that are inadequate to its essence.

We see thus what the idea of the unity of nature signifies and also what it excludes. First, it signifies the uniqueness of nature, which understands without limitation all that belongs to its kind, according to a causal chain identical in all its attributes. At the same time, it signifies the power of God, which acts within it, and exactly *not* on it, through the immanent necessity of its essence. Finally, it eliminates the representation of an internal unity, or of an Order of nature, which is only a product of reasoning, but which renders its real infinity incomprehensible in a fictive limitation.

We must conclude from this an absolute identity of the infinite and the finite: these are not like two independent orders, between which one could only establish a relationship of correspondence or subordination, but it must be said that they are nothing without each other, they are nothing outside of each other, other than from the abstract point of view of imagination that separates them. On this point, the

Hegelian interpretation of the notion of determination, which tends to isolate affections from substance, as if they were nothing but fictitious beings in relation to its immutable essence, is untenable.

Non Opposita Sed Diversa

The very specific position Spinoza occupies in philosophy expresses itself in particular in the overthrowal or corruption of traditional forms of "logic." Thus, in his system he makes an uncharacteristic use of the principle of contradiction. Does this modification tend toward a Hegelian logic, which is itself elaborated against this principle? It is not easy to answer this question, because in Hegelian philosophy, Logic makes an object of a theory that develops all its implications within itself, where for Spinoza "logic," if this term is still pertinent here, remains implicit. It exists only in deed, inextricably joined to singular demonstrations, which exclusively constitute its visible form. However, let us attempt to characterize it at least in certain of its effects.

To do this we must go through Descartes, because he gives us a very illuminating basis for comparison: it consists of his correspondence and his polemic with Regius, which contains the well-known theme that commentators frequently apply to Spinoza, *diversa sed non opposita*. Recall that Regius was a doctor who, beginning in 1638 at the University of Utrecht, gave a very controversial lecture related to the principles of Cartesian physiology. It soon became apparent that he interpreted these principles in a paradoxical, unilateral manner, which deviated from their meaning; this is why Descartes was actively preoccupied with demarcating his own doctrine from the thesis of this abusive disciple. Regius's error was to intervene recklessly in the delicate, and at once dangerous and complicated questions of metaphysics, advancing imprudent formulas that Descartes could not accept.

In the letter of July 1645, here is how he recapitulates the errors of Regius:

> At first, in considering the mind as a distinct substance from the body, you write that a man is an *ens per accidens*; but then, when you observe that the mind and the body are closely united in the same man, you take the former to be only a mode of the body. The latter error is far worse than the former.[57]

What makes this carelessness of Regius particularly intolerable is that it puts its finger on a particular difficulty of the Cartesian doctrine, which is the theory of the union of soul and body. In his correspondence with Elizabeth, Descartes himself attested to the contradictory nature of this theory, which affirms simultaneously the distinction of soul and body, returning to the theory of thinking substance and extended substance, and their substantial union in human nature:

> It does not seem to me that the human mind is capable of forming a very distinct conception of both the distinction between the soul and the body and their union; for to do this it is necessary to conceive them as a single thing and at the same time to conceive them as two things; and this is absurd.[58]

It seems that these doctrines, professed in succession by Regius, can be explained by the desire to escape this contradiction, that they resolve by retaining only a single term at a time: first Regius insists on the distinction of soul and body and on this basis characterizes the nature of man as accidental and composite, because it consists of the superposition of two distinct natures. Then, as summarized by Descartes himself in retracting this heretical concept, which could be suspected of Pelagianism, Regius adopts the opposite doctrine to the preceding one, refusing to grant the soul a nature distinct from body, for which it constitutes only a modification, and so he falls into an error, which is for Descartes more serious still than the preceding one, because he ends up professing materialism.

What interests us in this polemic is that it introduces the problem of contradiction in a particular way into the state of practice, which it illuminates in a very specific way. This question appeared fairly early in the correspondence of Descartes with Regius:

> You agree that thought is an attribute of a substance that contains no extension, and conversely that extension is an attribute of a substance that contains no thought. So you must also agree that thinking substance is distinct from extended substance. For the only criterion we have enabling us to know that one substance differs from another is that we understand one apart from the other. And God can surely bring about whatever we can clearly

understand; the only things that are said to be impossible for God to do are those that involve a conceptual contradiction, that is, that are not intelligible. But we can clearly understand a thinking substance that is not extended and an extended substance that does not think, as you agree. So even if God links and unites substances insofar as he can, he cannot thereby divest himself of his omnipotence and lay down his power of separating them, and hence they remain distinct.[59]

We must follow this reasoning in detail. We clearly understand thought without extension, and extension without thought, as two distinct substances. In effect, to define thought through extension and vice versa implies a contradiction. But this idea, which is clear in my mind, cannot impose itself on me with such evidence except if God had wanted it so; and because his perfection excludes the possibility that he would want to trick me, this idea must correspond to an effective content. Thought and extension are thus in reality two distinct substances. Thus the principle of contradiction functions as a criterion of the limits of what we understand, but we must be careful not to apply this, on the other hand, to the limits of our reason, which is narrowly limited by its nature. God, whose omnipotence is infinite, can easily do something that is for us incomprehensible, if it is absolutely necessary that he would do what we understand. Thus it is entirely possible, even if this new operation is for me a profound mystery, that God "links and unites substances insofar as he can." It is this which testifies exactly to the union of soul and body in my own nature: from the fact that I do not understand this union, because its idea indicates a contradiction for me, does not imply that it would be impossible, because in God a priori nothing is impossible, because his power [*puissance*] is by definition unlimited. All I can affirm is that God cannot, by linking these substances, intend and make them such that they are not at the same time as I understand them, that is, separate and distinct.

The principle of contradiction thus has the value of an absolute and objective criterion for all my ideas, but it loses this value for that which is outside my power to understand. Divine logic, if one might call it that, understands and guarantees human logic, but it is not reducible to it, and rather it surpasses it infinitely:

> As to the difficulty of conceiving how it was both free and indifferent for God to bring it about that it was not true that the three sides of a triangle were equal to two right angles, or in general that contradictories cannot both be true, it is easy to remove this difficulty by considering that the power of God can have no limits. Then we can also consider that our mind is finite and created with such a nature that it can conceive as possible the things that God willed to be truly possible, but not created in such a way that it can also conceive as possible things that he could have willed possible, but which nevertheless he willed to make impossible. For the first consideration makes us recognize that God cannot have been determined to make it true that contradictories cannot both be true, and that, consequently, he could have done the contrary. But the other assures us that, although this is true, we should not try to comprehend it, since our nature is not capable of such comprehension.[60]

It is altogether characteristic that these pointed arguments, which completely astonish Leibniz, depend on the attribution of God's free will, which makes him rule as a monarch over ideas and things with which he does what he wants, a conception of divine nature that Spinoza expressly rejects because, these pretentious declarations to the contrary, it imagines this nature beginning from ours, through projections into a relationship of eminence. Thus, for Descartes, God inspires a principle of contradiction, eminently but not formally; this principle is itself a consequence of his action and not an eternal principle that could limit and rule it. Is this not exactly the position of Hegel that Descartes takes here, by suspending the efficacy of a rational principle, when considering the absolute? It is true that, here, this suspension has the effect of rendering the infinite as such incomprehensible, thus noting that our finite reason is powerless to have access to a knowledge of the absolute, or of an absolute knowledge.

This preface was necessary to make us see what there is behind the argument Descartes proposes publicly to Regius in 1647, in his *Notae in Programma,* in response to a certain "placard" of his. Regius wrote in particular,

> As far as the nature of things are concerned, they seem to allow that the mind may be either a substance, or a mode of a corporeal substance; or, if we follow some new philosophers who state that extension and thought are attributes inherent in certain substances, as in subjects, then, since these attributes are not mutually opposed but different, there is no reason why mind should not be an attribute coexisting in the same subject with extension, though the one attribute is not included in the concept of the other. Whatever we can conceive of can exist. But mind can be conceived of, so that it can be any one of the aforesaid, for none of them involves a contradiction. Therefore it may be any one of these things. Hence those who assert that we conceive of the human mind clearly and distinctly, as though it were necessarily and really distinct from the body, are in error.[61]

This text is altogether characteristic of the manner of Regius, which, in its reliance on the principles borrowed from Descartes, struggles to justify conclusions that are exactly those that Descartes has rejected. Perhaps Regius has good reason to support different positions from those of Descartes, but without a doubt he is wrong to seek to defend them with proofs borrowed from Descartes, which confers on his reasoning the quality of a rather ambiguous compromise.

Regius's "demonstration" tries to establish that the mind and the body could belong to the same substance, even if diverse attributes depend without contradiction on a same subject. We are very far here from Spinoza, not only because Spinoza maintains a real distinction between thought and extension but above all because he rejects the grammatical conception of attributes, according to which the relationship between these and their substance could be equated to a relation of the type subject–predicate. But we will see that the refutation Descartes proposes to Regius has a much greater significance than the object that it immediately engages; in this sense, it illustrates very well a manner of reasoning that is exactly a point of rupture for Spinoza.

For Descartes, Regius has committed an initial error in confusing the notions of attribute and mode. Because these "new philosophers"—that is, Descartes himself—define thought as an attribute of incorporeal substance and extension as an attribute of corporeal substance, what they mean by the word *attribute* is "a thing that is immutable and inseparable from the essence of its subject," just as a substance has an attribute to exist through itself. Therefore, it does not consist of a mode that is, according to Descartes, a kind of variable being, which could be modified without changing the essence of the thing that it belongs to; thus extension considered in itself is in no way modified by the fact that it can take diverse forms (e.g., spherical, squared), and the same goes for thought. Once this is established, even if the principle *non opposita sed diversa* were acceptable, it would not apply here: the self-identity of a substance passing into its attributes, which are from this point on unchanging, excludes the possibility that these would even be "diverse" because this would introduce a principle of change into the substance on which they depend.

But the principle Regius relies on, *non opposita sed diversa,* is itself unacceptable. The objection Descartes sets himself against might surprise us, because it consists of a return to the principle of contradiction. But we have just seen that Descartes himself called into question the universality of this principle, by affirming that it could not be applied to all things in which the infinite perfection of God expresses himself directly, which escape our finite reason, but if the universality of this principle is undermined for everything that exceeds our power of understanding [*connaître*] and must remain incomprehensible for us, it remains nevertheless unassailable for everything that resides within the limits of the natural light, where it constitutes—as we have seen—a criterion of objective truth. The reasoning of Regius is thus faulty because it is contradictory:

He adds that "these attributes are not mutually opposed, but different." Again there is a contradiction in these words, for when the question concerns attributes that constitute the essence of substances, there can be no greater opposition between them than the fact that they are different. Once it is admitted that "this is different from that," it is equivalent to saying that "this is not

that"; but to be and not to be are contraries. . . . Of the other attributes that constitute the natures of things, it cannot be said that
those which are different, and of which neither is contained in the
concept of the other, are coexistent in one and the same subject,
for this is equivalent to saying that one and the same subject has
two different natures, and this involves a contradiction, at least so
long as the subject in question is simple and not composite—as
in the present case.[62]

In the case of a simple and noncomposite substance (as is exactly
the case of human nature, which is the union of a soul and a body), it
is absurd to think of distinct attributes in a same subject where they
must simply oppose one another as incompatible or mutually exclusive
"natures." From this argument it would be necessary, inversely, to conclude from this diversity attributes in distinction from the substances
on which they depend: these, being irreducible to each other, as with
subjects of two distinct grammatical propositions, could be said to be
diversa sed non opposita only in the exact measure where, being exterior
to each other, they offer no place for a contradiction.

The Spinozist conception of attributes, among which thought and
extension have without a doubt nothing to do with the elementary
and confused materialism of Regius, nevertheless comes under attack via Descartes's objections, not because it rejects a real distinction
between thought and extension but because from this distinction it
refuses to draw a conclusion about the distinction of substances. As
we have shown, for Spinoza the infinite diversity of attributes is the
other aspect of the unity of substance that it effectively constitutes, in
the active infinity of its essences, each of which they express in their
kind, identically and without opposition.

This signifies that substance, as Spinoza conceives it, has lost the
function of a subject that it still retains in Cartesian philosophy, and
this is why it is not determined in its intrinsic nature by the principle
of contradiction of traditional logic, which is powerless to determine
it. In this manner, Spinoza rejoins Descartes here: the principle of
contradiction does not appear to allow us to grasp all that concerns
the absolute. But this incapacity does not signify, for Spinoza as it does
for Descartes, that the absolute should remain incomprehensible for us

because the principles that guide finite reason are not applicable to it. On the contrary, it means that the rationality of true causes—which no longer have anything to do with "impenetrable ends" of an excessive God—is not reducible to formal principles of a logic, whose fundamental precariousness, on the contrary, it reveals: all that is general is also, for Spinoza, imaginary.

It is here that we see the extent to which we are at the same time close to and far away from Hegel: quite close because of this suspension of abstract rational criteria to which Descartes remains attached (this is why, if he admits the idea of the infinite in his philosophy, he rejects the possibility of deriving from it any knowledge whatsoever) but also very far because, with the principle of traditional contradiction and the automatic, rigid separation he installs between the true and the false, it is the thought itself of the contradiction that Spinoza apparently expels from philosophy, refusing in advance the Hegelian notion of a rationality of the negative and perhaps rejecting with it the possibility of a dialectic.

In a manner that is entirely remarkable, Spinoza thus reveals in Hegelianism an astonishing collusion with classical reason, from which he still retains a presupposition: this is the idea that the contradiction is a relation that cannot be contained and resolved within a subject or for a subject. In effect, for Descartes, it is the assimilation of substance to the subject of a proposition that permits him to apply the principle of contradiction and to disengage it from rationality. For Hegel, it is the presentation of the absolute as subject, returning it to itself in an exhaustive discourse, that makes it possible to develop within it all the contradictions of which it is capable and through them to lead the spirit to its effective completion. In these two cases, the method that leads to the truth is the resolution of contradictions, insofar as they belong to a subject.

And yet Hegel never tires of saying that Spinoza is the philosopher who thinks the absolute in the concept of a substance *that is not a subject*. This is why substance as he presents it is at the same time liberated from constraints of finite reason, as Descartes has established them, and also from the evolving model imagined by Hegel. At the same time as he prevents the introduction of a juridical subject into philosophy—God creator of eternal truths for which he carries a guarantee—Spinoza invalidates the function of a logical subject that serves to ground the true proposition and attests to its noncontradictory character or permits him to explain and thus to resolve all the contradictions it carries within itself.

Singular Essences

Spinoza takes a position vis-à-vis classical reason, whose unchanging and formal order he refuses, by making use of an aberrant, deviant, or at the very least different principle of contradiction. Let us explain this point a bit further. This principle of traditional logic is introduced in book III of *Ethics,* at a place and in a formulation that merits reflection:

> Things are of a contrary nature, that is to say unable to subsist in the same subject *(in eodem subjecto esse)* to the extent that one can destroy the other.[63]

This signifies that contraries exclude each other and that they cannot thus coexist, that is, as the demonstration indicates "agree with each other" *(inter se convenire),* to constitute together a same being or a same "subject."

Here the same divergence between Spinoza and Hegel reappears: for the latter, not only *can* contraries exist easily in the same subject, but it is this same unity of contraries that constitutes the nature of the subject, as such, insofar as it is the living and autonomous process of its own development. In expelling all internal negativity from the subject, Spinoza appears to do no more than manifest his powerlessness to think a dialectic of subject, that is, a dialectic that finds its conditions in the subject itself, in its subject: the point of view of the substance. Nevertheless, things are not that simple: could we not also say that what Spinoza refuses is to think the dialectic in a subject, which is exactly what Hegel does? Here a new route is opened, even if Spinoza does not actually take it: it poses the problem of a dialectic of substance, that is, a material dialectic that does not presuppose its completion in its initial conditions through the means of a necessarily ideal teleology. But such a dialectic is the Hegelian unthinkable.

Let us return to book III of *Ethics*: proposition 5 is expounded here in an absolutely general manner, and its "demonstration," which proceeds by the absurd in only making a reference to the preceding proposition as "evident in itself," shows very well that it consists of a kind of axiom, a formal principle that bears on no reality in particular but exposes a universal condition of all rational thought. It seems thus to have essentially a logical significance and could be equated with a traditional statement: "a thing cannot be at the same time itself and its contrary."

Nevertheless, the meaning of this proposition cannot be completely determined except in its context. Why does Spinoza recall this general principle, by giving it the form of a proposition, in the course of his argumentation? It is clear that propositions 4 and 5 of book III on *Ethics*, which are fundamentally axioms, serve as preamble to the presentation of the notion of conatus, whose significance is, on the contrary, entirely real and determined, to which the following propositions are consecrated:

- Each thing, insofar as it is in itself *(quantum in se est),* endeavors to preserve in its being *(in suo esse perseverare conatur)* (proposition 6).
- The effort *(conatus)* by which each thing strives to preserve in its being is nothing other than the actual essence of this thing *(nihil est praeter ipsius rei actualem essentiam)* (proposition 7).

Thus, a singular or finite thing, in which the power of God expresses itself in a certain and determined manner *(certo et determinato modo)* through the intermediary of one of his attributes, tends naturally to conserve its own being, and this tendency constitutes its essence, because it expresses everything that is within it *(quantum in se est).* In accordance with this essence, and the *conatus* that effectuates it, it opposes itself to all that could destroy it, or suppress its existence *(existentiam tollere),* as is indicated in the demonstration of proposition 6. In effect, "nothing can be destroyed except by an external cause" (proposition 4) because it is not possible that a same act affirms its essence and denies it at the same time. This is why, according to its own or actual essence, every thing tends to preserve its being indefinitely.

Once again, this line of argument apparently confirms Hegel's interpretation, to the extent that it shows that Spinoza remains attached to the classical concept of a "finite negative," an external negation that suppresses and excludes, outside all immanent discursivity or work of the negative, which returns to itself, precisely to constitute an essence: the *conatus* is an absolutely positive movement, in which an activity and a power [*puissance*] is expressed outside all limitation, all exclusion. Nevertheless, if we stop here, we do not understand very well why this reality asserts itself and effectuates itself *tendentially* in a *conatus*.

In addition, Hegel's reasoning is undermined on another point, because the movement through which a thing tends to conserve its own being is exactly its actual essence, or again, as Spinoza writes elsewhere, its "singular essence," which causes it to exist, not absolutely as only substance is able, but in a certain and determined manner, as a particular affection of substance, expressed in one of its kinds. The notion of *conatus* thus refers directly to that of determination, from which it removes all internal negativity: to the extent that a thing is determined as such *(quantum in se est)* through its immanent relation to substance, of which it is an affection, it opposes itself *tendentially* to all that limits its reality, by threatening to destroy it. It is thus certain that the determination is not *in itself* a negation but in contrast an affirmation; thus Hegel's argument, according to which Spinoza thinks of determination only through a lack, and thus as ineffective, withers like a leaf in fall.

There is thus in Spinoza a positive concept of determination that seems elsewhere to call into question the initial definitions that give the basis to the system:

- A thing is said to be finite in its own kind when it can be limited by another thing of the same nature (*E* ID2).
- By mode, I understand the affections of substance, that is, that which is in something else and is conceived through something else (*E* ID5).
- A thing is said to be necessary, or rather constrained, if it is determined by another to exist and produce an effect according to a finite and determined reason *(certa determinata ratione)* (*E* ID7 modified).
- For things that originate from external causes, whether they consist of several parts or a small number, owe whatever per-

fection or reality they have to the external cause, and thus their existence originates from the sole perfection of this cause, not in their own perfection (*E* IP11S modified).

In all these formulas, a thing is determined not specifically according to what there is *in it (quantum in se est)*, as in book III, but on the contrary externally, through other things that limit it and at the same time cause it to exist, in constituting it, itself, as an external cause for other effects. This reasoning is thus entirely different from that in book III: a finite thing is determined externally by another thing, and what is assembled in this exteriority is not the conditions that can destroy it but, on the contrary, those that make it possible or that necessarily produce it. These definitions lead to proposition 28 of book I, according to which a singular thing does not exist in itself but through another that is itself determined by another, in an infinite sequence.

And yet this difference, this contrast between two expositions of the notion of determination, "external" determination or "internal" determination, cannot be explained except by one obvious reason: these are not the same "things" that are determined in one or the other case, or at least the same things are determined from different points of view. In one case, a finite thing is determined according to its essence, following which it tends indefinitely to preserve its being; in the other case, it is determined according to its existence in the conditions that limit it. This is exactly the particular situation of singular things; they have their own essence, which is given within them and in which substance expresses itself *certo et determinato modo,* and they exist in exteriority in an interminable sequence that links them to all other things. We understand from this why, for the difference of the substance itself, these things do not exist necessarily. Said another way, their essence does not envelop their existence; it is that their existence and their essence are "determined" in completely different manners, *in se et in alio.* This is why the fact that singular things do not exist in eternity (but in the incessant and changing movement of extrinsic relations in the course of which they appear and disappear) has no effect at all on the eternity of their essence, that is, their immanent tendency to preserve their being.

Let us return to the example that serves as a pretext for Spinoza in his imaginary dialogue with the obscurantists (*E* IApp). A man dies from the fall of a tile carried by the wind, which falls on his head at the exact moment that he is meeting with his friends. His existence is eradicated by the concourse of exterior circumstances, which explains itself through an interminable sequence of determinations, all external to each other, without any immanent connection. But because of his own essence, exactly not because of his common belonging in the human race, but this actual and singular form that causes him to exist in person, nothing destines him to endure that which must thus be designated, in the strong sense, as an accident, that is, something that happens to him outside all predestination, outside all internal tendency, because this by contrast opposes it. It consists of a necessary accident, because it is explained by causes, and even by an infinite sequence of causes that determine it completely but without which no part in this sequence appears as the conditions of an internal unity, which links all these causes in the framework of an immanent development between them, that is, a final movement. This is why the interpretation of this event as providence or fate (which looks within itself, through inter-mediaries, for final causes, a hidden internal significance) is perfectly inadequate. It is beside the point, because it sees a completely different object than that which it attempts to explain; it exploits a circumstance and the ignorance in which we necessarily find ourselves, from the totality of its conditions, and uses it as a pretext to establish or reinforce superstition. The providentialist thesis, which serves as a vehicle for a religion of fear, relies on the confusion of these points of view of essence and existence.

Let us return to the problem of contradiction. What are two things that are contrary? They are two things for which one suppresses the *existence* of the other and which cannot thus agree with one another, that is, be in the same subject *(in eodem subjecto simul esse)*. But what does it mean to be in the same subject? Literally, it is to *coexist,* fol-lowing the same term used by Spinoza: two things are contrary when the existence of one excludes the other and carries in it the external conditions of its annihilation. From this a very important consequence results: the statement of a principle of contradiction here concerns ex-istences and not essences, and the "subject" that is made to intervene, and whose possibility it guarantees, is itself determined at the level of existence, not at that of essences. Would there be no contradiction except between existences and for existences and not between essences and for essences? The result would be that singular things, considered as they are in themselves *(quantum in se est),* according to their own essence, are not themselves determined as subjects, because a subject is no more than a "being" in which distinct existences coexist, that is, what Spinoza elsewhere calls an individual. The notion of the subject has no rational significance except if we relate it to existences and not to essences.

If there is a theory of the subject in the work of Spinoza, it takes a form that is first and foremost not logical but physical, in the sense that physics studies forms of coexistence between beings. This theory is set forth in the definition of proposition 13 of book 2 of *Ethics*:

> When a certain number of bodies of the same or different magnitudes are constrained by others in such a way to remain in reciprocal contact with each other, or for example if they set themselves in motion at the same or different speeds, in communicating their movements with each other following a fixed ratio, we say that these bodies are united and that together they compose a sole and same body, otherwise called an individual, which is distinguished from others by this union of bodies.[64]

This definition applies immediately to bodies, that is, to determinations of extension, but it applies indirectly to all other forms of unions of determinations that produce themselves as well as for other modes of being; this is why it is possible to use it to develop a general notion of the individual.

What is an individual? A "union of bodies," that is, a certain assemblage of elements of the same nature that agree among themselves, not only in terms of their essence, because all bodies agree among themselves in terms of their essence,[65] but in terms of their existence. They form thus "a sole and same body, otherwise called an individual," which distinguishes itself from others by a certain number of common properties. He resorts immediately to this definition, that individuals do not exist absolutely but relatively, according to circumstances or a point of view: "By singular things I mean things that are finite and have a determinate existence; but if several individuals concur in the same action in such a way that all together would be the simultaneous cause of the same effect, I consider them all in this regard *(eatenus)* as a same singular thing."[66]

"In this regard": the unity that constitutes an individual is nothing eternal, but it depends on conditions that make and unmake it. Where does this union come from? From an internal principle of assembly that would link diverse elements according to their own being, to constitute the singular and original reality of the individual? Thus the finalists "when they consider the structure of the human body are struck with a stupid astonishment, and ignoring the causes of such a beautiful arrangement conclude that it is decidedly not formed by mechanical arts, but through a divine or supernatural art, and *is so arranged that no one part causes harm to another,*"[67] as if they complete each other following a principle of immanent harmony. But singular bodies that compose individuals in extension are here "connected to each other," by a constraint that is necessarily external, and not by the internal necessity of an essence that tends indefinitely to perpetuate itself. To take up the expression of Guéroult, the genesis of individuals can be explained by the "pressure of ambient forces,"[68] that is, by a mechanical action, a sequence of determinations that articulate themselves or rather that are articulated among themselves, outside all intrinsic reason; this momentary encounter therefore takes the specific form of a "constraint."

The individual, or the subject, thus does not exist by himself in the irreducible simplicity of a unique and eternal being, but it is composed in the encounter of singular beings, who agree conjuncturally within him in terms of their existence, that is, who coexist there but without this agreement presupposing a privileged relationship, the unity of an internal order at the level of their essences, which subsist identically, as they were themselves before being thus assembled and without in so being in any way affected.

Let us take the example of such an association. We recall that the finalists have often taken the human body as an integrated model of organization, and its perfection has provoked their "stupid astonishment." Here is how Spinoza resolves this problem by relying on the definition of the individual we have just elaborated (proposition 13):

The parts that compose the human body only belong to the essence of the body itself, insofar as that they communicate their movements with each other according to a fixed ratio *(certa ratione),* and not in so far as they can be considered as individuals, an abstraction produced through their relation to the human body.[69]

Insofar as it is—like all individuals—a composite being, the human body is constituted of parts that can be considered in two ways: as the elements that coexist in it and together form its global organization, and as they are themselves, independent individuals, which exist themselves in their own entirety, making an abstraction of their belonging to the human body. Spinoza proposes the same distinction in his letter 32 to Oldenburg. But it is only the imagination that discovers an identity or convergence between these two aspects, as if each part constituted within itself a means of forming a harmonious and ordered totality with all the others. In response to this finalist conception that abstractly summarizes an infinite sequence of determinations in the fiction of a unique intention, we must substitute an integrally causal explanation, one that does not take into account anything but the external relations of bodies and is thus completely mechanistic. Each part of the body belongs to this global form that is the body taken in its entirety, not according to its own essence but in light of this external liaison, whose transitive necessity is one of constraint, which holds together all the elements of the human body until the moment when the ambient conditions have changed, and the relation between these elements is also modified: the assemblage comes apart, and the parts are returned to other combinations. There is thus no need to interpret the structure of the human body according to a divine and supernatural art, whose reasons are essentially mysterious, in taking as pretext the fact "that it is formed in this fashion that no one part causes harm to another" but by contrast agrees with it. The reason for this harmony is not found in an obscure predetermination of singular essences that inclines them to converge all together toward a unique essence (an ideal nature) but in the transitive relationship of determination that constrains them, provisionally, to associate.

We will have noticed that in the text we just analyzed, Spinoza himself presents the parts of the human body, considered outside their common belonging to the individual, in which they coexists as "individuals":

> The human body is composed of a very many individuals of a diverse nature *(de diverse nature),* each of which is extremely complex.[70]

> The parts of the human body (post. 1) are highly composite individuals, whose parts can be separated from the human body (lemma 4) without impairing its nature and specific reality *(forma)* in any way and can establish quite a different ratio of motion with other bodies (Ax 1 after lemma 3)....The same holds good for any part of an individual component part of the human body.[71]

The constitutive elements of an individual are thus themselves complex realities, composed of distinct parts that coexist within it and themselves are determined outside this relationship, and thus in an infinite sequence, because the analysis of reality is interminable, according to Spinoza, and can never lead to absolutely simple beings, from which a complex system of relations would be constructed. Not *existing,* strictly speaking, except as relations: this is why singular essences that are determined themselves are not affected by the exterior sequence of existence, and this is why they cannot be understood through an analysis that would discover the simple underneath the complex, as a terminal element, an irreducible unity. Essences are not unities that constitute a whole, any more than they are themselves totalities, unifying elements for eternity.

As we have already seen, this movement could be interpreted the other way: in the body, taken as individuals, there are always other bodies, which are themselves individuals; but also each body insofar as it is itself an individual belonging to another body, which is also another individual, and so on to infinity, until we arrive at the total individual, the infinite mediate mode of extension: "Nature in its totality is a single individual in which the parts, that is to say all the bodies, vary in infinite ways, without changing the total individual." We have indicated that it would be wrong to interpret this text in the sense of an organic conception of nature, inevitably associated with the representation of an immanent finality, as is nevertheless often done. Following such a conception, the parts of nature, that is, the ensemble of corporeal things (but equally the ensemble of things that constitute each of the other attributes), would be themselves constituted considering each in terms of their own essence, by an internal relation of solidarity that would make them all converge in the realization of a global form, inside of which they would be all disposed in relation to each other in a unitary manner. It would thus be possible to proceed [*conclure*] harmoniously from their own natures, linking them to each other according to a single rule, toward their infinite organization, and reciprocally: we would be doing nothing more than reading Leibniz in Spinoza.

And yet according to Spinoza such a representation of nature, like the knowledge of the human body it refers to as a model, belongs to the domain of imagination. This obscures or alters the adequate idea of an actual infinite, according to which substance expresses itself immediately and identically—without mediation of a principle of an inevitably hierarchical and finalized order—in each of its affections, whose singular essences it produces all at once, with no privilege accorded to any of them, by conferring on them this original tendency to preserve in their being that which belongs rightly to them and cannot be excluded from them. These tendencies are equivalent to the same extent that they cannot be compared, because they actualize themselves in the positive plenitude of their own nature. We must therefore definitively renounce the communal illusion according to which things agree with each other in such a manner as to effectuate a single order of perfection, by their reciprocal relations that situate them in relation to each other in an infinite chain of causes. Because such an interpretation "turns Nature completely upside down,"[72] it relates each part of nature to nature itself, considered as a whole, and as the final principle of their restitution, from which they are themselves determined; but we, on the contrary, must consider nature as the result of their coexistence, that is, as an ensemble that is not totalizable. Considered from this point of view, nature exactly constitutes an individual in the sense we have established: it realizes a necessary relation of *coexistence* between the beings that complete it, because all corporeal things find themselves by definition assembled, without this relationship being commanded by an order, much less an ideal one, of essences, of which it would be nothing more than a manifestation or materialization.

However, a new difficulty appears here: following the definition Spinoza gives the individual, the relationship of elements that constitutes this as a composite being is entirely determined in exteriority, in the exclusive form of a transitive causality, or following a principle of the "pressure of ambient forces" to return to the expression proposed by Guéroult. This causes no problems for anything in nature, which finds itself thus constrained externally by the infinite sequence of causes in which it is caught up. But can this also be said of nature itself, which contains, or at least consists of, everything in it, and for which nothing can remain outside? This apparently creates a setback for the principle of the pressure of ambient forces.

We are halted here because we have reintroduced, without realizing it, this notion of interiority that completely excludes the definition of the individual: if corporeal nature, grasped globally as *facies totius universi,* is an unlimited ensemble that cannot be totalized, this signifies that it exists in itself completely in exteriority. Nothing is external to it, precisely because all externality falls within it and finds itself, if not united and comprised (i.e., resolved according to an internal principle of unity), at least reunited and assembled in a relationship of immutable and unlimited coexistence; in this sense, its "order" excludes all contradiction, that is, it tends toward its resolution in a state of equilibrium that is moreover constantly called into question. The pressure of ambient forces, which holds together all corporeal beings and constitutes nature as their global form of individuality, is the infinite sequence of their causal determination. The exteriority of this sequence is interpreted by the imagination through the abstract fiction of *an* exterior, which would exist, itself, independently of that which it determines, but we must understand, on the contrary, that there is nothing "outside" these things that it determines. It is the sequence of transitive causes that is itself, in itself, so to speak, a sequence in exteriority. There is therefore no need to suppose a reality exterior to nature to understand that it is itself subordinate to an external determination, the very same that is the beings that compose it. All is *in* nature exactly because it cannot be explained through an ideal harmony, an integral order, which would establish a fictive limit between that which is internal and that which is external. This is why we find once more, at the level of nature itself considered in its entirety, just as with each of its parts, the same conception of the individual, considered as an external relation between existences.

Does this signify that we can no longer think any kind of unity at all in nature and that this nature is dispersed to infinity, in a circumstantial succession of encounters to a level at which no immanent necessity could be freed? To escape the illusion of a finalized order, however, it is not enough to substitute it with the representation of a contingent disorder of pure existences, which is nothing more, after all, than a mirror image. All that produces itself in nature is determined by universal laws of movement, according to which each thing expresses in a certain and determined manner the essence of substance, insofar as this is an extended thing; this signifies that there is for each thing a singular essence, which necessarily causes it to exist, not by the constraint of an exterior being but through the act of substance that affirms itself in it, as in all its other affections. In this sense, nature itself, considered as a unique being, possess a specific essence, which is the reason for its necessity and its unity: it is an infinite immediate mode, in which substance expresses itself directly, outside all relations to any other thing. But, considered thus, from the point of view of its essence, in which the power of God expresses itself immediately, it is no longer an individual or a subject, that is, the system of all constraints that gather within it, in an infinite series of existences that are external to each other. As we have seen, Spinoza discounts all attempts to conclude from the one these aspects of the other, because it reintroduces this hierarchical conception of the true [*le réel*] and the order of ends, which so astounds imbeciles and slaves.

In the same manner, as with all modal reality, the human body possesses a singular essence, distinct from its existence, according to which it tends to persevere in its being. But, considered from this point of view, it is no longer an individual, that is, a complex assemblage of parts that dispose themselves within it following the external constraints of their reciprocal relations, because it is determined by an internal disposition, which is not the finalized order of a composition or a totality but the indecomposable affirmation of substance that expresses itself within it in a certain and determined manner, in a unique act, incomparable and irreducible to an exterior determination, whatever that might be.

More generally, we must say that no singular essence can deduce itself directly as such from another singular essence, no more than it can from a common nature, that is, the attribute on which they all depend: "That which is common to all things and which is equally in one part as in the whole does not constitute the essence of any singular thing."[73] Universal necessity does not simply represent a common order between things, through which they might be understood [*comprises*] by abstraction; it is the concrete affirmation of substance that acts in all things, in an absolutely equal infinity, and absolutely diverse affections that express it identically to the extent that they escape all reciprocal comparison.

We are thus led to an important idea that we have already encountered before: substance itself, whose unity coincides with its infinite power [*puissance*], which can never be seen as a shortcoming and expresses itself in an infinity of essences, does not exist as an individual, according to the order from which all determination would be comprised [*comprise*]. As Spinoza indicated briefly in his *Letter 50* to J. Jelles—but the true idea, we know, suffices in itself—the unity of substance is not numerical, it is not that of a single being that would exist to the exclusion of all other examples we could imagine, but it is the absolutely infinite unity, which cannot be grasped as such from the outside, through a kind of elimination, in a movement that would conclude the real from the possible. Not only is God not an individual, but he is the only "thing" that can absolutely not be considered from this point of view, abstractly, following a principle of order or coexistence that would stamp out all intelligibility in him, because in God essence and existence coincide exactly, in the immanent necessity of *causa sui*. Even though all things in "nature," in whatever attribute they are, could be considered from this exterior and negative point of view, where their causal relation takes an exclusively transitive form, God is by definition entirely positive; he is also that which determines all things as such, positively.

Hegel is thus justified in declaring that, in Spinoza's reasoning, substance never "becomes" subject; we can even say it is what gives Spinozist thought its effective content, this very thing that Hegel perceived as its restriction and its limit. The God of *Ethics* is not a totality of determinations, arranged in a rational order by the logic of their development or of their system. For Spinoza, the intelligibility of a whole [*un tout*] is that of an individual form, which explains itself relatively through a mechanical and transitive sequence, in a series of interminable constraints; it thus distinguishes itself radically from a singular essence, which is determined on the contrary through its necessary relationship to substance. Thus, it is the idea of totality, which is, in the context where it appears, abstract and negative; it in no way represents the positive reality of a being that tends, according to its own nature, to persevere indefinitely in its being, but rather this reciprocal limitation that situates individual forms in relation to one another and explains their appearance and their disappearance, through causes that remain exterior.

This is where contradictions and conflicts—but also equilibriums and compromises—present themselves, in the transitive succession of individual constraints, whose existence is explained by an order of negative determinations, which remains exterior to essences. But the absolute knowledge of things, which consists of the "intellectual love of God," rejects this model of knowledge and separates itself from it absolutely: it eliminates all contradiction from its object, not in the illusory movement of its internal resolution but in recognizing that real necessity consists of the exclusive relationship of all reality to the substance that is affirmed in it and outside of all contradiction.

In *Metaphysical Thoughts* Spinoza had already written,

> In the comparison of things with one another there arise certain notions, which nevertheless are nothing outside of the things themselves except simple modes of thought. This is apparent in the fact that if we want to consider them as things posed outside of thought, we thus render confused the clear concept that we previously had of them. Such are the notions of Opposition, Order, Agreement, Difference, Subject, Adjunct, and other similar concepts that one could add to these.[74]

As with order and agreement, opposition is nothing but a way of representing not even the things but their relations; these notions depend in effect on their "comparison." It thus consists of abstract

formal notions, which do not actually correspond to any content. Not only is there no order within itself, there is no opposition within itself; that is, it is impossible to adequately know what pertains to these notions. Nevertheless, it is not enough to notice that they are formal and illusory; it is more necessary to know where they come from and what makes them so credible. "To compare things," even if this teaches us nothing about their real nature, is an operation that is not entirely without consequences to the extent that it represents the transitive sequence of beings who authorize such a comparison, because they themselves measure the objects in relation to one another, in an indefinite relation of their reciprocal determination. As a mode of thought, this opposition thus corresponds equally to a certain mode of being: that which makes finite things *coexist* in an unlimited series where they limit one another. But this representation completely ignores the positive determination of affections that unites them directly to substance. This is why it gives no place to a rational principle whose validity would be effectively universal.

The result of all this is that the mechanism of the principle of contradiction, which still regulated the function of rational thought in the classical age, even if at this time it was beginning to be called into question (as with Pascal), is found to deviate or become unsettled in a way with Spinoza. Returned to the abstract order of existence, which constitutes individuals through external relationships, it permits all the more to measure, or rather to record, the precarious durée of their survival, but it tells us nothing more about this essential reality that confers on things their immanent relationship with substance, that is, this positive necessity that causes them to exist and to persevere. For Spinoza, nothing is intrinsically determined by its contradictions, exactly as Hegel has noted; in this sense, the dialectic is effectively absent from Spinozism. But we must insist on the fact that, in the same instance, the contradiction has lost its negative power of refutation from which it derives, again for Descartes, an essentially logical function: not so much that it does not establish a being in its reality, it does not even allow it to refuse a reality, because its discourse is completely outside the essence of things. Whereas Hegel does nothing more after all this than reverse the principle of contradiction, by drawing conclusions from it that are inverse to those that would confirm an earlier tradition in its entirety, Spinoza displaces it completely from the domain of enquiry [*champ d'application*] by withdrawing from it as with all other formal principles this universal power that allows its uniform application to all reality. But should not a dialectic, if we developed it to the limit of its immanent tendency, be just as able to think against contradiction?

Force and Conatus

Spinoza still accords a rational significance to the principle of contradiction, but in fact, he eliminates its power to think the real nature of things, that is, he limits its use, by refusing its pretense to universality. On this point, it seems, he anticipates the critical philosophy that takes a position in an apparently analogous fashion against formalism. Is this link between Spinoza and Kant relevant?

Following the "Amphibology of Concepts of Reflection," which in *Critique of Pure Reason* constitutes the appendix of "Analytical Principles," the application of the principle of contradiction does not give rise to knowledge except from the point of view of pure intellect, which considers a thing in general without determining it within a particular phenomenon:

> When reality is represented by nothing except pure understanding (*realitas noumenon*), no opposition can be conceived between realities; that is, no such relation that if these realities were connected in one subject, they should mutually destroy their consequences and take a form such as $3 - 3 = 0$.[75]

A thing cannot be at the same time itself and its contrary: the universality of this principle is abstract and universal, because it treats its object as a thing of unspecified nature, independent of all empirical character, which intellect poses solely within itself, in the manner of a purely logical subject that cannot admit opposing predicates. The question then arises whether the same principle can also be applied to things that are actually present in experience and whether it is enough to provide a rational explanation for them.

And yet in these relations between phenomena contradictions appear, or rather oppositions, whose movement cannot be reduced to this formal determination:

On the contrary, these realities in the phenomenon can very well be in mutual opposition and if connected in one subject, one can destroy in whole or in part the consequences of the other, as in the case of two forces moving in the same straight line, insofar as they are drawing or pushing a point in opposite directions, or even the pleasure that counterbalances grief.[76]

Scientific knowledge of nature cannot resolve these contradictions in a speculative manner, by reducing them to the impossible or to nothingness, but it must explain their consequences, which signifies that it recognizes their existence or their reality. Is there not a conflict, then, between logic and experience?

Kant introduces this problem in the *Critique of Pure Reason,* in a very precise polemical perspective: his remark is directed against the Leibnizian tradition, which resolved this conflict by "intellectualizing the phenomena," that is, by subordinating nature and experience directly to conditions of pure intellect, for which existence is a logical predicate that can be extracted from its subject through analysis:

The principle that these realities (as simple affirmations) do not repel each other is an entirely true proposition as regards the relation of these concepts, but it has no meaning in relation to nature, and above all in relation to a thing in itself (of which we have not the slightest concept). . . . Even if Leibniz did not announce this proposition as a new principle, he nevertheless made use of it for new affirmations, and his successors introduced it expressly in their Leibnizian–Wolfian doctrine. According to this principle, all evils, for example, are merely the consequence of limits of created beings, that is, negations, because these negations are the only things that conflict with reality (and it is effectively the case in the concept of a thing in general, but not in things as phenomena). The followers of Leibniz find likewise that it is not only possible but even natural to reconcile all reality in one being, without fear of opposition, because they recognize no other opposition except that of contradiction (through which even the concept of the thing disappears), but they do not recognize the opposition of reciprocal destruction, which arises when a real principle destroys the effect of another. We encounter conditions necessary to represent this opposition or contrariness only in sensibility.[77]

From the point of view of universal harmony, the necessity of things leads to a relationship of agreement, which links them to each other and expresses itself [*s'explique*] completely through it; a sort of objective logic thus permits us to deduce the real from the possible, through a homogeneous and continuous reasoning, which allows no external determination to intervene, no principle of autonomous existence. The order of the real from this moment on finds itself guaranteed by its conformity to a purely intellectual principle, according to which, in particular, all that contradicts itself in the same instance suppresses its right to exist; reciprocally, contradictions find themselves effectively absent from all that exists.

Kant refuses this direct manner of deriving the sensible from the intelligible, which makes an economy of a veritable transcendental deduction, because it never leaves this sphere of idealities with which it has identified all reality for once and for all. The synthesis of determinations that is the basis of an empirical knowledge, which guarantees its legitimacy, cannot be reduced to formal conditions of pure intellect, which reasons through the analysis of concepts, but it supposes the concept of a thing in particular, as it is given through experience. And yet, from this point of view—in nature—the principle according to which realities (considered as simple affirmations) cannot repulse or deny each other, that is, enter into a conflictual relationship, no longer applies universally. We must then develop a new concept of contradiction and negation, which are no longer determined by strictly logical conditions.

This is what Kant undertook in 1763 in *The Attempt to Introduce the Concept of Negative Magnitude into Philosophy,* in which he already took a position of Newtonian "realism" against the "conceptualism" of the Cartesians and Leibniz. Negative magnitudes, whose concept belongs to physics and not to logic, result from real oppositions, as are given in experience, through which a thing affirms itself positively by denying [*en niant*] another, at least by "suppressing the consequences." A new relationship of positive and negative appears here, which is not, in a strict sense, contradictory.

To take note of this entirely particular phenomenon [*phénomète*] that is the negative magnitude, we must point out the distinction between a logical contradiction and a real opposition:

> Two things are opposed to each other when the fact of positing one suppresses the other. This opposition is two-fold: either logical (through a contradiction) or real (without contradiction). Until now we have considered only the first opposition or logical opposition. It consists of affirming and denying something from a same subject. This logical connection is without consequence *(nihil negativum repraesentabile)* as the principle of contradiction asserts. . . . The second opposition, the real opposition, is such that the two predicates of a subject are opposed but without contradiction. Here too, a thing equally destroys that which was posed by another, but here the consequence is something *(cogitable).*[78]

In the two forms of opposition, the relation that is established between conflicting determinations presents itself as the relation between predicates that belong to the same subject. But the nature of this relationship is, in the two cases, completely different. Because in a logical contradiction the predicates are not envisaged in themselves, in their real existence, but only according to their reciprocal relation, in this common subject that cannot support antagonistic determinations: thus the contradiction can be resolved by a simple analysis, internal to the subject itself. This analysis removes all positivity from the predicates, because it concludes the impossibility of thinking them together: "We will consider only the relationship through which the predicates of a thing and their consequences suppress each other reciprocally through contradiction. Which of the two predicates is truly affirmative *(realitas)* and which truly negative? We do not care the least in the world."[79]

We must practically [*à la limite*] say that they are both negatives: they are nothing in themselves, to the extent that each one defines itself, in an abstract and relative manner, through the exclusion of the other. Recall that Hegel takes this into account, to conclude something entirely different: here he discovers a reason to affirm the immanent character of a relationship of the negative to the positive.

On the contrary, in a real opposition, the predicates must be really and positively determined, outside their antagonism, that is, independently of this negativity (annihilation or diminishment), which manifests itself in their encounter; they are thus not in themselves exclusive of one another, and in order to enter into conflict there must be an occasion that reunites them in a same "subject" where they coexist, in a sense that is no longer logical but physical. This conflict thus cannot be resolved by a simple conceptual analysis but through a synthesis of external determinations, whose conditions are given by experience: "That which is affirmed by a predicate is not negated by another, because this is impossible: on the contrary, the predicates A and B are two affirmatives: but as the consequences of each of them taken individually would be a and b, neither can coexist in the subject in such a way that the consequence is zero."[80]

In this case the discord is thus not between "predicates" themselves but what results from them: these are their effects, which annul or counteract each other reciprocally, in a state of equilibrium. This signifies that the predicates are not, as in the preceding case, logical predicates, determined according to their subject whose intrinsic nature they express, but they are themselves autonomous "subjects," each defined in themselves by their properties, or what Kant calls their "consequences." Real opposition is in fact an extrinsic relationship, a coexistence, in the strictly physical sense of the term, between independent beings.

To present this form of opposition, Kant resorts first to the example of mechanical movement: a ship subjected to the contrary forces of the winds that blow in opposing directions does not enter into a contradiction with itself, like the subject of a predicative judgment, but it is caught in the tension of inverse effects that confront each other within it, because they take it for the object of their antagonistic actions. None of these actions is, in itself, negative, because "it would be absurd to imagine a particular kind of object and call it negative."[81] Rather, a negativity would appear only in the reciprocal relation that establishes itself on the occasion of their encounter: "One of these opposites is not the contradiction of the other, and if one is something positive, the other is not a pure negation, but is opposed to the first as something positive."[82]

Here "contradiction" takes the form of an opposition between causes, which act on each other in a relation of empirically determined forces and which reciprocally modify their effects.

In his *Attempt* of 1763 Kant intends "to apply the concept (of the negative magnitude) to objects of philosophy," that is, to transpose the study of mechanical oppositions from the natural world to the spiritual world. This attempt, which elsewhere produces singular results (in discovering conflicts of forces in the soul as well), would be abandoned in the critical period. But the same concept of opposition, strictly limited to the domain of physics, lends authority to the *Metaphysical Foundations of Natural Science* in 1786, where its significance is explained more completely.

In this text, Kant takes the position against a geometrical mechanism inherited from Descartes, which presumes the reduction of material reality to abstract extension, in the absence of a physical principle of determination that applies itself not to the intelligible world but to the reality of experience; it substitutes for this the physics of real opposition applied to a metaphysical concept of force. The science of nature does not limit itself to a "phoronomy" that interprets phenomena according to the sole principles of the figure and movement, for which "matter is the movable in space,"[83] but it corrects this through a "dynamic" for which "matter is the movable insofar as it fills a space."[84] The movement cannot be explained therefore solely by geometric properties but by the intervention of a real "force" that acts on the movement, either as an incitement or as a resistance to movement.

On this occasion, Kant engages in a polemic with Lambert, in terms that are altogether characteristic:

> According to their notion, the presence of something real in space should imply this resistance already by virtue of its very concept, first according to the principle of contradiction, and arises in such a way that nothing else could coexist in the space with these things. But the principle of contradiction does not repel any matter advancing to penetrate a space where it encounters other matter. Only when I attribute to that which occupies a space, a force to repel all exterior movement that approaches it, do I understand how a contradiction is involved when the space that a thing occupies is penetrated by another thing of the same kind.[85]

Here again, Kant refuses all confusion between a logical determination and a physical determination: "The principle of contradiction does not repel matter." It has here no effectively causal value; at the very most it could, once the movement was completed, express certain of these properties, by describing in them formally, a result. But to make this abstract interpretation pass for the rational explanation of the phenomenon is to renounce, on the contrary, the physical reality, which is determined by the antagonistic relationship of forces: "the impenetrability of a physical basis."[86] Physics is no longer subordinated here to a presupposed logic but it finds its guarantee in a metaphysical principle.

In effect, these primitive forces whose concept takes experience into account are as such unassignable in experience and cannot be represented except "metaphysically." Neither attractive force nor repulsive force can be reduced to an empirical movement that effectuates itself in a determinate place through a determinate body; this movement is nothing but their effect, the physical manifestation of a principle that is not itself physical. Thus the idea of a real opposition between forces is at its basis an experimental rationality, but it does not confound itself with real relations between bodies that effectively constitute material nature. This signifies that the "forces" do not belong to the parts of matter whose essential nature they would express but that they are forces of nature itself, considered in general from a metaphysical point of view. The concept of antagonistic forces permits thus a "construction of matter." Phenomena must be interpreted from a real opposition of forces, not the inverse. As we know from elsewhere, for Kant the return to experience implies not the submission to experience but its determination according to rational principles, which apply to experience without being given within it.

As we have seen, these principles develop not in the sense of an analysis but of a synthesis. They suppose thus that the reduction of matter to extension is refuted: "Space is a concept that does not contain anything at all existent but merely the necessary conditions of external relations of possible objects of external senses."[87]

How does a body fill a space in extension? Not through the qualities that belong to extension itself or could be deduced from it: "Here is the general principle of the dynamics of material nature, that all that is real in objects of external senses and that are not simply

determinations of space (place, extension, and figure) must be re-
garded as moving force."[88]

In introducing the category of metaphysics of force into the representation of nature, Kant thus eliminates the mechanistic conception,
"which explains all the diversities of matter through the combination
of the absolute void with absolute plenitude,"[89] because such a conception finally leads to a corpuscular philosophy that determines nature
through the abstract relationship between full elements and empty
extension in which they are in movement. It limits itself to a physics
of shock, whose rationality is incomplete and arbitrary, because it
depends on the presupposition of an initial impulsion and thus leads
to a natural theology:

> Everything that relieves us of the necessity of having recourse
> to these empty spaces is an actual gain for the science of nature,
> because these spaces give too much play to the imagination to
> replace the deficiencies of an intimate science of nature with crude
> dreams. Absolute emptiness and the absolute density correspond
> more or less in this science to what, in metaphysical philosophy,
> are blind chance and blind destiny, that is, a barrier for a trium-
> phant reason such that fantasy takes its place or it is lulled to rest
> on the pillow of occult qualities.[90]

The positivity of this geometric or mechanical interpretation, which
expels all real action from its object, engenders all the more, in its
margins, the poetic fiction of a possible world.

The metaphysical point of view on nature, which on the contrary
introduces a dynamic investigation of phenomena, determines matter
through a combination of primordial forces. And yet this explanation

> conforms much more to experimental philosophy and is more
> useful for it, since it leads directly to the discovery of the mov-
> ing forces proper to matter and their laws while restricting the
> freedom of assuming empty intervals and fundamental particles
> of diverse shapes, because neither of these two things can be
> determined or discovered through experiment.[91]

Whereas the mechanistic representation of nature (whose abstract determinations can be developed through analysis) is of no value except for a possible world, the metaphysical hypothesis of forces has a concrete signification, an experimental validity; it permits us to know, through construction, the real world.

Following this hypothesis, the relations between the bodies that constitute nature are explained by the antagonism between two fundamental forces, repulsion and attraction, which act on one another in a synthetic relationship.

This relationship is fundamental [*primitive*]. If repulsive force is immediately accessible to representation because the existence of a body, whatever it is, coincides with the resistance that it puts up to all external intrusions, it appears immediately that this force can be thought of only as a principle that is unique to the existence of matter, because if it is only constituted through this expansive tendency, this tends not only to occupy a space to defend this against external aggressions but expands through all space, in an unlimited manner. "This is to say that it disperses itself to infinity, and no assignable quantity of matter would be found in an assignable space. Consequently, if there were only repulsive forces in matter, all space would be empty, and strictly speaking, there would be no matter at all."[92]

Repulsive force is thus not an intelligible principle for nature considered in its entirety except if it is in some way balanced by a contrary principle, an attractive force: we must accept a fundamental force of matter that acts in opposite magnitude to the repulsive force that produces the relationship, thus a force of attraction.[93] Theorem 6 of the dynamic ("No matter is possible only by the force of attraction without the force of repulsion") takes up the same demonstration in the opposite sense: to explain nature only by an attractive force would submit it to a movement of infinite contraction, which would equally cause matter to vanish, into a single point of space. The result is that that which is fundamental [*primitif*] and constitutes a genuine principle of the knowledge of nature is the original conflict of opposing forces, which determines all movement of matter in space.

This conflict is original to the extent that it cannot be reduced to a more profound determination. Giving its principle to the entire science of nature, this principle cannot itself be explained, that is, analyzed, and this is why it is a metaphysical principle:

> All natural philosophy consists of the reduction of these given forces, in diverse appearances, to a smaller number of forces and powers, adequate to the explanation of the effects of the former; but this reduction extends only to the fundamental forces beyond which our reason cannot proceed.... This is all that metaphysics can achieve in relation to the construction of the concept of matter.[94]

Thus the conflict of forces is the ultimate threshold that a rational explanation of nature can reach, but this does not mean in the least that it constitutes it, as it is in itself, according to its final destination. The metaphysical principles of a science of nature do not emerge from anything but this knowledge to which they assign their conditions, but in no way do they lead us to a metaphysics of nature that (if their undertaking has any sense at all) could implement other concepts and other proofs. In the Kantian doctrine, it harks back to a philosophy of history, which relies from the beginning on the same concepts of antagonistic forces (see for example the notion of "unsocial sociability" in the *Idea for a Universal History*) to resolve the conflict within it in an ultimate determination that reconciles nature and reason in a rule of law [*état de droit*]; it is because there is an end of history that such a "solution" is possible and that it conforms necessarily to the "design of nature."

In the domain of nature, it is easy to understand why this original conflict is irreducible, and in particular why it cannot lead to an analytic relation: if this were the case, the antagonistic forces could be related to each other as adversarial or inverse forms of the same primitive force, in the manner of élan vital, or a fundamental energy, which would constitute a sort of general model of interpretation of nature. Then an unsolvable problem would arise: why does this force enter into conflict with itself at the level of its manifestations? But such a reduction is impossible, except through abstraction, because the antagonistic forces, even in principle, are irreducible to each other: "the two motive forces are wholly different in kind, and there is not the least reason to make one dependent on the other or to deny its possibility without the intervention of the other."[95]

The two forces are thus inseparable, because they act on each other, or else through each other's intervention, and yet their relationship is synthetic and it supposes their real exteriority. It is here that we rediscover the concept of negative magnitude, because it is only convention or the game of illusion that tells us that one is the negative of the other.

Let us take up the coordinated movement of this reasoning as summarized in the "General Observation on Dynamics."[96] The point of departure is provided by the repulsive force as immediate determination in real space: the body presents itself first to representation as a solid, through the phenomenon of resistance. The attractive force is presented next, in opposition to the preceding one, but this opposition is then contained within the order of representation that reveals "that which in relation to this real, the proper object of external perception, is negative, that is to say, the force of attraction."[97] There is no negativity in itself in this case but only following the immediate conditions of our apprehension of the real, which decomposes the relations within it, in following the order of succession that is proper to it. This is why the opposition of two forces is given only after the fact, as a relation of reciprocal limitation, which is the condition of intelligibility of nature. We see the advantage of this representation, which is immediately comprehensible because it relies on the spontaneous representation of physical reality: it rightly causes the synthetic character of the antagonistic relation to appear, because it opposes attraction to repulsion after the fact. But in making attraction an intrinsically negative force, it actually reverses the rational physical order that should arise from the conflict of forces and not from one or the other of these, to understand actually and not formally the necessary relations between the phenomena. But what then becomes problematic is the real independence of these forces and the originally synthetic character of their relation.

In his remark in paragraph 262 of the *Encyclopedia,* Hegel indicates that Kant "had opened the way, thanks to his essay, through what he calls a construction of matter, towards a concept of matter, and thanks to this essay roused the concept of a philosophy of nature from its slumber."[98] Nevertheless, according to Hegel, Kant was not able to follow this undertaking through to its limit, because he restricted the determination of material reality to the consideration of forces, between which there exists only a synthetic relation of exteriority "as being firmly positioned one facing the other."[99] Reduced to this relation of forces, matter remains unknowable in itself; as we have seen, it is precisely in order to respect this limitation of knowledge that Kant presents the conflict of forces as irreducible. But it results in a paradoxical consequence: the relation of forces, given as a real opposition, whose existence is de facto impassable [*indépassable*], is nevertheless not accessible except from a metaphysical point of view, because it never manifests itself as such in experience. To get out of this "contradiction," it is necessary to give a new content to the concept of matter, no longer by constructing it synthetically with the help of its "reflexive determinations,"[100] which are primitive forces, but by producing it actually from the development of its internal contradictions. There is what in effect separates contradiction and opposition. In the latter, the antagonistic terms are exterior and independent; in the movement of the contradiction, contraries are united with each other in the same immanent process. Hegel develops this distinction completely in book II of *Logic*.[101]

Hegel thus overthrows the Kantian position: attraction and repulsion are no longer irreducible elements that permit only a rational representation of nature. They are manifestations or moments of a unique material process, in whose development they appear as intrinsically linked: "These moments are not to be taken for themselves as autonomous moments, or in other words, as forces; matter does not result from them, insofar as they are conceptual moments, but matter is that which is presupposed in order that it manifests itself phenomenally."[102]

We see the routes of the dialectic, which here take over metaphysics, returning Hegel to a strictly logical analysis of reality. But it uses means other than those of Leibniz, and in particular it makes use of means completely opposed to the principle of contradiction.

The same argument can be found in a more developed form in the first section of book I of *Logic,* in the form of a remark in the chapter on "Being for Itself."[103] For Kant, the construction of matter departs from attraction and repulsion considered as autonomous forces, "as self-subsistent and therefore as not connected with each other through their own nature; that is, they are considered not as moments, each of which is supposed to pass into the other, but rather as fixed in their opposition to each other."[104] These forces are thus juxtaposed abstractly, and matter is nothing but the result of their conflict. Material reality is not really known, to the extent that it is represented through external determinations, which are external to each other and external to it. The metaphysics of forces forbids the comprehension of internal movement, of "passage," which unifies the constitutive elements of matter while it brings them into existence.

Kant has thus failed in his objective of providing a rational deduction of matter. The appreciation of this fact leads Hegel to a surprising conclusion: "Kant's method is basically analytical, not constructive."[105] In effect, the concept of primitive forces is obtained through an immediate representation of matter, given in intuition, whose presuppositions he explains:

> Repulsion is at once thought in the concept of matter because it is immediately given therein, whereas attraction is added to the concept syllogistically. But these syllogisms, too, are based on what has just been said, namely, that matter which possessed repulsive force alone, would not exhaust our conception of matter.[106]
>
> It is evident that this is the method of a cognition which reflects on experience, which first perceives the determinations in a phenomenon, then makes these the foundation, and for their so-called explanation assumes corresponding basic elements or forces which are supposed to produce those determinations of the phenomenon.[107]

The concept of primitive forces thus stems from the analysis of empirical representation; they are only abstract and objective elements of this representation. Their differences, their real exteriorities, are thus nothing but an externality, a difference in representation projected in the form of a real opposition. The "forces" are not the actual properties of nature but "determinations taken from perception," formally realized and artificially isolated.

On this point, Kant is thus an inconsequential thinker for Hegel, who did not know how to go to the limits of his critique of mechanism. In determining matter from forces that determined the real movement of bodies, Kant eliminated the abstract concept of an inert matter, analyzable through exclusively geometric means; he thus opened the way to a new conception of matter, not only dynamic but dialectical, which leads it to the rational process of attraction and repulsion, united intrinsically in their contradiction. But of this consequence, which is the real construction of matter, that is to say its actual genesis, Kant remains completely unaware (bewusstlos).[108] He did not grasp it because he falsified the "nature of the thing" in an abstract and at the same time empirical representation of force.

If we leave aside the liberties that it takes with Kant's text, Hegel's critique has merit above all in highlighting the ambiguity of the concept of real opposition and the artificial character of the distinction that separates it from logical contradiction. What, in fact, does the term real signify in the expression real opposition? It signifies a characteristic that is irreducible to a logical determination, other than through the operation of a formal intellect. But does the "real" also have a positive rather than a critical significance, here, indicating (independent from thought) the material existence of an objective reality that is not immediately adequate to it and remains exterior to itself? Certainly not, because the "reality" of the original conflict of forces, which can be affirmed only metaphysically, is posited for thought, insofar as it aims to appropriate objects for itself through knowledge, and it is thus subjected to transcendental and no longer formal conditions of reason.

The opposition of forces is the concept that reason has need of in order to explain nature theoretically, and this concept is provided to it through a metaphysics that gives the sciences of nature their conditions of possibility. Kant opposes Leibniz, we have seen, to the extent that he refuses a continuous deduction that immediately identifies existence with a predicate, the sensible with the intelligible. But he agrees with him much more deeply, in retaining the idea of a deduction (even if this is no longer only formal) that leads from the possible to the real, in terms of a complex synthesis taking into account the diversity of sources of knowledge instead of immediately situating them in the fiction of an intuitive intellect. And the real that aims for such a deduction, whatever the conditions, can only be the *realization* of rational conditions that anticipate its actual movement and carve out within it a priori a domain open to understanding [*connaissance*].

Lucio Colletti believed it was possible to recognize in Kant "the only classical German philosopher in whom it is possible to detect at least a grain of materialism."[109] This materialist "critique" is contained exactly in the distinction that situates itself between real opposition and logical contradiction, a distinction that guarantees "the priority of existence and its extralogical character,"[110] that is, "the heterogeneity of thought and being."[111] But this interpretation overlays the distinction of intuition and concept, which conditions the internal functioning of reason by diversifying the sources of knowledge, and that of the thing in itself and the phenomenon, which limit the power of reason from the outside. But in these two cases the relationship of real and thought designate completely different and precisely irreducible contents. The real that restores the physical concept of opposition results from a metaphysical construction, or, to use an expression we have used before, it is the realization of a possible. In this sense, it is determined from conditions that are first given in reason; it thus remains outside the constitution of material reality as such.

This long digression leads us finally back to Spinoza. We have set out the major lines of Kant's argument, because we believed we would find a certain connection between the new logic that is sketched out there and a mode of thought that also appears in *Ethics*, and which, without turning the principle of contradiction against itself, as Hegel does, institutes a new usage of this principle.

At least two points seem to support this connection between Spinoza and Kant: on one hand, the claim to a sort of absolute positivity, which expels all internal negativity from reality and limits the concept of contradiction to the reflection of an abstract intellect, and on the other hand, an attempt to explain physical reality through tendencies that affirm it in an absolutely positive manner: *conatus* in the Spinozist sense, *force* in the Kantian sense. We can now see the superficial aspects of this connection.

Following Kant, "forces" are not thinkable except from the point of view of their reciprocal confrontation, outside which they have no assignable reality, at least for reason. That is, the tension through which they assert themselves together is produced in a sequence of physical determinations within a phenomenal series that entirely exhausts the concept. With Spinoza, by contrast, the conatus that constitutes a singular essence unites it without intermediary to infinite substance that expresses itself within it, in a determination that is at the same time finite and infinite, and cannot therefore be restrained by the conditions of a possible knowledge. From this point of view, knowledge of the third kind rejects the consideration of real opposition and that of logical contradiction to the extent that they prohibit, under whatever form they present themselves, all pretense of deducing the real from the possible.

Here we find the confirmation of an idea we have already encountered: the "passage" of substance to the mode in which it affirms itself is not the movement of a realization or a manifestation, that is, something that can be represented in a relationship of the power to act [*puissance à l'acte*]. Substance does not precede its modes or lie behind their apparent reality, as a metaphysical foundation or a rational condition, but, in its absolute immanence, it is nothing other than the act of expressing itself immediately in all its modes, an act that is not itself determined through the relations of modes to each other but that is on the contrary their effective cause. There is therefore nothing more, nothing less either, in substance than in its affections: it is that which expresses the immediate identity between the unity of nature and the infinite multiplicity of beings that constitute it without "composing" it, and it is irreducible to the formal principle of an order.

The *conatus,* which are the expression of substance in its affections, are thus not forces: in fact, they exercise no action on each other. Inversely, their tendency to preserve their being, that is, the eternity that they are in themselves, of their essence, should be thought outside all temporal development. This tendency leads them nowhere except to what they are; we cannot even say that it is completed in its beginning, because it no more begins than it ends. In this sense, it is absolutely causal, that is, it excludes all ends and all mediation; these would not be thinkable except in the perspective of a sequence, whether rational or not. As we have clearly demonstrated, singular essences are not "subjects" centered on themselves, intending to realize themselves, because they are pure substantial acts with neither object nor subject, without content or form; that is, they are immediately beyond these distinctions posed through an abstract reflection.

As we have also demonstrated, the Spinozist theory nevertheless concedes a place for the notion of subject, which it defines as a relation, no longer between essences but between existences. At the level of existences, that is, of all that composes *natura naturata*, does the analogy with Kant's doctrine of forces make sense anymore?

Spinoza's physics actually poses a certain number of correlations between "individuals," which can be treated as a game of actions and reactions and which is explained completely through mechanical principles, in the absence of all interventions, external or internal, of a purpose: "If two contrary actions are instigated in the same subject, a change must necessarily take place in both or in one of them, until they cease to be contrary."[112]

Are we not dealing here with a "metaphysical principle of nature," in the manner of Kant?

Before answering this question, we must clearly grasp the importance of this connection. If the doctrine of equilibrium of forces effectively describes the system of relations that constitutes a "subject," whatever kind it might be, without being able to represent a positive determination (the absolutely affirmative act that immediately unites all singular essences to the infinite that is expressed within them), then it would seem that the distance established by Spinoza between the order of essences and that of existences announces the critical distinction between the phenomenon and the thing in itself, which also forces us to identify the different kinds of knowledge for the faculties or for the uses of reason.

But for Spinoza there are not two orders of reality, one substantial and infinite and the other modal and finite, but one single and same reality, continuous and indivisible, determined by one unique law of causality, through which the finite and the infinite are indissolubly linked. It is no less possible to cut this reality into two distinct modal regions, in which one is the world of essences and the other is a world of existences; this is precisely what we learned in the difficult theory of infinite modes. What is perceived in its essential eternity, following general laws of movement and of rest, is also what can be represented according to its existence, as *facies totius universi*, the global individual that conserves itself identically as itself in an unlimited *durée*, without beginning or end, which no longer falls under the concept of eternity.

It is a sole and same nature that grasps all the kinds of knowledge: following points of view that are irreducible because they are in a certain sense differently aligned [*décalés*] in relation to each other, according to whether they grasp the elements of reality as they are in themselves, or according to their sequence, and in this later case, according to the order in which they construct this sequence. But as we have seen, each of these knowledges is "true" in its way, that is, it obeys laws according to the point of view on which it depends: they all have the capacity for explanation that conceals their cause, and this is not to be found in the nature of reason or human intellect that would fix its conditions to reality in order to represent it. In any case, it is not possible to affirm that one of these genres is more "true" than the other (if we take care to distinguish between truth and adequation) because they are equally necessary in the system of their functioning: it is only from a practical perspective, whose domain is precisely delineated in *Ethics,* that a hierarchical relationship can be established between them, which places the intellectual love of God in a supreme place, above the knowledge of natural sequences and the distractions of imagination. But, we might add, these diverse forms of knowledge point to the same reality, which they present in the internal diversity of its nature, in the relationship of the infinite to the finite, of the finite to the infinite, or of the finite to the finite.

This is why, as seductive as it might appear, we must reject the attempt to relate the open perspective of Spinoza to the one that Kant would follow. But it is not clear that Hegel has not fallen into this confusion himself: the objections he launches at Spinoza and at Kant speak to each other with a secret resonance. Is this not the key to his scorn for Spinozism? Everything happens as if Hegel has read Kant in Spinoza, because he was not able to read Spinoza himself, in the revolutionary singularity of his philosophical position.

Teleology

In thinking the relationship of substance to its affections is an immediate identity that does not need to be mediated by contradictions, Spinoza wanted neither to realize the infinite in Being in one fell swoop nor to conceive it as the process of realization of a tendency that satisfies itself in its own development. Neither absolute object nor absolute subject, the Spinozist substance invalidates precisely these categories of representation, which Hegel, in turn, gambles on, with the pretense of resolving their contradiction once and for all.

Thus the Spinozist substance is not a *subject*. But, in truth, neither is the Hegelian spirit *a* subject: it is subject, which is altogether different. Hegelian logic invalidates the traditional position of subject, as it is assigned to it through a logic of the intellect, the fixed position of a subject in relation to an object or a predicate. In its immanent movement the concept that grasps itself as Self in the concept identifies itself with "the thing itself," that is, with the content of which it is the presentation, and not just the representation. In this presentation, *Geist* [*l'Esprit*] reemerges not as a subject but as absolute subject, which expresses itself in the totality of its process. To return to the expression of L. Althussser, it is "process without subject," which is the proper subject of itself, or again, process–subject. This is the meaning of the "subjective logic," which is not a logic of subject, and even less the logic of a subject.

The ordinary function of a subject, the one that this subject possesses in a predicative judgment, is thus undone. Where it emerges in rational discourse, the concept is at the same time subject and predicate, or rather it is their unity, that is, the movement of their reciprocal determination:

> Similarly when it is said: "the real is the universal", the real, qua subject, passes away in its predicate. The universal is not only meant to have the significance of a predicate, as if the proposition stated that the real is universal: the universal is meant to express the essential nature of the real. Thinking therefore loses that fixed objective basis which it had in the subject, just as much as in the predicate it is thrown back on the subject, and therein returns not into itself but into the subject underlying the content.[113]

For abstract intellect, the truth of a proposition is uniformly determined by a formal system of relations in which the rules must be respected. But the activity, the life of a concept, lays bare this rigid relation, this construction, erasing the limits it imposes on reason from the outside, decomposing every form in another form, which is nothing in turn but a step in the evolution that carries it toward its actual realization.

True rationality, which is concrete, requires thus that we put aside the traditional model of predicative thought:

> In that which concerns dialectical movement, its element is pure concept; it thus has a content that is, in its own self, subject, through and through. There is thus no content that would present itself as underlying subject and whose significance is due to it as a predicate; the proposition as it stands is nothing but empty form.[114]

The proposition is an empty form to the extent that it separates subject from predicate by assigning them fixed positions. But the true [*le vrai*] is not subject for a predicate that would be exterior to it, but to the extent that it is also content, it exposes itself as rational in every moment of its presentation. This is what is expressed in the phrase "it is subject in itself through and through." This is the key to its autonomy and its infinity.

In its immediate development, the living mind contradicts [*dément*] the exigencies of an abstract logic, and this is why it makes a place for the negative in its own system. Absolute negativity, or negation of the negation, is nothing other than the irresistible pressure of the concept that does not allow it to stop in any limited determination, in any form, because these are only provisional and incomplete forms for it, which it must dismantle [*défaire*] itself to discover and realize its identity in itself:

> Living substance, further, is being which is truly subject, or what is the same is truly realised and actual solely in the process of positing itself in mediating with its own self its transitions from one state or position to the opposite. As subject it is negativity pure and simple, and for this very reason a process of splitting up what is simple and undifferentiated, a process of duplicating and setting factors in opposition, which in turn is the negation of this

indifferent diversity and of its opposition. It is only this sameness reinstated, this reflection within itself of the other being, which is the true and not an original unity as such or an immediate unity as such.[115]

The concept is "in its own self, subject, through and through" to the extent that positing its other in itself, it reflects itself: it does not recognize itself in the determination except to suppress itself immediately within it, and at the same time suppressing it as a singular and finite determination, incapable of gathering within itself the infinite rationality of all. It is the movement of the negative that returns to itself and thus serves the realization of the true, its rational becoming.

Additionally, unlike the abstract subject of a finite logic, which excludes all negativity from itself and cannot enter into a contradiction with itself, the Hegelian subject (infinitely concrete because it is "subject through and through") contains all contradictions within itself: it is at the same time the condition for and the result of their integral development. It is through the intermediary of this internal negativity that the true is precisely not *a* subject but subject of itself, and it presents itself as such.

All the same, we can ask ourselves, proceeding from the opposite direction to this classical rationality whose abstraction and limitation Hegel constantly denounces, whether it does not achieve the same effect. In one case, the contradiction is rejected from the beginning, following formal conditions and rules that are a precondition to the exposition of the true; in the other, it is finally overcome, through a complicated and laborious route, in the course of which the contradiction turned against itself, resolves itself in the affirmation of a subject of truth, which is actual [*effectif*] because it has derived [*tiré*] all possible limits from itself, and infinite because it has overcome them. It has thus become absolute position of self. In the two cases, there is rationality in relation to a subject that finds in itself that which suppresses all negativity and thus guarantees the preeminence of the true. However, in the previous representation Hegel struggles against, this subject is a finite subject that is already entirely constituted from the beginning, realized in a completely positive principle, and it is its permanence that ensures the coherence, or the order of the demonstration, whereas in the Hegelian development it is an infinite subject that is not itself except at the end of a process that it completes, whose movement refutes all preconditions.

Is the Hegelian "subject" thus not the mirror image of the subject of classical reason? A critical image, to be sure, that exposes and analyzes the insufficiencies of an abstract rationality. But it is nothing other than an image, still attached to a model on which it depends and through which it reproduces, in its own way, its essential characteristics. Thus, in comparison to the traditional thought he denounces, Hegel only proceeds through a displacement, installing in an end, no less absolute than the beginning from which it was extracted, the illusion of an ideal rationality, purified of all materiality to the extent that it admits no element that is external to it. In this "reversal" something of the essential is conserved: it is the idea of the mind as subject of self, master of truth that controls the rational process in which it appears identical to self.

This connection might appear arbitrary, but it brings to light something of the essential that is the function of Hegelian teleology: it is this teleology that retains, for an idealist dialectic, the traditional criteria that establish the coherence or the permanence of the true. The infinity of the concept, the irresistible movement of its return to itself, tends toward an end, and (in the manner of the truthful God of Descartes, who upholds the entire order of truths, which the labor of the concept does not undertake in vain but which it inscribes in a progressive development) this tendency guarantees an evolution that is at the same time continuous and broken, which leads the spirit from uncertain beginnings to its necessary completion. Thus Hegel can write that "reason is a teleological [*zweckmäßige*] operation,"[116] taking his concept of finality explicitly from Aristotle.

Across all these vicissitudes, the becoming of the true is the return to self of the concept: it has a meaning, and thus it is rational. These preliminary steps, as distant as they are from this completion, constitute within it its anticipation and its arrival. And it is this, specifically, that comprises Hegelian idealism, in this guarantee that mind gives to itself, in engendering itself as its own content, that its movement goes somewhere, or it maintains itself already in some manner, because it is subject that actualizes itself, returning to itself across the cycle of all its manifestations. Through this guarantee, a certain number of possibilities are immediately rejected, which shows that this infinite process is nevertheless limited, because it depends on an orientation. For example, it excludes the possibility that the process has no meaning, because it would cease to be rational in itself, and it would no longer have its unity in itself. Or, an even less acceptable possibility, it excludes that it would have multiple meanings at the same time, remaining indefinitely in a confrontation of antagonistic meanings, between which no equilibrium could definitively establish itself, because it would not be able to clarify a unitary and dominant tendency. The true would enter into insurmountable contradictions, or at least ones in which nothing would ensure that they be resolved once and for all.

The other name for this teleology is the negation of the negation, that is, the concept of a negation that is not finite. Finite negation is the negation that is no more than negation, negation of something that it suppresses from the exterior and that thus in some way escapes it; as with all limits, this is essentially relative. Absolute negation on the contrary is the power of overriding all limits, which cannot be achieved except in the infinity of a completely developed system, carrying its limits within it and suppressing them as limits. Finite negation is a stopping point: it goes nowhere. Infinite negation is necessarily oriented toward the end that it tends to achieve through the intermediary of contradictions it resolves.

It is precisely on this point where Hegel pretends to break with prior tradition, that we can equally say he renews it. Through this guarantee that gives him the negation of the negation, the condition of its "completion," the Hegelian dialectic (exactly like the logic of representation whose limits, moreover, it denounces) is a way of thinking *against* contradiction, because it does not conceive of it except through recurrence, through the promise of its resolution, thus from the point of view of its disappearance. This is explained in a commentary from the *Encyclopedia*:

Contradiction is the very moving principle of the world: and it is ridiculous to say that contradiction is unthinkable. The only thing correct in that statement is that contradiction is not the end of the matter, but cancels itself. But contradiction, when cancelled, does not leave abstract identity; for that is itself only one side of the contrariety.[117]

To think contradiction is to think its suppression, because "contradiction is not the end of the matter." To hold on to the contradiction is a symptom of arrested thought, incapable of completing its goal, caught within the contradiction without being able to escape it.

We have seen that Hegel reproaches Spinoza for his negativity, his "acosmism." In a noteworthy manner, in the historical remark of book II of *Logic,* dedicated to Spinoza, Hegel writes in relation to his "oriental intuition": "Thus being increasingly obscures itself and night, the negative, is the final term of the series, which does not first return into the primal light."[118]

That the process of the absolute completes itself through a negative term signifies that it is marked once and for all by this end toward which it tends; its progression is thus nothing but regression, or a degradation, and it is obscured in the irrational.

From this "negativism" that Hegel imputes to Spinoza he constitutes nevertheless his own "positivism." A philosophy of absolute affirmation, which discovers the conditions of its reversal, of its abolition, within the contradiction itself, because if everything passes necessarily through contradiction these are no more than intermediaries or indispensable auxiliaries to the accomplishment of the true, the contradiction is still the best means to emerge from contradictions, and the "labor of the negative" has for its object the negative itself, which it eradicates. Against impatient philosophies and incomplete logics that suppress contradiction in their foundation or in their beginning, it is necessary to wager on the triumph of the contradiction over itself, which makes it disappear in this end, of which it is no more than the manifestation. For the concept, the open path through absolute negation is also the promise of access to the infinite.

Through this recurrence, which turns the contradiction against itself, the true announces itself throughout the process that brings it into being: mind that remembers itself remains present to itself across the totality of forms of its actualization. This is why its "history" knows no past, but it deals only with the eternal actuality of mind that moves within itself:

The universal that philosophical history seeks should not be understood as one very important aspect of historical life, alongside
which we might find other determinations. This universal is the
infinitely concrete, which contains all and which is present every-
where because mind remains eternally beside itself—the infinitely
concrete for which the past does not exist but which always remains the same in its force and its power.[119]

Identical to itself throughout its process, mind has no history in itself,
because this process "is absolute movement and at the same time
absolute rest."[120] And again, "It is thus not really a history, or else it is
a history at the same time as it is not one, because the thoughts, the
principles, the ideas that offer themselves to us are of the present; they
are determinations of our own mind. That which is historical, that is,
past, is no longer, is dead."[121]

In its immanent development, mind places itself, ultimately, above
all history, to the extent that it situates itself immediately at its end, in
relation to that which is nothing more than an exterior manifestation.
To understand a history rationally is precisely to make it return to the
concept that is at the same time its motor and its truth, that is, to suppress in it that which is historical and to affirm the triumph of living
thought over the dead past, which has done away with itself within it.

Passing through its own history to return to itself, mind remains
eternally "beside itself" in the course of this achieved identity. Doesn't
this "eternity" have something in common with the Spinozist eternity,
which also characterizes it from the point of view of the infinite?

For Spinoza, eternity is the property of something eternal; it coincides with "its infinite existence in act."[122] It belongs to this existence
that is immediately essence, substance in which all of nature is not
limited by a common condition of duration. In fact, all duration is
limited, to the extent it is composed of parts, and becomes the object
in this analysis of enumeration. But infinite substance necessarily
escapes such an analysis, because "by attributing a duration to it, we
would be dividing into parts that which of its own nature is infinite
and can never be conceived except as infinite."[123] Eternity is thus not
a particular form of duration; in particular, it is not a duration pro-
longed beyond all assignable limit, "even if duration be conceived as

without beginning and end."[124] We return here to a reasoning that already has helped us to understand the nature of the infinite in act, that is, an infinite that excludes from itself all potentiality and thus does not allow itself to be understood by composition, or construction, through the finite.

Eternity in the Spinozist sense is essentially causal: it belongs to the infinite that has its cause in itself, outside any possibility of a finalized development. Substance differs fundamentally, then, from Hegelian mind: one cannot say that it "remains beside itself" to the extent that it is nothing other than the act through which it simultaneously affirms itself, outside all temporal determination, in all its affections, without these constituting, as we have seen, the ordered system of its manifestation. This act is eternal because it does not depend on any process of actualization, which would lead its unfolding back to the conditions of a would-be infinity [d'un infini en puissance]. Eternity is the absence of end.

This concept of eternity is crucial if we want to understand the real stakes of the debate that confront Spinoza and Hegel. The self-identity of substance excludes all mediation, and in this sense it effectively casts negativity outside itself. But this rejection is not a manifestation in an exterior: the negative, the finite, which substance does not admit as part of its own nature, it does not project either into its affections, as is the intention of the formula omnis determinatio est negatio. Because between substance and modes, no "passage" can be thought, which would signify a necessarily inadequate decomposition of the infinite in the finite. This is why substance is eternally present in its affections and cannot be thought outside of them, no more than they can be thought without it. And yet the immediacy of this relation of the infinite to the finite is exactly what prevents us from understanding this relation as a completed relation [un rapport finalisé] and substance as absolute subject that accomplishes itself within it.

The self-identity of substance thus refutes a teleological interpretation of the act through which it expresses itself in self-determination. Such an interpretation revives the illusion of a subjective that envisages an ideal reality, from the point of view of its "creation"; this is what the appendix to book I of Ethics clearly demonstrates. From the point of view of eternity, there is no longer a place for a consideration of ends, nor, equally, for the intervention of a free "subject" who would impose his own order over and above that of things; this is exactly the point of opposition between Spinoza and Descartes. But Hegel himself also refutes the Cartesian subject that is nothing but a subject and remains thus as an abstraction, but this refutation, the inverse of Spinoza's, reveals itself finally as less decisive, because by withdrawing subject to the finiteness of its unicity, it again reinforces this internal orientation, this projection of self toward ends that characterize, for all idealist thought, a rational, that is, intentional, process. But as we have seen, by applying the notion of *conatus* to singular essences, Spinoza eliminates the conception of an intentional subject, which is not adequate either to represent the absolute infinity of substance or to understand how it expresses itself in these finite determinations.

Hegel was thus not ill advised to notice the absence of the concept of subject and also of negation of negation in Spinozist thought; for that matter, they are two different names for the same thing. In Spinoza's system this is glaringly absent. Does this signify, as Hegel himself interprets this absence, that this concept is his "shortcoming" from which he concludes the inferiority of Spinozism that cannot rise to his level?

We know that Hegelian teleology reappears in his conception of the history of philosophy: present as a succession of systems related one to another hierarchically and transformed through their own internal contradictions, through which they cause their own downfall, constraining them to make way for superior forms that are ever closer to the true philosophy, which has denied all history within itself. This point of view demonstrates an incontestable bias: it permits us to study philosophies in their internal movement, and according to their reciprocal relations, by staving off the attempt at a formal comparison. It specifies a philosophical position derived from their contradictions and not an indifferent order. But, and this is the price to be paid for disengaging this rationality, these contradictions are presented following the principle of absolute negativity, as resolving themselves through one another in an irresistible sequence that explains itself entirely in terms of its end [*fin*]. Thus Hegel has introduced into the history of philosophy what we might call, anachronistically, an evolutionism. In this conception, one philosophy is necessarily superior because it follows another and nourishes itself on the previous one's failure. This is what authorizes Hegel to characterize philosophies according to the principle of a negative rationality, thus oriented: according to his position in history, the philosophy of Spinoza is necessarily insufficient or defective, and it is on this basis that it must be interpreted.

But, on the contrary, if we eliminate Hegelian teleology in applying ourselves to the Spinozist demonstrations, this evolutionary conception of the history of philosophy disappears as well. The real relation between philosophies is no longer measurable solely in terms of their degree of hierarchical integration; it is no longer reducible to a chronological line that arranges them in relation to one another in an order of irreversible succession. In this history, which is perhaps not material but is no longer ideal, a new kind of contradiction appears: the struggle of tendencies that do not carry within themselves the promise of their resolution. Or again, a unity of contraries, but without the negation of the negation.

From this point of view, the absence of the negation of the negation in Spinozist thought can no longer simply be interpreted by default, as a lack to be overcome, as a lack that will certainly be overcome. On the contrary, it represents the positive sign of an anticipated resistance (but no less real for all that) to an aspect of the Hegelian dialectic that we will call, to summarize quickly, his idealism. Thus the very surprising phenomenon that we have encountered several times is explained: Hegel's intense sensitivity to certain fundamental themes of Spinozism, which express themselves *a contrario* in the common form of repulsion through interpretations that, even if they are aberrant, are no less pertinent. Thus, no longer taking the "laws" of chronology into consideration, we can say that if Hegel seems to not have always properly understood Spinoza or to have not wanted to understand him, it is because Spinoza himself understood Hegel very well, which, from the point of view of a teleology, is evidently intolerable.

The most obvious perspectives are thus reversed: it is Spinoza who refutes the Hegelian dialectic. But does that also mean that he refutes all dialectics? Could we not equally say that what he refutes in the Hegelian dialectic is that which is exactly not dialectical, what Marx himself called his idealism? Because we must put aside (as absolutely devoid of philosophical interest) the idea that all dialectics are idealist in themselves or reactive; for a historical materialism of thought the expression "all dialectics" is completely without meaning. The real question is, What is the limit that separates an idealist dialectic from a materialist one? Under what conditions can a dialectic become materialist? We recognize that Spinoza helps us ask this question and that he gives it a content: What is or what would be a dialectic that functioned in the absence of all guarantees, in an absolutely causal manner, without a prior orientation that would establish within it, from the beginning, the principle of absolute negativity, without the promise that all the contradictions in which it engages are by rights resolved, because they carry within them the conditions of their resolution?

When Marx wrote the famous sentence, "Humanity only poses for itself problems that it can resolve," he was still completely part of the lineage of Hegelian evolutionism. The subsequent history of Marxism would demonstrate exactly in the course of events that a question is not resolved simply by the fact that it is asked. But it is already something significant to pose a question, even if it can promise nothing as its answer. To read Spinoza following Hegel, but not according to Hegel, allows us to pose the question of a non-Hegelian dialectic, but we must also admit, and this is also a way of being Spinozist, that this does not enable us at the same time to answer it.

Abbreviations

THE FOLLOWING standard abbreviations appear in the text and end-notes:

App	Appendix
Ax	Axiom
C	Corollary
Def	Definition
D	Demonstration
E	*Ethics*
Exp	Explanation
Lem	Lemma
P	Proposition
Pref	Preface
S	Scholium

Thus, for example, the citation for *Ethics* Book II, Proposition 13, Lemma 3, Axiom 2 appears as *E* IIP13Lem3Ax2.

Notes

Translator's Introduction

1 Warren Montag, "Introduction by Warren Montag," in *In a Materialist Way: Selected Essays by Pierre Macherey*, ed. Warren Montag (London: Verso, 1998), 13.

2 Ibid.

3 Jason Read, "The Order and Connection of Ideas: Theoretical Practice in Macherey's Turn to Spinoza," *Rethinking Marxism* 19 (2007): 500–20, 500.

4 Pierre Macherey, "Althusser and the Concept of the Spontaneous Philosophy of Scientists," *Parrhesia* 6 (2009): 14–27, 20.

5 Pierre Macherey, "Soutenance" in *In a Materialist Way: Selected Essays by Pierre Macherey*, ed. Warren Montag, trans. Ted Stolze (London: Verso, 1998), 17–27, 25.

6 See Ted Stolze, "Macherey and the Becoming Real of Philosophy," *The Minnesota Review* 26 (1986): 112–17.

7 Michael Kelly, "The Post-War Hegel Revival in France: A Bibliographical Essay," *Journal of European Studies* 13 (1983): 199–216, 213.

8 Alexandre Matheron, *Entretien avec Alexandre Matheron: A Propos de Spinoza*, vol. 3, Multitudes (2000), accessed May 19, 2011, http://multitudes.samizdat.net/A-propos-de-Spinoza.

9 Pierre Macherey, "Spinoza 1968 (Guéroult ou/et Deleuze)," presentation to *Groupes d'Etudes la Philosophie au Sens Large* (11/26/2008), http://stl.recherche.univ-lille3.fr/seminaires/philosophie/macherey/macherey20082009/macherey26112008.html.

10 Read, "The Order and Connection of Ideas." At the time of the publication of *Hegel ou Spinoza* there were already several works by French scholars exclusively on Spinoza. See Martial Guéroult, *Spinoza, Analyse et Raisons* (Paris: Aubier-Montaigne, 1968); Gilles Deleuze, *Spinoza et le Problème de l'Expression, Arguments* (Paris: Éditions de Minuit, 1968); and Alexandre Matheron, *Individu et Communauté chez Spinoza, Le Sens Commun* (Paris: Éditions de Minuit, 1969). In fact, Macherey argues that Spinoza also constituted something of an absent presence in the

work of several well-known scholars, specifically Heidegger, Adorno, and later Foucault, whose respective concerns about the relationship between being and essent (Heidegger), the dialectic (Adorno), and the ethical subject (Foucault) resonated with Spinoza's framework, a connection sometimes obscured by the intervening presence of Hegel. See Pierre Macherey, *In a Materialist Way*, 135.

11   Michael Hardt, *Gilles Deleuze: An Apprenticeship in Philosophy* (Minneapolis: University of Minnesota Press, 1993), x–xi.

12   A second, less sustained line of thought that drew on Hegel in this period was promoted by Vacherot, a disciple of Cousin. Vacherot studied at the École Normale from 1827 to 1829 and became a professor there in 1839. He proposed a dualism and a separation—between God and the world, the real and ideal—that was "even more strict than that of his teacher." For Vacherot, Hegel's philosophy constituted the summit of philosophical thinking, prefigured by the Alexandria school and emerging as a "new form of Spinozism." Vacherot was responsible for the brief if highly contested popularity of Hegel's *Metaphysics of Science* and *Principles of Positive Metaphysics,* which were hailed on one hand as a "philosophical event of the greatest significance" and castigated on the other as a dangerous pantheism challenging the precepts of the Catholic church. See Morgan Gaulin, "Refonder la Philosophie en 1860: Ernest Renan Critique de Vacherot," *Nineteenth-Century French Studies* 38, nos. 1 and 2 (2009–2010): 52–66.

13   Although not fluent in German, Cousin went to Berlin in the 1820s and maintained correspondence (in French) with Hegel. He was appointed to the Sorbonne in the 1830s, at the young age of twenty-three, a position that gave him "considerable influence over French philosophy." Cousin chose to elaborate the position of his advisor and predecessor, Royer-Collard, reviving the significance of common sense against a Cartesian vision of the primacy of doubt, a Cartesian vision that in France at the time supported a spiritualism. Pierre Macherey, "Les Débuts Philosophique de Victor Cousin," *Corpus* 18–19 (1991): 29–49.

14   Ibid.

15   Pierre Macherey, "Entre Philosophie et Histoire de la Philosophie: Le Hegel de Jean Hyppolite," Communication présentée par P. Macherey, ENS Ulm: Journée d'études consacrée à Jean Hyppolite (salle des Actes, samedi 27 mai 2006), accessed May 19, 2011, http://stl.recherche. univ-lille3.fr/sitespersonnels/macherey/accueilmacherey.html.

16   Macherey, *In a Materialist Way*. Indeed, Macherey remarked later that

Hegel "haunted" French philosophy in the nineteenth century, surfacing only occasionally in marginalized readings by "professional philosophers and literary hacks" such as Villiers de l'Isle Adam and Mallarme; see Macherey, "Entre Philosophie et Histoire." And particularly after the Franco-Prussian war, a growing aversion in French scholarship precluded any explicit reference to Hegel's thought: an aversion to all things German, an aversion to Hegel's rejection of mathematized science, and a sense that Hegel was synonymous with pan-Germanism. See A. Bohm and V. Y. Mudimbe, "Hegel's Reception in France," *Bulletin de la Société Américaine de Philosophie de Langue Française* 6, no. 3 (1994): 5–33.

17 Macherey, "Entre Philosophie et Histoire."

18 Judith Butler, *Subjects of Desire: Hegelian Reflections in Twentieth Century France* (New York: Columbia University Press, 1999), 62.

19 Although arguably post–World War II humanism took a slightly different form, sharing some but not all of the coordinates that characterized humanism in the 1930s, in a different relation to other conceptual coordinates: understandings of the individual and class, particular arguments about agency, teleology, totality, or anthropologizing of the dialectic. And the contexts of the philosophical and political struggles of the 1950s through the early 1960s were markedly different than the specifics of the mal de siècle that spurred the rise of an indigenized Hegelian philosophy in France between the wars, in the 1920s and 1930s, and increasingly after World War II.

20 Butler, *Subjects of Desire*, 62.

21 Ibid.

22 Pierre Macherey, *The Object of Literature*, trans. David Macey (Cambridge: Cambridge University Press, 1995), 60–62.

23 Macherey, "Althusser and the Concept of the Spontaneous Philosophy of Scientists."

24 Macherey, *The Object of Literature*, 62n16.

25 Macherey, *In a Materialist Way*, 58.

26 Macherey, *The Object of Literature*, 59–63. Pierre Macherey, "Lacan et le Discours Universitaires," Groupe d'études animé par Pierre Macherey, *Groupes d'Etudes la Philosophie au Sens Large* (12/2/2009), accessed May 19, 2011, http://philolarge.hypotheses.org/87.

27 Montag, "Introduction," 8.

28 Note the distinction between the appropriation of Hegel by Kojève and a more productive engagement by Hyppolite, which "instead of

introducing Hegel into a French reading, by instead introducing the French into a reading by Hegel . . . broke open a torrent of concrete philosophical problems . . . expos[ing] the innumerable difficulties and obscurities presented by this text, rather than degenerating into a tyrannical reading which authorised the 'real content' of Hegel." See Georges Canguilhem, "Jean Hyppolite (1907–1968)," *Revue de Métaphysique et de Morale* 2 (1969): 129–30, cited in Macherey, "Entre Philosophie et Histoire." By the 1930s, the steady translation of Hegel's work into French, in particular by Giblet and Hyppolite, marked for subsequent scholars an "event" that was to transform Hegelian studies in France. It was to give the public "a means to engage Hegel on its own terms" (ibid.).

29   Bruce Baugh, "Hegel in Modern French Philosophy: The Unhappy Consciousness," *Laval Théologie et Philosophique* 49, no. 3 (1993): 423–38.

30   Butler, *Subjects of Desire,* 61–62.

31   Perry Anderson, *Arguments within English Marxism* (London: Verso, 1980), 106–7.

32   Michael Sprinker, "The Legacies of Althusser," *Yale French Studies Depositions* 88 (1995): 201–25.

33   Montag, "Introduction."

34   There are conflicting accounts of this event; see Julian Bourg, "The Red Guards of Paris: French Student Maoism of the 1960s," *History of European Ideas* 31 (2005): 472–90.

35   The humanist position maintained an effective distinction between what was viewed as the idealism of thought and the materialism of practice. Antihumanism (with a Spinozist inflection) countered that theoretical practice had its own materiality, expressed not least in the institutional structures in which ideas emerged, the context of their consumption. The point was not to produce a world free of ideology—as Althusser argued, "an organic part of every social totality"—but to understand the context that produced it. See Louis Althusser, *For Marx* (London: New Left Books, 1977), 232. Theoretical practice, then, was a necessary feature of all practice, because ideology was not a "position" to be excoriated once and for all but was endemic to the social field. And theoretical practice was as necessary in that period, to develop the science of Marxism, as it would be in ours to develop its philosophy. See Stolze, "Macherey and the Becoming Real of Philosophy."

36   Bourg, "The Red Guards of Paris."

37   As Montag argues, Macherey, in correspondence with Althusser, ex-
      pressed great reticence about the spiritualist inflection of the concept
      of a structured whole. Montag, "Introduction."

38   After the publication of *Hegel ou Spinoza*, Macherey produced a cor-
      pus that includes a five-volume commentary on Spinoza's *Ethics*, *Avec
      Spinoza*; and a series of articles that discuss Spinoza in relation to the
      work of Pascal, Descartes, Deleuze, and Boyle and include discussions
      of Spinoza's monism and his concept of action. Macherey remarked
      later in his "Soutenance" that "I have attempted to situate the Spinozist
      doctrine in the context of its own history: that of successive readings
      which have in some sense reproduced it by adapting it to theoretical
      and ideological configurations sometimes very far from the conditions
      in which it was actually produced." Macherey, *In a Materialist Way*, 24.

39   Pierre Macherey, "On the Rupture," *The Minnesota Review* 26 (1986):
      118–27, 120, 119.

40   Edward Palmer Thompson, *The Poverty of Theory and Other Essays*
      (New York: Monthly Review Press, 1978), 112.

Translator's Note and Acknowledgments

1   Pierre Macherey and Warren Montag, *In a Materialist Way: Selected
     Essays* (London: Verso, 1998), 174.

The Alternative

1   Georg Wilhelm Friedrich Hegel, *Lectures on the History of Philosophy*,
     trans. Elizabeth S. Haldane and Francis H. Simson, 3 vols., vol. III
     (London: Kegan Paul, Trench, Trübner and Company, 1896), 253–54,
     modified.

2   Jacques Derrida, "L'âge de Hegel," in *Receuil Collectif du G.R.E.P.H.:
     Qui a Peur de la Philosophie?* (Paris: Flammarion, 1977), 106.

3   Martial Guéroult, *Spinoza I: Dieu* (Paris: Aubier-Montaigne, 1968), 468.

4   Louis Althusser, *Essays in Self-Criticism*, trans. Grahame Lock (London:
     New Left Books, 1976), 187. [In Lock's translation this passage reads,
     "Hegelian critique is already present in Spinoza."—*Trans.*]

1. Hegel Reads Spinoza

1   [My translation. Compare Georg Wilhelm Friedrich Hegel, *Lectures
     on the History of Philosophy*, trans. Elizabeth S. Haldane and Francis H.
     Simson, 3 vols., vol. III (London: Kegan Paul, Trench, Trübner and

Company, 1896), 283. For this text Macherey relied largely on his own translations from the German.—*Trans.*]

2   Georg Wilhelm Friedrich Hegel, Pierre-Jean Labarrière, and Gwendoline Jarczyk, *Science de la Logique,* trad., présentation, et notes par Pierre-Jean Labarrière et Gwendoline Jarczyk, Bibliothèque Philosophique (Paris: Aubier, 1972), t. I, 249, my translation. [See Georg Wilhelm Friedrich Hegel and George Di Giovanni, *The Science of Logic,* Cambridge Hegel Translations (Cambridge: Cambridge University Press, 2010), 212. Labarrière's text is closest to the 1832 revised edition of *Logic.*—*Trans.*]

3   Georg Wilhelm Friedrich Hegel, *G. W. F. Hegel: Science de la Logique ("Wissenschaft der Logik"),* traduction par S. Jankélévitch (Paris: Aubier, 1949), my translation. [The French here is closer to the German. Georg Wilhelm Friedrich Hegel, *Science of Logic,* trans. A. V. Miller (London: George Allen and Unwin, 1969), uses the term "immanent dialectic," but Georg Wilhelm Friedrich Hegel, *Wissenschaft der Logik,* zweiter teil, "Die subjektive Logik oder Lehre vom Begriff" (Leipzig: Duncker and Humboldt, 1841), does not.—*Trans.*]

4   Georg Wilhelm Friedrich Hegel, *Encyclopédie des Sciences Philosophiques 1: La Science de la Logique,* trans. Bernard Bourgeois, Bibliothèque des Textes Philosophiques (Paris: J. Vrin, 1970), remark §151, 584. See also §159, 405, my translation.

5   Georg Wilhelm Friedrich Hegel, *Encyclopedia of the Philosophical Sciences,* trans. William Wallace (Oxford: Oxford University Press, 1873), §76, modified.

6   Hegel, *Science of Logic,* §1180.

7   Hegel, *Lectures on the History of Philosophy,* 259, modified.

8   Martial Guéroult, *Spinoza I: Dieu* (Paris: Aubier-Montaigne, 1968), 41.

9   Hegel, *Science of Logic,* §1179.

10   Hegel, *Lectures on the History of Philosophy,* 257, modified.

11   Georg Wilhelm Friedrich Hegel, *L'Encyclopédie des Sciences Philosophiques,* trans. Bernard Bourgeois (Paris: Vrin, 1970), §151, my translation.

12   Hegel, *Lectures on the History of Philosophy,* 252, modified.

13   Georg Wilhelm Friedrich Hegel and Jean Gibelin, *Leçons sur l'Histoire de la Philosophie Introduction, Système et Histoire de la Philosophie,* trad. de l'Allemand par J. Gibelin, Idées (Paris: Gallimard, 1970), 74, my translation.

14   Ibid., 76, my translation.

15   Georg Wilhelm Friedrich Hegel, *La Théorie de la Mesure,* traduction et

commentaire par André Doz, Epiméthée Essais Philosophiques (Paris: Presses Universitaires de France, 1970), 22, my translation. [See Hegel, *Science of Logic*, §703, modified.—*Trans.*]

16   My translation. [Compare Hegel, *Lectures on the History of Philosophy*, vol. 1, 252. "Omnis" appears in the original German but not in Haldane's translation.—*Trans.*]

17   Hegel, *La Théorie de la Mesure*, 22–23, my translation. [Compare Hegel, *The Science of Logic*, trad. Di Giovanni, 284—*Trans.*]

18   Hegel, *Lectures on the History of Philosophy*, 253, modified.

19   Hegel, *Science of Logic*, §152, modified.

20   Ibid., §803, modified.

21   Ibid., Book II, "The Essence," §3, "Actuality," chapter 1, "The Absolute."

22   Ibid., §861, modified.

23   Ibid. Remark: Leibniz and Spinoza, §1168. [The French text includes a typographical error, reading "l'absolu dans un determinite ou il est absolut."—*Trans.*]

24   Ibid., §1170.

25   Ibid., §1173, modified.

26   Hegel, *Science de la Logique*, 291, my translation. [Compare *Logic*, §703.—*Trans.*]

27   Hegel, *Logic*, §702.

28   Unless otherwise noted I have translated *savoir* as "understanding" and *connaissance* as "knowledge."

29   Hegel, *Lectures on the History of Philosophy*, 288, modified.

30   Ibid., 254, modified.

31   The orientalist interpretation of Spinozism is a common link with German philosophy. One can read in the opuscule of Kant on *The End of All Things*, "The good sovereign is nothingness; one pours oneself into the abyss of divinity; one immerses oneself there, and personality disappears. To know the foretaste of this happiness, the Chinese philosophers close themselves off in obscure locales, compel themselves to keep their texts closed, they try to meditate, to sense their nothingness. From there again, the pantheism of Tibetans and of other oriental peoples, then later through a metaphysical sublimation, Spinozism: two doctrines closely affiliated to one of the oldest systems, that of emanation, according to which all the human spirits after having emerged from divinity finish by reentering and being reabsorbed by it. All this expressly [*uniquement*] in order that at all costs men could in the end enjoy this eternal rest, which constitutes

in their eyes the blissful end of all things, a conception that is nothing less than an abolition of all intelligence, this cessation even of all
thought." Emmanuel Kant, *Pensées Successives sur la Théodicée et la
Religion,* traduction et introduction par Paul Festugière (Paris: Vrin,
1931), my translation. Hegel, as we see, has invented nothing.

2. *More Geometrico*

1 Georg Wilhelm Friedrich Hegel, *Lectures on the History of Philosophy,*
   trans. Elizabeth S. Haldane and Francis H. Simson, 3 vols., vol. III
   (London: Kegan Paul, Trench, Trübner and Company, Ltd., 1896),
   283, modified.
2 Ibid., 263–264, modified.
3 Georg Wilhelm Friedrich Hegel, *G. W. F. Hegel: Science de la Logique*
   ("Wissenschaft der Logik"), Traduction par S. Jankélévitch (Paris: Aubier,
   1949), t. 1, 35, my translation.
4 Georg Wilhelm Friedrich Hegel, *L'Encyclopédie des Sciences Philosophiques,* trans. Bernard Bourgeois (Paris: Vrin, 1970), add. au §20,
   421, my translation. [See Georg Wilhelm Friedrich Hegel, *Encyclopedia of the Philosophical Sciences,* trans. William Wallace (Oxford: Oxford University Press, 1873), part 1, section II. "Preliminary Notion,"
   §20n.—*Trans.*]
5 Georg Wilhelm Friedrich Hegel, Pierre-Jean Labarrière, and Gwendoline Jarczyk, *Science de la Logique,* trad., présentation, et notes par
   Pierre-Jean Labarrière et Gwendoline Jarczyk, Bibliothèque Philosophique (Paris: Aubier, 1972), t. 1, 35, my translation. [Compare Georg
   Wilhelm Friedrich Hegel, *Science of Logic,* trans. A. V. Miller (London:
   George Allen and Unwin, 1969), §61.—*Trans.*]
6 Georg Wilhelm Friedrich Hegel, *The Phenomenology of Mind,* trans. J.
   B. Baillie, Library of Philosophy (London, New York: Sonnenschein,
   Macmillan, 1910), §48, modified.
7 Ibid.
8 Hegel, *Science of Logic,* §62, modified.
9 Ibid., §63, modified.
10 Hegel, *Encyclopedia of the Philosophical Sciences,* part 1, §243, modified.
11 Hegel, *The Phenomenology of Mind,* Preface §48, modified.
12 Georg Wilhelm Friedrich Hegel, "Introduction to the History of Philosophy," in *Hegel's Idea of Philosophy,* ed. Quentin S. J. Lauer (New
   York: Fordham University Press, 1971), 100.
13 Ibid., 124.

14   Hegel, *The Phenomenology of Mind*, §40, modified.

15   Gérard Lebrun, *La Patience du Concept Essai sur le Discours Hégélien*, Bibliothèque de Philosophie (Paris: Gallimard, 1972), 78.

16   Hegel, *The Phenomenology of Mind*, §42, modified.

17   Lebrun, *La Patience du Concept Essai sur le Discours Hégélien*, 77.

18   Hegel, *The Phenomenology of Mind*, §38, modified.

19   Hegel, *Science of Logic*, §1179.

20   Hegel, *Encyclopedia of the Philosophical Sciences*, §151, modified.

21   Ibid., §229, modified.

22   Ibid., modified.

23   Baruch Spinoza, *Spinoza: Complete Works*, trans. Samuel Shirley (Indianapolis: Hackett Publishing, 2002). *Letter* 37 to Bouwmeester, modified.

24   Ibid. *Treatise on the Emendation of the Intellect*, §106, modified.

25   Ibid. *Treatise*, §38, modified.

26   Ibid. *Letter* 37 to Bouwmeester, modified.

27   Ibid. *Treatise on the Emendation of the Intellect*, §36, modified.

28   On the conditions under which this preface was written, according to Spinoza, cf. the *Letter* 13 to Oldenberg.

29   [Rene Descartes, *Objections to the Meditations and Descartes's Replies*, trans. Jonathan Bennett (2010), in the version by Jonathan Bennett presented at http://www.earlymoderntexts.com, 35, modified.—*Trans.*]

30   [Unless otherwise noted, *puissance* has been translated as "capacity" and *pouvoir* has been translated as "power."—*Trans.*]

31   Spinoza, *Spinoza: Complete Works*, E 1P36.

32   Ibid. *Treatise on the Emendation of the Intellect*, §85, modified.

33   Ibid.

34   Ibid. *E* IIP40S1.

35   Ibid. *Treatise of the Emendation of the Intellect*, §93, modified.

36   Ibid., §99, modified.

37   Spinoza, *Spinoza: Complete Works*, E IIP36, modified.

38   [In Spinoza, *Spinoza: Complete Works*, this appears as *Letter* 60; it appears as 50 in Macherey's text.—*Trans.*]

39   Spinoza, *Spinoza: Complete Works*, E IID4, modified.

40   Ibid., *E* IIP5, modified.

41   Ibid., *E* IIP6C, modified.

42   Ibid., *E* IIP32.

43   Ibid., *E* IIP33.

44   Ibid., *E* IIP35.

45   Ibid., *E* IVP1S.

46   Léon Brunschvicg, "Section I. Pensées sur l'Esprit et sur le Style," *Pensées de Pascal* (1897), P335, my translation.

47   Hegel, *Encyclopedia of the Philosophical Sciences,* §24n, modified.

48   *Preface* to Hegel and Hyppolite, *G. W. F. Hegel: La Phénoménologie de l'Esprit,* traduction de Jean Hyppolite, . . . t. I, §39, my translation. [See Hegel, *The Phenomenology of Mind,* §39, modified.—Trans.]

3. The Problem of Attributes

1   Baruch Spinoza, *Spinoza: Complete Works,* trans. Samuel Shirley (Indianapolis: Hackett Publishing, 2002), *E* ID6Exp, modified.

2   Georg Wilhelm Friedrich Hegel, *Science of Logic,* trans. A. V. Miller (London: George Allen and Unwin, 1969), §805, modified.

3   Ibid. *Remark: The Philosophy of Spinoza and Leibniz,* §1181.

4   Spinoza, *Spinoza: Complete Works,* *E* ID4.

5   Georg Wilhelm Friedrich Hegel, *Lectures on the History of Philosophy,* trans. Elizabeth S. Haldane and Francis H. Simson, 3 vols., vol. III (London: Kegan Paul, Trench, Trübner and Company, 1896), 256–57, modified.

6   Ibid., 259–60, modified.

7   Spinoza, *Spinoza: Complete Works,* *E* ID4.

8   Ibid. *Letter* 2 to Oldenburg, modified.

9   As does André Doz, "Remarques sur les Onze Premières Propositions de l'Éthique," *Revue de Métaphysique et de Morale* 2 (1976): 221–61.

10   Spinoza, *Spinoza. Complete Works, Letter* 10 to Simon de Vries, modified.

11   Martial Guéroult, *Spinoza I: Dieu* (Paris: Aubier-Montaigne, 1968), 109.

12   Spinoza, *Spinoza: Complete Works,* *E* ID6, modified.

13   Ibid. *Letter,* 60 to Tschirnhaus, modified.

14   Ibid. *Principles of Cartesian Philosophy,* IP7S, modified.

15   As in the reading by Deleuze. See Gilles Deleuze, *Expressionism in Philosophy: Spinoza,* trans. Martin Joughin (New York; Cambridge, Mass.: Zone Books; Distributed by MIT Press, 1990), 45.

16   Spinoza, *Spinoza: Complete Works, Letter* 2 to Oldenburg.

17   Ibid. *Letter* 4 to Oldenburg, modified.

18   Ibid. *E* IP19D, modified.

19   Ibid. *E* IP6C, modified.

20   Ibid. *Letter* 4 to Oldenburg, modified.

21   Ibid. *Letter* 36 to Hudde, modified; see also *Letter* 4 to Oldenburg.

22   Ibid. *Letter* 35 to Hudde.

23 Guéroult, *Spinoza I: Dieu,* 169.

24 Spinoza, *Spinoza: Complete Works,* E IP8D.

25 Guéroult, *Spinoza I: Dieu,* 150.

26 Spinoza, *Spinoza: Complete Works, Letter* 64 to Schuller, modified.

27 Ibid. *Letter* 50 to Jelles, modified.

28 Ibid. *E* IP14C, modified.

29 Ibid. *E* IIP1, IIP2.

30 Ibid., modified. [In the translation by Shirley, p. 46, this is rendered as "one limits [not] the other." Shirley adds the word *not.* But we can see from Macherey's prior argument that Shirley's modification is incorrect: Spinoza's point is that Desire, acting from the point of view of imagination, precisely *does* see the relationship as one of limitation, where reason sees it correctly.—*Trans.*]

31 Ibid. *E* IIP7.

32 Hegel, *Science of Logic,* §1182.

33 Ibid., §151.

34 Ibid., §1179.

4. *Omnis Determinatio Est Negatio*

1 Georg Wilhelm Friedrich Hegel, *Science of Logic,* trans. A. V. Miller (London: George Allen and Unwin, 1969), §1184.

2 Georg Wilhelm Friedrich Hegel, *Encyclopédie des Sciences Philosophiques 1: La Science de la Logique,* trans. Bernard Bourgeois, Bibliothèque des Textes Philosophiques (Paris: J. Vrin, 1970), §151, my translation. [Compare Georg Wilhelm Friedrich Hegel, *Encyclopedia of the Philosophical Sciences,* trans. William Wallace (Oxford: Oxford University Press, 1873), §151.—*Trans.*]

3 Hegel, *Science of Logic,* §1179, modified.

4 Georg Wilhelm Friedrich Hegel, *Leçons sur l'Histoire de la Philosophie,* trans. J. Gibelin, vol. 1 (Paris: J. Vrin, 1937; Reprint, Paris, 1946), my translation. [See Georg Wilhelm Friedrich Hegel, *Lectures on the History of Philosophy,* trans. Elizabeth S. Haldane and Francis H. Simson, 3 vols., vol. III (London: Kegan Paul, Trench, Trübner and Company, Ltd., 1896), 286–87.—*Trans.*]

5 Ibid., my translation. [See Hegel, *Lectures on the History of Philosophy,* 259.—*Trans.*]

6 Georg Wilhelm Friedrich Hegel, *La Relation du Scepticisme avec la Philosophie suivi de l'Essence de la Critique Philosophique,* Traduction et notes par Bernard Fauquet, préface de Jean-Paul Dumont, Bibliothèque des

Textes Philosophiques (Paris: J. Vrin, 1972), 38, my translation. [See Georg Wilhelm Friedrich Hegel, "On the Relationship of Skepticism to Philosophy, Exposition of Its Different Modifications and the Comparison of the Latest Form with the Ancient One," in *Between Kant and Hegel: Texts in the Development of Post-Kantian Idealism,* ed. George di Giovanni and H. S. Harris (Indianapolis: Hackett Publishing Company, 2000), 324.—*Trans.*]

7   Hegel, *La Relation du Scepticisme avec la Philosophie,* 39, my translation. [See Di Giovanni, *Between Kant and Hegel,* 325.—*Trans.*]

8   Ibid., 63, my translation. [See Di Giovanni, *Between Kant and Hegel,* 339.—*Trans.*]

9   Hegel, *Leçons sur l'Histoire de la Philosophie,* my translation. [Compare Hegel, *Lectures on the History of Philosophy,* 258–59.—*Trans.*]

10   "Enthusiasm which starts straight off with absolute knowledge, as if shot out of a pistol, and makes short work of other points of view simply by explaining that it is to take no notice of them." Georg Wilhelm Friedrich Hegel and Jean Hyppolite, *Préface de la Phénoménologie de l'Esprit,* trad., introd., notes par Jean Hyppolite (Paris: Aubier-Montaigne, 1966), §27, compare as well §31, my translation. [See Georg Wilhelm Friedrich Hegel, *The Phenomenology of Mind,* trans. J. B. Baillie, Library of Philosophy (London, New York: Sonnenschein, Macmillan, 1910), §27.—*Trans.*]

11   Ibid.

12   Baruch Spinoza, *Spinoza: Complete Works,* trans. Samuel Shirley (Indianapolis: Hackett Publishing, 2002), E ID6Exp.

13   Hegel, *Lectures on the History of Philosophy,* 262, modified.

14   Spinoza, *Spinoza: Complete Works,* Letter 36 to Hudde.

15   Lewis Robinson, *Kommentar zu Spinozas Ethik* (Leipzig: F. Meiner, 1928), 103, my translation.

16   Spinoza, *Spinoza: Complete Works,* Letter 50 from Spinoza to Jelles, modified.

17   Spinoza, *Spinoza: Complete Works,* Letter 32 from Spinoza to Oldenberg, modified.

18   Ibid., *Letter* 81 of Spinoza to Tschirnhaus, modified.

19   Spinoza, *Spinoza: Complete Works,* Letter 12 from Spinoza to Meyer, modified.

20   Hegel, *Science of Logic,* §401.

21   Spinoza, *Spinoza: Complete Works,* E IP15S, modified.

22   My translation. [Compare ibid., *Letter* 12 to Meyer.—*Trans.*]

23   Ibid., *Letter* 12 to Meyer, modified.

24   Ibid., *Letter* 12 to Meyer, modified.

25   Georg Wilhelm Friedrich Hegel, *Science de la Logique, I: La Doctrine de l'Être* [1812], trad. Pierre-Jean Labarrière and Gwendoline Jarczyk, Bibliothèque Philosophique (Paris: Aubier-Montaigne, 1972), 249–50, my translation.

26   Georg Wilhelm Friedrich Hegel, *Science de la Logique, I: La Doctrine de l'Être* [2nd ed., 1831–1832], trad. Samuel Jankélévitch (Paris: Aubier-Montaigne, 1972), my translation. [Compare Di Giovanni, *Between Kant and Hegel*, 212–13.—*Trans.*]

27   Hegel, *Leçons sur l'Histoire de la Philosophie,* my translation. [Compare Hegel, *Lectures on the History of Philosophy,* 262–63.—*Trans.*]

28   Martial Guéroult, *Spinoza I: Dieu* (Paris: Aubier-Montaigne, 1968), 523.

29   Yvon Belaval, *Leibniz Critique de Descartes,* Bibliothèque des Idées (Paris: Gallimard, 1960), 329–38, my translation.

30   Gilles Deleuze, *Expressionism in Philosophy: Spinoza,* trans. Martin Joughin (New York; Cambridge, Mass.: Zone Books; Distributed by MIT Press, 1990), 201–5.

31   Spinoza, *Spinoza: Complete Works, Letter* 4 to Oldenburg.

32   Deleuze, *Expressionism in Philosophy: Spinoza,* 60.

33   Spinoza, *Spinoza: Complete Works,* E IP35.

34   Ibid., *E* ID2.

35   Ibid., *Letter* 36 to Hudde, modified.

36   Ibid., *Treatise on the Emendation of the Intellect,* §88, modified.

37   Ibid., *E* IP26, modified. [The French text is *produire un effet*; in the English translation of Shirley it is "to act."—*Trans.*]

38   Ibid., *E* IP26D, modified.

39   My translation.

40   Ibid., *E* IIP13S, modified.

41   Martial Guéroult, *Spinoza II: L'âme* (Paris: Aubier-Montaigne, 1974), 177.

42   Ibid., 188.

43   Spinoza, *Spinoza: Complete Works, Letter* 63 from Schuller to Spinoza, modified.

44   Ibid., *Letter* 64 from Spinoza to Schuller, modified.

45   Ibid., *Treatise on the Emendation of the Intellect,* §101, modified.

46   Ibid., *E* IIP13.

47   Ibid., *E* IIP13S.

48   Ibid., *E* IP15S, modified.

49   Ibid., *Treatise on the Emendation of the Intellect*, §41.

50   Ibid., *E* IIP13Lem3Ax2.

51   Guéroult, *Spinoza II: L'âme*, 156.

52   [In Macherey's text this reads "de choses fixes et changeantes"; in Shirley's, "particular mutable things."—*Trans.*]

53   Spinoza, *Spinoza: Complete Works, E* IIP13S LemVII, modified.

54   Gilles Deleuze, *The Logic of Sense*, trans. Charles Stivale, European Perspectives (New York: Columbia University Press, 1990), 267.

55   Spinoza, *Spinoza: Complete Works, Theologico-political Treatise*, chapter 6, 444, modified.

56   Ibid., *E* IApp, modified.

57   René Descartes, *Oeuvres Philosophiques de Descartes, Publiées d'après les Textes Originaux, avec Notices, Sommaires et Éclaircissements, par Adolphe Garnier* (Paris: L. Hachette, 1835), t. III, 583. René Descartes, *The Philosophical Writings*, vol. III: *Correspondence*, trans. John Cottingham, Robert Stoothoff, Dugald Murdoch, and Anthony Kenny (Cambridge, England: Cambridge University Press, 1991), 255.

58   Ibid., *Lettre à Elizabeth*, June 28, 1643, t. III, 46. See Descartes, *Philosophical Writings* ¶ 694, 227.

59   Descartes, *Oeuvres Philosophiques, Lettre à Regius*, October 6, 1642, t. II, 934. Descartes, *Philosophical Works* 214 ¶, 567, modified. [In this text the letter is referenced as *Letter to Regius* June 1642.—*Trans.*]

60   Ibid., *Descartes à Mesland*, May 2, 1644, t. III, 74. Descartes, *Philosophical Writings* ¶ 119, 235.

61   Ibid., trad. Clerselier, t. III, 789. René Descartes, *Philosophical Essays and Correspondence*, ed. Roger Ariew (Indianapolis, Ind.: Hackett, 2000), ¶ 343, 281.

62   Ibid., Descartes, *Notae in programma*, t. III, 798. Descartes, *Philosophical Essays*, ¶ 350, 284.

63   Spinoza, *Spinoza: Complete Works, E* IIIP5.

64   Ibid., *E* IIP13D, modified.

65   Ibid., *E* IIP13Lem2.

66   Ibid., *E* IID7, modified.

67   Spinoza, *Spinoza: Complete Works, E* IApp, modified.

68   Guéroult, *Spinoza II: L'âme*, 166, my translation.

69   Spinoza, *Spinoza: Complete Works, E* IIP24D, modified.

70   Ibid., *E* IIP13Post1, modified.

71   Ibid., *E* IIP24D, modified.

72   Ibid., *E* IApp.

73   Ibid., *E* IIP37, modified. [The reference appears as prop. 7 in the French text.—*Trans.*]

74   Spinoza, *Spinoza: Complete Works, Metaphysical Thoughts,* part 1, chapter 5, modified.

75   Immanuel Kant et al., *Critique de la Raison Pure,* traduction Française avec notes par A. Tremesaygues et B. Pacaud; préface de C. Serrus, Quadrige (Paris: P.U.F., 1965), 234. Immanuel Kant, *Critique of Pure Reason,* trans. F. Max Müller (London: MacMillan, 1881), 230, modified.

76   Kant, *Critique of Pure Reason,* 230, modified.

77   Ibid., 273–74, modified.

78   Immanuel Kant and Roger Kempf, *Essai pour Introduire en Philosophie le Concept de Grandeur Négative Traduction et Notes par Roger Kempf,* 2e éd., Bibliothèque des Textes Philosophiques (Paris: J. Vrin, 1972), 79, my translation. [See Immanuel Kant, *Theoretical Philosophy 1755–1770,* trans. and ed. David Walford (Cambridge, England: Cambridge University Press, 1992), 211.—*Trans.*]

79   Ibid., 80. [See Kant, *Theoretical Philosophy,* 211.—*Trans.*]

80   Ibid. [See Kant, *Theoretical Philosophy,* 212.—*Trans.*]

81   Ibid., 84. [See Kant, *Theoretical Philosophy,* 216.—*Trans.*]

82   Ibid. [See Kant, *Theoretical Philosophy,* 217.—*Trans.*]

83   Immanuel Kant, *Premiers Principes Métaphysiques de la Science de la Nature,* trans. Jean Gibelin (Paris: J. Vrin, 1971), 25, my translation. [See also Immanuel Kant and Ernest Belfort Bax, *Kant's Prolegomena, and Metaphysical Foundations of Natural Science,* Bohn's Philosophical Library (London: G. Bell, 1883) 150.—*Trans.*]

84   Ibid., 52. [See Kant, *Kant's Prolegomena,* 169.—*Trans.*]

85   Ibid., 53–54. [See Kant, *Kant's Prolegomena,* 170–71.—*Trans.*]

86   Ibid., 59. [See Kant, *Kant's Prolegomena,* 175.—*Trans.*]

87   Ibid., 61. [See Kant, *Kant's Prolegomena,* 176.—*Trans.*]

88   Ibid., 95. [See Kant, *Kant's Prolegomena,* 199.—*Trans.*]

89   Ibid., 112. [See Kant, *Kant's Prolegomena,* 200.—*Trans.*]

90   Ibid., 111. [See Kant, *Kant's Prolegomena,* 210.—*Trans.*]

91   Ibid., 113–14. [See Kant, *Kant's Prolegomena,* 211.—*Trans.*]

92   Ibid., 71. [See Kant, *Kant's Prolegomena,* 183.—*Trans.*]

93   Ibid., 74. [See Kant, *Kant's Prolegomena,* 212.—*Trans.*]

94   Ibid., 115–16. [See Kant, *Kant's Prolegomena,* 213.—*Trans.*]

95   Ibid. [Kant, *Kant's Prolegomena,* 188–89.—*Trans.*]

96   Ibid. [Kant, *Kant's Prolegomena*, 199.—*Trans.*]

97   Ibid. [Kant, *Kant's Prolegomena*, 199, modified.—*Trans.*]

98   Georg Wilhelm Friedrich Hegel, *Encyclopédie des Sciences Philosophiques en Abrege, 1817–1827*, trans. Maurice de Gandillac (Paris: Gallimard, 1970), 253, my translation. [See Georg Wilhelm Friedrich Hegel, Friedhelm Nicolin, and Otto Pöggeler, *Enzyklopädie der philosophischen Wissenschaften im Grundrisse (1830)*, 6. Aufl. ed., Philosophische Bibliothek (Hamburg: F. Meiner, 1959), Vorrede zur ersten Ausgabe [1817], §262.—*Trans.*]

99   Ibid.

100   Ibid.

101   Hegel, *Science of Logic*, chapter 2, "Determinate Being."

102   Hegel, *Encyclopédie des Sciences Philosophiques en Abrege, 1817–1827*, 253, my translation. [See Hegel, Nicolin, and Pöggeler, *Enzyklopädie der Philosophischen Wissenschaften im Grundrisse (1830)*. "Deswegen sind sie nicht als Selbständig oder als Kräfte für sich zu nehmen; die Materie resultiert aus ihnen nur als Begriffsmomenten, aber ist das Vorausgesetzte für ihre Erscheinung." Zweiter teil, "Die Naturphilosophie B. Materie und Bewegung. Endliche Mechanik," §262.—*Trans.*]

103   Hegel, *Science of Logic*, vol. 1.

104   Ibid., "Remark: The Kantian Construction of Matter from the Forces of Attraction and Repulsion," §373.

105   Ibid., §377.

106   Ibid.

107   Ibid.

108   Ibid., §384.

109   Lucio Colletti, *Le Marxisme et Hegel*, trans. Jean-Claude Biette and Christian Gauchet (Paris: Champ Libre, 1976), 106. Lucio Colletti, *Marxism and Hegel*, trans. Lawrence Garner (London: Verso, 1979), 105.

110   Colletti, *Le Marxisme et Hegel*, 104, my translation. [See Colletti, *Marxism and Hegel*, 92.]

111   Colletti, *Marxism and Hegel*, 104.

112   Spinoza, *Spinoza: Complete Works*, E VAx1.

113   Georg Wilhelm Friedrich Hegel, *The Phenomenology of Mind*, trans. James Black Baillie (London: George Allen and Unwin, 1961), Preface, §62.

114   Georg Wilhelm Friedrich Hegel and Jean Hyppolite, Préface de la *Phénoménologie de l'Esprit*, trad., introd., notes par Jean Hyppolite (Paris:

Aubier-Montaigne, 1966), IV, 153, my translation. [See Hegel, *The Phenomenology of Mind,* §66.—*Trans.*]

115 Ibid., 49, modified. [See Hegel, *The Phenomenology of Mind,* Preface, §18.—*Trans.*]

116 Ibid., 55, my translation. [Ibid., Preface, §22. In this translation Miller uses *purposive* where Macherey uses *téléologique.*—*Trans.*]

117 Georg Wilhelm Friedrich Hegel, *Encyclopédie des Sciences Philosophiques 1: La Science de la Logique,* trans. Bernard Bourgeois, Bibliothèque des Textes Philosophiques (Paris: J. Vrin, 1970), §119. Hegel, *Encyclopedia of the Philosophical Sciences,* §119.

118 Hegel, *Science of Logic,* §1184.

119 Georg Wilhelm Friedrich Hegel, *La Raison dans l'Histoire, Introduction à la Philosophie de l'Histoire,* trans. Kostas Papaïoannou, Le Monde en 10/18, 235/236 (Paris: Union Générale d'Éditions, 1965), 52, my translation. [This work is a French translation of Georg Wilhelm Friedrich Hegel, *Die Vernunft in der Geschichte,* ed. Johannes Hoffmeister (Hamburg: Felix Meiner Verlag, 1955). This text used both Hegel's manuscripts and a number of notebooks of his students as its sources, which were then differentiated in the text. The passage quoted is drawn from Hegel's own manuscripts.—*Trans.*]

120 Georg Wilhelm Friedrich Hegel, *Leçons sur l'Histoire de la Philosophie,* trans. J. Gibelin, vol. 1 (Paris: J. Vrin, 1937; reprint, Paris, 1946, Paris, 1967), t. I, 131, my translation.

121 Ibid., 156.

122 Spinoza, *Spinoza: Complete Works, Principles of Cartesian Philosophy, Appendix Containing Metaphysical Thoughts,* II, ch. 1, 191, modified.

123 Ibid., 190, modified.

124 Spinoza, *Spinoza: Complete Works,* E 1D8Exp.

Index

101; immobile, x, 79; infinite, 64, 90, 115, 130, 140, 147, 200, 211; intellect and, 83, 86, 87, 88; living, 204–5; manifestation of, 79–80; negative movement of, 29; perception of, 83–84, 87; points of view of, 13–19, 30, 81; real/distinct, 98; reality of, 145, 149; self-production of self-constitution of, 99–100; self-sufficiency of, 26, 80; Spinozist, 24, 91, 116, 203; subject and, 129, 182; thought and, 163; unity of, 19, 30, 31, 82, 85, 98, 109; universality of, 117

system, reconstruction of, 24–32

teleology, xviii, 12, 18, 202–13
Theological-Political Treatise (Spinoza), 44
things, 156, 160; absolute knowledge of, 183; corporeal, 179; extended, 104; fixed/eternal, 153, 157; ideas and, 106; objective essence of, 45; order/connection of, 104–7
thinking, 36, 104, 218n12
Thompson, E. P., xvii
thought, ix, 73, 108, 123, 224n31; absolute and, 13, 110; abstract, 59–60; attribute of, 77, 106; beginning for, 49; being and, 16, 199; dogmatic form of, 40; extension and, 83, 93, 110, 126, 164; immediate, 23; movement of, 45, 59; predicative, 204; rational, 23, 24, 39, 74, 144; real and, 77; self-determination of, 75; substance and, 77, 163; truth and, 73
totality, 36, 83, 129, 153, 158, 159, 183
Treatise on the Emendation of the

Intellect, The (Spinoza), 9, 43, 44, 46, 65, 152, 157
true idea, true path of, 45
truth, x, 76, 202; absolute, 36; abstract problematic of, 71; classical conception of, 86; error and, 62, 70, 71; falsehood and, 66, 71, 72; God and, 61, 165, 169–70; Hegelian conception of, 72; historical, 40; mathematical, 40; method and, 38; order of, 62; philosophical, 33; positive, 62; production of, 49; relationship to itself of, 70; search for, 48; theory of, 66; thought and, 73
Tschirnhaus, Ehrenfried: letter to, 63, 133, 136, 140

understanding, 43, 84, 118, 167, 199, 209, 223n28; deployment of, 38; negative, 30; original, 49; pure, 185
unicity, 98, 102, 103, 211
Union des Étudiants Communistes, xvi
unity, 175, 180; absolute, 103, 108; diversity and, 98; infinite, 182; nature and, 181
universal, 12, 33, 39, 182, 185, 187, 203, 209
universe, of the Stoics, 158
University of Berlin, Hegel and, 7, 8
University of Heidelberg, Hegel and, 7, 8

Vacherot, Étienne, xii, 218n12

Wahl, Jean: Hegel of, xii
Weil, Eric, xiv
whole, 37, 75, 155, 159, 161; corporeal nature as, 158; intelligibility of, 183

Pierre Macherey is a philosopher, Marxist literary critic, and professor emeritus at the Université Lille Nord de France. He is the author of *Theory of Literary Production,* and his other works on Spinoza include *Avec Spinoza* and a five-volume exposition of *Ethics.* He is also the coauthor of *Lire le Capital* with Louis Althusser.

Susan M. Ruddick is associate professor of geography at the University of Toronto.